BUYING A HOME IN IRELAND

by

Joe Laredo

SURVIVAL BOOKS • LONDON • ENGLAND

First published 1999
Second edition 2001

Survival Books Limited, Suite C, Third Floor
Standbrook House, 2–5 Old Bond Street
London W1X 3TB, United Kingdom
☎ (+44) 020-7493 4244, ▤ (+44) 020-7491 0605
✉ info@survivalbooks.net
💻 www.survivalbooks.net

British Library Cataloguing in Publication Data.
A CIP record for this book is available from the British Library.
ISBN 1 901130 86 X

Printed and bound in Italy by LegoPrint

ACKNOWLEDGEMENTS

M y sincere thanks to all those who contributed to the successful publication of this book, in particular the many people who took the time and trouble to read and comment on the draft versions, including Ron and Pat Scarborough, David Hampshire, Karen Verheul (proof-reader), Kerry Laredo and Gill Mildenhall and everyone else who contributed in any way and whom I have omitted to mention. Also a special thank you to Jim Watson (☎ UK 01788-813609) for the superb cover, illustrations, cartoons and maps.

By the same publisher:

The Alien's Guide to Britain
The Alien's Guide to France
Buying a Home Abroad
Buying a Home in Britain
Buying a Home in Florida
Buying a Home in France
Buying a Home in Greece & Cyprus
Buying a Home in Italy
Buying a Home in Portugal
Buying a Home in Spain
Living and Working Abroad
Living and Working in America
Living and Working in Australia
Living and Working in Britain
Living and Working in Canada
Living and Working in France
Living and Working in Germany
Living and Working in Ireland
Living and Working in Italy
Living and Working in London
Living and Working in New Zealand
Living and Working in Spain
Living and Working in Switzerland
Rioja and its Wines

What Readers and Reviewers

When you buy a model plane for your child, a video recorder, or some new computer gizmo, you get with it a leaflet or booklet pleading 'Read Me First', or bearing large friendly letters or bold type saying 'IMPORTANT – follow the instructions carefully'. This book should be similarly supplied to all those entering France with anything more durable than a 5-day return ticket. It is worth reading even if you are just visiting briefly, or if you have lived here for years and feel totally knowledgeable and secure. But if you need to find out how France works then it is indispensable. Native French people probably have a less thorough understanding of how their country functions. – Where it is most essential, the book is most up to the minute.

Living France

We would like to congratulate you on this work: it is really super! We hand it out to our expatriates and they read it with great interest and pleasure.

ICI (Switzerland) AG

Rarely has a 'survival guide' contained such useful advice This book dispels doubts for first-time travellers, yet is also useful for seasoned globetrotters – In a word, if you're planning to move to the USA or go there for a long-term stay, then buy this book both for general reading and as a ready-reference.

American Citizens Abroad

It is everything you always wanted to ask but didn't for fear of the contemptuous put down – The best English-language guide – Its pages are stuffed with practical information on everyday subjects and are designed to complement the traditional guidebook.

Swiss News

A complete revelation to me – I found it both enlightening and interesting, not to mention amusing.

Carole Clark

Let's say it at once. David Hampshire's Living and Working in France is the best handbook ever produced for visitors and foreign residents in this country; indeed, my discussion with locals showed that it has much to teach even those born and bred in l'Hexagone – It is Hampshire's meticulous detail which lifts his work way beyond the range of other books with similar titles. Often you think of a supplementary question and search for the answer in vain. With Hampshire this is rarely the case – He writes with great clarity (and gives French equivalents of all key terms), a touch of humour and a ready eye for the odd (and often illuminating) fact – This book is absolutely indispensable.

The Riviera Reporter

The ultimate reference book – Every conceivable subject imaginable is exhaustively explained in simple terms – An excellent introduction to fully enjoy all that this fine country has to offer and save time and money in the process.

American Club of Zurich

Have Said About Survival Books

What a great work, wealth of useful information, well-balanced wording and accuracy in details. My compliments!

Thomas Müller

This handbook has all the practical information one needs to set up home in the UK – The sheer volume of information is almost daunting – Highly recommended for anyone moving to the UK.

American Citizens Abroad

A very good book which has answered so many questions and even some I hadn't thought of – I would certainly recommend it.

Brian Fairman

A mine of information – I may have avoided some embarrassments and frights if I had read it prior to my first Swiss encounters – Deserves an honoured place on any newcomer's bookshelf.

English Teachers Association, Switzerland

Covers just about all the things you want to know on the subject – In answer to the desert island question about the one how-to book on France, this book would be it – Almost 500 pages of solid accurate reading – This book is about enjoyment as much as survival.

The Recorder

It's so funny – I love it and definitely need a copy of my own – Thanks very much for having written such a humorous and helpful book.

Heidi Guiliani

A must for all foreigners coming to Switzerland.

Antoinette O'Donoghue

A comprehensive guide to all things French, written in a highly readable and amusing style, for anyone planning to live, work or retire in France.

The Times

A concise, thorough account of the DOs and DON'Ts for a foreigner in Switzerland – Crammed with useful information and lightened with humorous quips which make the facts more readable.

American Citizens Abroad

Covers every conceivable question that may be asked concerning everyday life – I know of no other book that could take the place of this one.

France in Print

Hats off to Living and Working in Switzerland!

Ronnie Almeida

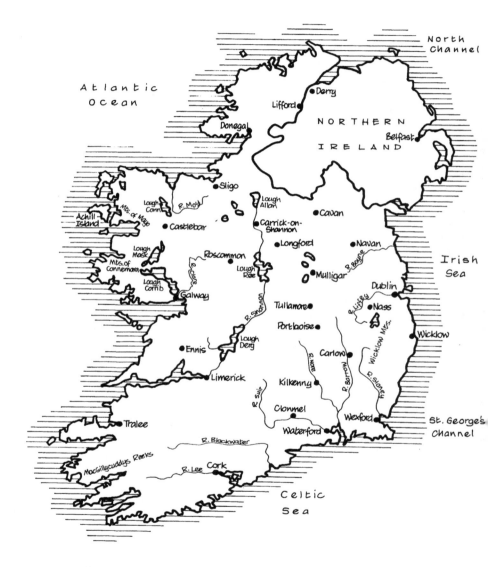

North
Channel

Atlantic
Ocean

• Derry

Lifford •

NORTHERN

Donegal •

IRELAND

Belfast •

• Sligo

Lough
Allon

• Cavan

Irish
Sea

Mts.of Mayo

R. Moy

Achill
Island

Lough
Conn

Carrick-on-
Shannon

• Castlebar

• Longford

• Navan

R. Boyne

Lough
Mask

Roscommon

Lough
Ree

Dublin •

Mts.of
Connemara

Mulligar •

R. Clare

Lough
Corrib

Tullamore •

R. Liffey

Naas •

Galway •

Wicklow Mts.

• Ennis

Lough
Derg

Portlaoise •

Wicklow •

R. Shannon

Carlow •

R. Barrow

R. Slaney

Limerick •

Kilkenny •

R. Suir

• Tralee

Clonmel •

Wexford •

St. George's
Channel

R. Blackwater

Waterford •

MacGillycuddys Reeks

R. Lee

Cork •

Celtic
Sea

CONTENTS

4. FINDING YOUR DREAM HOME 103

5. ARRIVAL & SETTLING IN 181

6. APPENDICES 193

INDEX 209

ORDER FORMS 215

IMPORTANT NOTE

Readers should note that the laws and regulations regarding buying property in Ireland aren't the same as in other countries and are also liable to change periodically. **I cannot recommend too strongly that you check with an official and reliable source (not always the same) and take expert legal advice before paying any money or signing any legal documents. Don't, however, believe everything you're told or read, even, dare I say it, herein!**

To help you obtain further information and verify data with official sources, useful addresses and references to other sources of information have been included in all chapters and in appendices A and B. Important points have been emphasised throughout the book **in bold print**, some of which it would be expensive or foolish to disregard. **Ignore them at your peril or cost**. Unless specifically stated, the reference to any company, organisation, product or publication in this book *doesn't* constitute an endorsement or recommendation. Any reference to any place or person (living or dead) is purely coincidental.

AUTHOR'S NOTES

- The book covers buying property in the Republic of Ireland (*Poblacht na hÉireann* or simply *Éire*) and doesn't include the counties of the province of Ulster (Antrim, Armagh, Down, Fermanagh, Londonderry and Tyrone) that comprise the region known as Northern Ireland, which remained part of the United Kingdom when the Republic was established in 1921.

- Frequent references are made throughout this book to the European Union (EU), which comprises Austria, Belgium, Denmark, Finland, France, Germany, Greece, Ireland, Italy, Luxembourg, the Netherlands, Portugal, Spain, Sweden and the United Kingdom and to the European Economic Area (EEA), which includes the EU countries plus Iceland, Liechtenstein and Norway.

- All prices are shown in Irish pounds or punts (IR£) unless otherwise noted. To convert to euros, multiply by 0.787564. Prices should be taken as estimates only, although they were mostly correct at the time of publication. Unless otherwise stated, prices quoted usually include value added tax (VAT) at 2.8, 12.5 or 20 per cent.

- His/he/him (etc.) also mean her/she/her (no offence ladies!). This is done simply to make life easier for both the reader and, in particular, the author, and **isn't** intended to be sexist.

- Irish words and titles are shown in *italics*.

- Warnings and important points are shown in **bold** type.

- The following symbols are used in this book: ☎ (telephone), 🖹 (fax), 🖥 (Internet) and ✉ (e-mail).

- Lists of **Useful Addresses** and **Further Reading** are contained in **Appendices A** and **B** respectively.

- A **Map of Ireland** showing the counties is included in **Appendix C** and a map showing the major cities and geographical features is on page 6.

- For those unfamiliar with the metric system of **Weights and Measures**, imperial conversion tables are included in **Appendix D**.

- A list of property, mortgage and other terms used in this book is included in a **Glossary** in **Appendix E**.

INTRODUCTION

If you're planning to buy a home in Ireland or even just thinking about it – this is **THE BOOK** for you! Whether you want a mansion, farmhouse, cottage or an apartment, a holiday or a permanent home, this book will help make your dreams come true. The aim of *Buying a Home in Ireland* is to provide you with the information necessary to help you choose the most favourable location and most appropriate home **to satisfy your individual requirements**. Most important of all, it's intended to help you avoid the pitfalls and risks associated with buying a home in Ireland, which for most people is one of the largest financial transactions they will make during their lifetimes.

You may already own a home in your home country; however, buying a home in Ireland (or any foreign country) is a different matter altogether. One of the most common mistakes many people make when buying a home in Ireland is to assume that the laws and purchase procedures are the same as in their home country (which is unlikely to be the case). Buying property in Ireland is, however, generally very safe, particularly when compared with certain other countries. Nevertheless, if you don't follow the rules provided for your protection, a purchase can result in serious financial loss, as some people have discovered to their cost.

Before buying a home in Ireland you need to ask yourself *exactly* why you want to buy a home there. Is your primary concern a good long-term investment or do you wish to work or retire there? Where and what can you afford to buy? Do you plan to let your home to offset the running costs? What about capital gains and inheritance taxes? *Buying a Home in Ireland* will help you answer these and many other questions. It won't, however, tell you where and what to buy, or whether having made your decision you will be happy – that part is up to you!

For many people, buying a home in Ireland has previously been a case of pot luck. However, with a copy of *Buying a Home in Ireland* to hand you'll have a wealth of priceless information at your fingertips. Information derived from a variety of sources, both official and unofficial, not least the hard won personal experiences of the author, his friends, colleagues and acquaintances. This book doesn't, however, contain all the answers (most of us don't even know the right questions to ask). What it *will* do is reduce the risk of making an expensive mistake that you may regret later and help you make informed decisions and calculated judgements, instead of costly mistakes and uneducated guesses (forewarned is forearmed!). **Most importantly of all, it will help you save money and will repay your investment many times over.**

The world recession in the early '90s caused an upheaval in world property markets, during which many so-called 'gilt-edged' property investments went to the wall. However, property remains one of the best long-term investments (particularly in Ireland) and it's certainly one of the most pleasurable. Buying a home in Ireland is a wonderful way to make new friends, broaden your horizons and revitalise your life – and it provides a welcome bolt-hole to recuperate from the stresses and strains of modern life. I trust this book will help you avoid the pitfalls and smooth your way to many happy years in your new home in Ireland, secure in the knowledge that you have made the right decision.

Good luck!

David Hampshire (Editor)
May 2001

1.

WHY IRELAND?

If you're seeking a retreat from the noise and stresses of modern life, open spaces and stunning scenery, simple, traditional pleasures and a slower, gentler way of life, as well as a wide choice of homes at affordable prices, Ireland could be just what you're looking for. Perhaps you also wish to avoid unfamiliar languages (it isn't necessary to speak Gaelic!), strange customs, exotic food and sweltering climates, and want a place where you'll be readily accepted into the community and can relax and feel at home, in which case you'll find Ireland hard to beat. It's the least densely populated country in Western Europe (outside Scandinavia), with just 51 people per km^2 compared, for example, with 245 in the UK. There isn't only space but also time in Ireland (an old Irish saying goes: "When God made time, he made plenty of it."), where there are hardly any motorways and few bustling cities. What Ireland *does* have is an abundance of tranquil countryside, rivers and lakes, a rugged, beautiful coastline and some of the greenest vegetation in the world.

However, there's more to the Emerald Isle than beautiful scenery. Although the modern state is politically less than 80 years old, Ireland can trace its roots to an ancient civilisation almost undisturbed by history: the country was virtually untouched by the Romans, the Reformation, the Industrial Revolution and two world wars. Ireland nurtures its links with the past, and its people are proud of their cultural heritage, their myths and legends, their writers and music – not forgetting their famous beer and whiskey! Catholics comprise over 90 per cent of the population and their religion is all pervasive: divorce has only recently been made legal and even schooling is mostly church-controlled. However, the traditional antipathy towards Protestants (a legacy of centuries of British rule) has largely disappeared and most Irish people are tolerant of other religions and beliefs. The capital, Dublin, is a sophisticated cultural centre and Dubliners have a reputation for knowing everything about everything (just as northerners are said to be direct and the people of the south-west poetic), although everywhere in Ireland you'll find those distinctive features of Irishness: friendliness, loquacity and irreverent humour.

Ireland is a virtually classless society, and pastoral life survives as almost nowhere else in Western Europe. Ireland's towns, including Dublin, are still essentially country towns and it isn't unusual to find horse-drawn carts in the streets. While it's a place of refuge for those seeking peace and relaxation, it's also a lively country for the young. Ireland has the youngest population in Europe (over 40 per cent are under 25, almost 70 per cent under 44) and, at more than 14 per thousand annually, the highest birth rate in the European Union (EU). The population is expected to rise by more than 20 per cent (to 4.5 million) by the year 2006, which would be its highest since before the famines of the mid-19th century.

It's important to bear in mind when buying a property in Ireland that you aren't simply buying a home, but a lifestyle, so you shouldn't be under any illusions as to what you can expect from a home there. The first and most important question you need to ask yourself is exactly why you want to buy a home in Ireland. For example, are you seeking a holiday or a retirement home? If you're seeking a second home, will it be used mainly for weekends or for longer stays? Do you plan to let it to offset the mortgage and running costs? If so, how important is the rental income? Are you primarily looking for a sound investment or do you plan to work or start a business in Ireland?

There's a variety of reasons for buying a home in Ireland: for example, many people buy a holiday home with a view to living there permanently or semi-permanently when they retire. If this is the case, there are many more factors to take into account than when 'simply' buying a holiday home which you plan to occupy for just a few weeks a year – when it's usually wiser not to buy at all!. If, on the other hand, you plan to work or start a business in Ireland, you'll be faced with a completely different set of criteria. Can you really afford to buy a home in Ireland? What of the future? Is your income secure and protected against inflation and currency fluctuations? Buying a home abroad can be a good long-term investment, but in the last decade many people have had their fingers burnt in the volatile property market in many countries (although Ireland suffered less than most in this respect).

Home ownership in Ireland is an astonishing 80 per cent, which is the highest in Europe (compared with some 65 per cent in the UK and just 35 per cent in Germany) and one of the highest in the world. The country boasts a million homeowners out of a population of 3.6 million, and the growth in property investment (by both nationals and foreigners) in the '90s was phenomenal. In recent years, immigration has reached record levels, around 45,000 people making Ireland their home in 1996/97. Not surprisingly, Britons make up the largest expatriate community. Ireland has also traditionally been popular with the British for holiday homes, particularly among outdoor sports enthusiasts (e.g. the hunting, shooting and fishing fraternity), but it's becoming increasingly popular with continental European homebuyers (especially Germans and Dutch, but also Swedes, Swiss, French and Italians), as well as Japanese and Americans. In the counties of Westmeath and Cavan, for example, there's a growing enclave of Italians, while Americans seem to prefer the west coast and the river Shannon area as well as Dublin (where there's a substantial American community).

If you're looking for an urban property, demographic statistics show that towns with more than 10,000 people are growing fastest. Since the early '50s, these larger towns have increased their share of Ireland's population from 3.5 to 10.5 per cent. Galway is the fastest growing city in Ireland, having increased its population by over 10 per cent in the last decade (it's estimated that a quarter of all homes in Galway have been built since 1960). In comparison, Dublin has grown by just 1 per cent in the same period, although its satellite towns have expanded rapidly.

Economically, Ireland is currently enjoying a period of greater prosperity than at any time since its formation. In fact, it's Europe's fastest expanding economy, with a growth rate three times the EU average (between 1988 and 1994, GNP grew at an annual average of around 5 per cent, rising to 9.8 per cent in 1999 and 10.5 per cent in 2000), earning it the nickname 'the Celtic Tiger'. Exports totalled IR£57 billion in 1999, having more than doubled in value since 1994. Current predictions are that the economy will continue to grow, albeit at a slower rate: GDP is expected to increase by 8.2 per cent in 2001, 7.1 per cent in 2002 and thereafter at an average of 6 per cent per year until around 2007 (barring global recessions). This rapid growth has inevitably had an effect on inflation, which rose from an all-time low in 1996/97 to 5.5 per cent in 2000 (its highest rate for 15 years), although it's predicted to fall to just over 4.7 per cent in 2001 and just over 3 per cent in subsequent years. These figures, however, are strongly influenced by the continued rise in house prices (see page 128), the 1999 increase in the 'consumer price index' being a mere 1.6 per cent.

Despite these price rises, the rate of construction of new houses in Ireland has also increased in recent years. Compared with 26,600 new houses built in 1995, more than 43,000 were constructed in 1999, the great majority in Dublin and neighbouring counties, a substantial number in the three other major cities (Cork, Limerick and Galway), in the south-west (Counties Clare and Kerry) and, more surprisingly, in Counties Mayo, Sligo and Donegal in the north-west, where the rate of house building has more than doubled in the last five years (in Co. Sligo planning permission for more than 1,000 new houses was sought in the first six months of 2000 alone).

You'll find plenty of properties to choose from in Ireland, whether you're seeking an imposing castle or stately home, a simple cottage or farmhouse, or a modern bungalow or apartment. However, you shouldn't expect to make a fast buck when buying property in Ireland; you should look upon it as a long-term investment in your family's happiness, rather than merely in financial terms.

As in all countries, there are both advantages and disadvantages to buying a home in Ireland, although for most people the benefits far outweigh the drawbacks. Among the many advantages are good value for money, easy and inexpensive access (at least for most western Europeans), good rental possibilities (in many areas), excellent local tradesmen and services (particularly in the more popular areas), fine food at reasonable prices, a slower and more relaxed pace of life, the friendliness and warmth of the Irish people, and the dramatic and rugged beauty of Ireland on your doorstep. There are other positive aspects to buying a home in Ireland: purchase fees are relatively low for new houses; there are no rates or community charges and mains water is free; and the cost of maintaining a property is small compared with many other European countries.

Among the disadvantages are the relatively high purchase costs associated with buying resale property, overcrowding in popular tourist areas during the summer season, and the expense of getting to and from Ireland if you own a holiday home there and don't live in a nearby country (or a country with good air connections). As when buying property in any country, there's also the danger of buying a property with debts and other problems (if you don't take legal advice), and, if you purchase an old property, there can be unexpected renovation and restoration costs (if you don't do your homework).

Unless you know exactly what you're looking for and where, it's best to rent a property for a period until you're more familiar with an area. As when making all major financial decisions, you should never be too hasty. Some people make expensive errors when buying homes in Ireland, usually because they do insufficient research and are in too much of a hurry, often setting themselves ridiculous deadlines such as buying a home during a long weekend break or a week's holiday. Not surprisingly, most people wouldn't dream of acting so rashly when buying property in their home country. It isn't uncommon for buyers to regret their decision and wish they'd purchased a different property in a different region – or even in a different country! Some people become so dissatisfied with their home that they resell within a few years.

Too many buyers also assume that the buying process is the same in Ireland as in their home country. Before deciding to buy a home in Ireland, it's wise to do extensive research and read a number of books especially written for those planning to buy a home or live there (like this one). It also helps to study the advertisements in specialist property magazines such as *World of Property* and *International Property* (see **Appendix A**), and to visit overseas property exhibitions such as those organised by Outbound Publishing in Britain. Bear in mind that the cost of investing in a few books or magazines (and other research) is tiny compared with the expense of making a big mistake. However, don't believe everything you read!

This chapter provides information about permits and visas, retirement, working, starting a business, communications, getting to Ireland and getting around, including the vagaries of Irish driving!

DO YOU NEED A PERMIT OR VISA?

Before making any plans to buy a home in Ireland, you must check whether you'll need a visa or residence permit and ensure that you'll be permitted to use the property when you wish and for whatever purpose you have in mind. If there's a possibility that you or a family member will want to live permanently or work in Ireland, you should enquire whether it will be possible before making any plans to buy a home there. If you were born in a European Economic Area (EEA) country (Austria, Belgium, Denmark, Finland, France, Germany, Iceland, Ireland, Italy, Liechtenstein, Luxembourg, Netherlands, Norway, Portugal, Spain, Sweden and the UK) or can show that at least one of your parents or grandparents was born in Ireland, you're free to live in the country without restrictions, provided that you're able to support yourself (and any dependants) without state assistance. However, non-UK nationals must register with the police within three months and obtain a residence permit.

Unless you're retired or otherwise financially independent, the duration of a residence permit is governed by the length of your employment or course (in the case of students) up to a maximum of five years. If you're employed in Ireland, the permit must be completed by your employer, who must also submit a letter detailing the nature and period of your employment. If you're a student, retired or financially independent, you must have private health insurance. In addition, anyone applying for a residence permit may be required to undergo a medical examination. You'll need to produce your passport or national identity card, marriage and children's birth certificates (as applicable), and four passport-size photographs. If you intend to stay for less than a year but more than three months, you'll be issued with a temporary residence permit.

Apart from the requirement to obtain a residence permit, the authorities prefer that EEA citizens register with the Aliens Registration Office (ARO) in Dublin (part of the Department of Justice). Although three out of four EEA nationals don't bother, it can be in your interest to do so (unless you don't want anyone to be able to track you down!). You'll need to go to the ARO in person with your passport.

Non-EEA nationals wishing to stay in Ireland for more than three months must register with the *Garda Síochána* (police) in the area where they intend to stay – e.g. in the Dublin area you must report to the ARO (☎ 01-666 3652). If you're coming to Ireland to work, you'll require a work permit or at least written confirmation from the

Department of Enterprise, Trade and Employment (DETE) that a work permit is being processed. Those planning to set up a business must obtain business permission from the Department of Justice, Equality and Law Reform. You'll also need your passport, documentation relating to your entry into Ireland and four passport-size photographs. There's no registration fee.

Registration gives you permission to live in Ireland, but the period is determined by the duration of your work permit (or course, if you're attending a school or college). On registration, you'll be given a Certificate of Registration (also called an Alien's Registration Book or Green Book), which you must keep up-to-date for the duration of your stay in Ireland. Note that it isn't usually possible to enter Ireland as a tourist and change your status to that of an employee, student or resident, nor indeed to remain in Ireland for any purpose other than that for which your visa and permission to remain were originally granted. If you want to change your residence status, you must usually return to your country of residence and re-apply for a visa.

Once you've been legally resident for ten years, you can apply for a 'residence stamp' allowing you to reside permanently. However, unless you become naturalised, you'll still require visas, work permits, etc. Non-EU nationals can acquire Irish citizenship in two ways: the first is to take up residence for five years with an undertaking to live in Ireland for at least 50 days in the two years following naturalisation; the other is to buy an Irish home and make an investment of at least IR£1 million (spread over seven years) in job-creation in Ireland.

Visitors

Visitors from EEA countries (including British dependent territories) don't need a visa to visit Ireland; neither do visitors from Andorra, Argentina, Australia, Bahamas, Barbados, Botswana, Brazil, Brunei, Canada, Chile, Costa Rica, Croatia, Cyprus, the Czech Republic, El Salvador, Estonia, Grenada, Guatemala, Honduras, Hong Kong, Israel, Jamaica, Japan, Republic of Korea, Latvia, Lesotho, Lithuania, Malawi, Malaysia, Malta, Mexico, Monaco, Nauru, New Zealand, Nicaragua, Panama, Paraguay, Poland, San Marino, Singapore, Slovakia, Slovenia, South Africa, Swaziland, Switzerland, Tonga, Trinidad & Tobago, the USA, Uruguay, Venezuela, Western Samoa and Zimbabwe. All other nationalities require at least a 'short-visit visa' (valid for a maximum of 90 days) to visit Ireland. Most visitors require a full passport, although EEA and Swiss nationals can enter Ireland with a national identity card only.

If you require a visa, you should apply to the Irish embassy or consulate in your country of permanent residence and you may be required to attend an interview. If there's no Irish embassy or consulate in your country of residence, you may apply to one in another country or to the Visa Office in Dublin (☎ 01-478 0822). You'll need to submit your passport, which must be valid for at least six months after the intended date of departure from Ireland. You'll also need to send three passport-size photographs and documents relevant to your planned visit, e.g. an invitation from an Irish company or conference organiser if you're visiting on business, a letter of registration from a school or college if visiting for educational purposes, or confirmation of a hotel booking or a letter of reference from an Irish resident who's to accommodate you if you're planning a holiday. Children under 16 years of age who are accompanying a parent or guardian don't require a visa to enter Ireland, provided they have their own passports or are named on those of a parent or guardian.

Note that the granting of a visa doesn't necessarily give you permission to enter the country and that Irish immigration officials have the authority to deny you admission. You should therefore ensure that you take with you the originals or copies of all documents submitted with your visa application. You must have a visa each time you enter Ireland, even if you travel to the UK. This also applies if you have permission to reside in Ireland, when you may apply for a re-entry visa at the Visa Office in Dublin.

The visa fee varies according to your country of residence; your local Irish embassy or consulate will inform you. If you're married to an EU citizen, there's no fee. You should allow at least three weeks (five weeks if you apply by post) for your visa application to be processed, although certain applications are decided more quickly, e.g. those of government officials, 'well-travelled' business people, and those with residence rights in Ireland or another EU country or with valid visas for other EU countries. For an additional fee you can have your application speeded up. There's also an appeals process for those whose visa applications are refused, which is handled by the Department of Justice, Equality and Law Reform (☎ 01-602 8202).

An Irish visa doesn't grant permission to stay in Ireland for any set period. The date of validity shown on the visa indicates only the date by which it must be presented to immigration. The length of stay is decided by immigration officers at the port of entry, who grant 'permission to remain' for up to three months by way of a stamp in your passport. You'll need to produce a valid passport and evidence that you have sufficient funds to support yourself and any dependants. Students need confirmation of registration with a school or college and evidence that the necessary fees have been paid. Employees and the self-employed must present a work permit or confirmation from the DETE that a work permit will be issued. If you require a visa and are coming from the UK, you won't be subject to immigration control on arrival in Ireland, but you may not stay longer than one month without obtaining permission to remain.

RETIREMENT

Retired, financially independent EEA nationals can obtain a residence permit in the normal way (see above), but all non-employed residents must provide proof that they have an adequate income or financial resources to live in Ireland without becoming a burden on the state. There's no specified minimum income for EEA nationals, but it must be more than you'd be paid if you were in receipt of Irish social welfare payments. The minimum income for non-EEA pensioners is under review and details should be sought from the Department of Justice (☎ 01-602 8202).

WORKING

If there's a chance that you or any member of your family will wish to work in Ireland, you must ensure that this will be possible before buying a home. Work permits aren't required by nationals of an EEA country, although they must apply at their local *Garda* (police) station for a residence permit if they plan to stay longer than three months. However, non-EEA nationals who carry out any activity for monetary gain in Ireland require a work permit as well as a residence permit (issued simultaneously for the same duration). If you don't qualify to live and work in Ireland by birthright, family relationship or as a national of an EEA country, obtaining a work permit may be difficult or even impossible.

Applications for work permits must be made by a prospective employer to the Work Permits Section of the Department of Enterprise, Trade and Employment (DETE) in Dublin. Some companies are under the impression that their employees need to apply for their own permits and may need reminding that this isn't the case. Indeed, it's important to note that work permits are specific not only to a company but also to a particular position within that company. If you wish to move to another company or even obtain promotion within a company, you must apply for a new work permit and there's no guarantee that it will be granted. Work permits should be obtained before your arrival in Ireland, or at least an application must be submitted; otherwise, you may be refused entry. Ideally, applications should be made at least six weeks before employment is due to start or before a current permit expires; the current processing time for applications is four weeks. The fees for a work permit are IR£25 per month for the first four months and IR£125 for the next eight months. Further information about working in Ireland can be found in our sister publication, *Living and Working in Ireland* (see page 213).

Many people turn to self-employment or start their own business (see below) to make a living, although this path is strewn with pitfalls for the newcomer and most foreigners don't do sufficient homework before moving to Ireland. While hoping for the best, you should plan for the worst and have a contingency plan and sufficient funds to last until you're established (this also applies to employees).

SELF-EMPLOYMENT

If you're an EU national or a permanent resident with a residence permit, you can work as a self-employed person or as a sole trader in Ireland. If you wish to be self-employed in a profession or trade in Ireland, you must meet certain legal requirements and register with the appropriate organisation. Members of some professions and trades must possess qualifications and certificates recognised in Ireland and are usually required to sit a written examination. You're subject to any professional codes and limitations in force, e.g. a medical practitioner must have his qualifications accepted by the Irish Medical Council. In certain professions, such as the law, it's unusual to be permitted to practise in Ireland without Irish qualifications. You must also show that you're in good standing with the professional authorities in your home country.

If you're thinking of setting up your own business, whether as a sole trader or a limited company, you should seriously consider obtaining quality certification. Certification is becoming increasingly important in Ireland. In fact, in some areas of business it's essential, and the ISO 9000 standards (incorporating the quality assurance standards 9001, 9002 and 9003) are a minimum requirement if you want to supply many foreign-owned multi-nationals. ISO 9000 standards (which are currently being updated) are awarded by the National Standards Authority (☎ 01-807 3800). Another recognised scheme in Ireland is the Q-Mark Based on Business Excellence, awarded by Excellence Ireland, formerly the Irish Quality Association (☎ 01-269 5255; 🖥 www.excellence-ireland.ie), which is important in certain areas. Note that both the Small Firms Association and the Irish Small and Medium Enterprises Association operate group ISO schemes to alleviate the cost of certification.

If you set up as a self-employed person, you should inform your local tax office. You won't need to pay any tax until after your first year of trading. Two months before the year ends, you'll be sent a preliminary tax notice informing you when your first tax payment is due. You must register for VAT if your taxable supplies are likely to exceed certain levels (see below). Unlike many other European countries, Ireland doesn't require new businesses to be registered with the Chamber of Commerce, although doing so can be useful. The address of your local chamber can be obtained from Chambers of Commerce in Ireland (☎ 01-661 2888).

As a self-employed person you won't have the protection of a limited company should your business fail, although there are certain tax advantages. On the other hand, it may be advantageous to operate as a limited company. Always obtain professional advice before deciding whether to operate as a sole trader or form a company in Ireland, as it has far-reaching social security, tax and other consequences (see **Chapter 3**). Anyone with an income in Ireland requires a PPSN (Personal Public Service Number) – previously called a Revenue and Social Insurance (RSI) number – and must register with the Department of Social, Community and Family Affairs (formerly the Department of Social Welfare) using form SE3, available from local Social Welfare Offices or from the Self-Employment Section of the Social Welfare Services Office (☎ 01-874 8444 or 051-874177).

Social Insurance: If you're employed or self-employed in Ireland, you must be registered for Pay Related Social Insurance (PRSI). There's a special scheme for self-employed workers, most of who are liable for what are called PRSI Class S contributions. In addition to covering social insurance, these include a health contribution and an employment and training levy when your income reaches a certain level. In general, PRSI contributions for the self-employed are lower than for salaried employees, but you receive fewer benefits. Unlike an employee, who's entitled to dental and optical treatment, as well as sickness and unemployment benefit, you'll receive little more than an old age pension. Self-employed women are also entitled to maternity benefits, but the wives or partners of self-employed men aren't. Note that, if a relative such as your husband or wife, mother or father, brother or sister, son or daughter helps with a business without being an official partner, they're exempt from PRSI contributions. On the other hand, if they're paid a salary, they should contact the Scope Section of the Department of Social, Community and Family Affairs to find out whether they can be insured.

Tax Registration: As a self-employed person, you must register with the Taxes Central Registration Office (TCRO). If your turnover is expected to be less than IR£100,000 per year, you should use the Small Traders' Registration (STR) form to register for income tax, PAYE/PRSI (if you're an employer) and VAT.

Value Added Tax (VAT): You must register for VAT if your taxable supplies are likely to exceed IR£40,000 (in the case of goods) or IR£20,000 (in the case of services). If your turnover is expected to be below those limits, you may still register for VAT, although you aren't obliged to. It's worth taking advice, however, before doing so. Registration for VAT is done on form TR1 or TR2; it must be declared and paid every two months and an annual return of sales and purchases submitted. You must keep a record of all sales and purchases for six years. You can pay VAT by direct debit or, in certain cases, annually. The Revenue Commissioners publish a guide to *VAT for Small Businesses* (IT49), available from the Revenue's Forms and Leaflets Service (☎ 01-878 0100).

STARTING A BUSINESS

Entrepreneurs were once disparaged in Ireland, although this is far from the case today. It's estimated that there are more than 180,000 small and medium-size businesses (SMEs) in Ireland and that the number is increasing by 10 per cent a year. Details of how to get started in business can be found in *Living and Working in Ireland* (see page 213). Non-EU nationals must obtain 'business permission', for which they must be able to demonstrate that they'll be creating jobs on a long-term basis for EU nationals (e.g. by showing a commitment to training) and that their business will fulfil a need and won't displace an indigenous business. In other words, they must have a USP (unique selling point) and find a niche market. Businesses that create jobs are welcomed with open arms, particularly in areas with high unemployment.

Avoiding Problems: In addition to any problems you may have with the Irish authorities, you may have to contend with people of doubtful business ethics, although these are far less common in Ireland, where trust is an important part of doing business, than in some other countries. However, it's probably wise to have a healthy suspicion of the motives of anyone you do business with (unless it's your mother or spouse), particularly your fellow countrymen. It's usually best to avoid partnerships, as they rarely work and can lead to disaster. In general, you should trust nobody and shouldn't sign anything or pay any money before having a contract checked by a solicitor. It's a sad fact of life that there are foreigners in most countries who prey on their fellow countrymen. In most cases, you're better off dealing with a long-established Irish company with roots in the local community (and therefore a good reputation to protect) rather than your compatriots. Note that, if things go wrong with a 'foreign' partnership, you may not be protected by Irish law.

Research: BEWARE! If you aren't prepared to thoroughly research the market and obtain expert business and legal advice, you shouldn't even think about starting a business in Ireland (or anywhere else for that matter). The key to starting or buying a successful business in Ireland is exhaustive research, research and yet more research (plus innovation, value for money and good service). It's an absolute must to check out the level of competition in a given area. Note that, even when competition is light, there may be insufficient business to sustain another competitor. In some areas, there's already a saturation of trades and services and your chances of making a living are practically zero.

If you're convinced that you have what it takes, don't burn your bridges and sell up abroad, but rent a home in Ireland and spend some time doing research before taking the plunge. You should also lease your business premises (at least initially) rather than buying them outright. Before doing so, however, it's imperative to ensure that you fully understand your rights regarding possible future rent increases and the renewal and termination of a lease.

Some foreigners start businesses in Ireland on a whim and a prayer with little business acumen or money. They're simply asking for trouble. It's no good following your dream of living in Ireland if you end up working all hours of the day and night struggling to make a living from a business that's doomed to failure. Also bear in mind that when a couple operate a business together it can put an intolerable strain on their relationship and many marriages fail under the pressure.

Wealth Warning: Whatever people may tell you, working for yourself isn't easy and requires a lot of hard slog (self-employed people generally work much longer hours than employees), a sizeable investment and sufficient operating funds (under-funding is the major cause of business failure), good organisation (e.g. book-keeping and planning), excellent customer relations, and a measure of luck (although generally the harder you work, the more 'luck' you'll have). Don't be seduced by the apparently relaxed way of life in Ireland – if you want to be a success in business, you cannot play at it.

However, although there are numerous failures for every success story, many foreigners run successful businesses in Ireland. Those who make a go of it do so as a result of extensive market research, wise investment, excellent customer relations, and most important of all, a lot of hard work.

KEEPING IN TOUCH

A recent US$5 billion investment in a state-of-the-art telecommunications network has ensured that communications, both within Ireland and with other countries, are not only modern and efficient (with all the latest technology such as ISDN, VPN, SMDS, etc.) but also among the cheapest in Europe. Postal services too are up to the highest European standards.

Telephone

Until recently, the Irish telephone service was operated exclusively by *Telecom Éireann* (TE). Although a state-controlled company, TE was floated on the stock market in mid-1999 when up to 30 per cent of the company was sold and TE became known as Eircom. Since then its share price has plummeted and only its mobile phone subsidiary Eircell is making a profit. The business sector was deregulated in 1994 and two new telecommunications companies were started by Irish entrepreneurs: TCL (recently taken over by the US telecom giant WorldCom) and Esat Telecom (now part of British Telecom), which has already established a national fibre optic network along CIÉ railway lines and has recently launched an 'Esat Home' scheme offering cheap international calls to domestic customers. Another Irish company, ITL, already provides discounts on international calls and calls to mobile phones, and has set up the country's first local call alternative to Eircom, offering savings of up to 20 per cent. Alcatel, Cable & Wireless, GTS, the ITG Group, Nevada Tele.com and Siemens have entered the business market, and private customers can now choose between providers: ESAT, Ocean, Spirit, Switchcom and Swiftcall, as well as Eircom. Cable companies NTL and Irish Multichannel are also joining the fray by offering telephone services as part of their entertainment packages. ITG have recently set up payphones in major towns but, in early 2001, all domestic services were still provided by Eircom.

Nevertheless, competition has already benefited Eircom customers in better quality service. On average, new customers are connected within ten days (Eircom aims to reduce this to five days), and 97 per cent of faults are remedied within two working days. Impending deregulation has also inevitably brought down prices. Over the past few years, Eircom has dramatically reduced its long-distance and international call charges and no doubt further cuts will be offered as competition increases.

Installation: When moving into a new home in Ireland with a telephone line, you must have the account transferred to your name. If you're planning to move into a property without an existing telephone line, you'll need to have one installed (although it isn't compulsory!). You can have a telephone installed or reconnected without even visiting your local Eircom office. All they need to know is your name and address and the existing telephone number of the property (if there is one). If you're renting, you must pay a deposit or find someone with an Eircom account to act as a guarantor. If you're taking over a property from the previous occupants, you should arrange for the telephone account to be transferred to your name from the day you take possession. Before buying a property, check that all previous telephone bills have been paid, or you may find yourself liable for them.

It can take up to five weeks to get a telephone line installed in Ireland, although it usually takes just five to ten working days in most areas. The cost of having a private telephone line installed is IR£99 and the charge for taking over an existing line (which takes up to a week) is IR£35. Unless you set up a direct debit for bill payments, a deposit of IR£200 is required or a guarantee from someone with an Eircom account.

Using the Telephone: Main towns and their surrounding areas have area codes consisting of two, three or four digits, as listed below:

Arklow	0402	Enniscorthy	054	Roscommon	0903
Athlone	0902	Galway	091	Rosslare	053
Ballina	096	Kilkenny	056	Shannon	061
Bandon	023	Killarney	064	Sligo	071
Bundoran	072	Letterkenny	074	Thuries	0504
Carlow	0503	Limerick	061	Tipperary	062
Castlebar	094	Longford	043	Tralee	066
Cavan	049	Mallow	022	Tuam	093
Clonmel	052	Monaghan	047	Tullamore	0506
Cork	021	Mullingar	044	Waterford	051
Donegal	073	Naas	045	Westport	098
Drogheda	041	Navan	046	Wexford	053
Dublin	01	Nenagh	067	Wicklow	0404
Dundalk	042	Portlaoise	0502	Youghal	024
Ennis	065	Rathluire	063		

Numbers beginning 01 indicate the Dublin area. Numbers starting 02 denote areas in Cork city and county, those beginning with 04 eastern areas, 05 the south-east, 06 the south-west and mid-west, 07 and 09 the west and north-west. Each of these seven areas is covered by a 'white pages' telephone book published by Eircom. Dublin's Golden Pages classified directory is published as a separate volume. In all other areas, the Golden Pages are included with the white pages in a single book. A separate fax directory for Ireland is available from Eircom at a cost of IR£2.25 (☎ 01-660 8488), although many fax numbers are also listed in telephone books. Eircom also publishes a CD-ROM containing all phone and fax numbers in Ireland, which is updated annually and costs around IR£20 (it's obtainable by calling the above number). Telephone and fax numbers, as well as e-mail and website addresses, are now also available via the Internet (🖳 www.goldenpages.ie). Business numbers can be found in the *Europages Online Directory* and the *Kompass Directory*.

Touch-tone dialling is universally available on the Irish public telephone network. Eircom uses the European caller-id standard, so telephones and other devices operating on the North American caller-id standard won't deliver caller-id information when used in Ireland. When making a domestic call to a place with the same area code as the number you're calling from, you don't need to dial the code. However, to make a call to somewhere with a different code, the appropriate area code must be dialled. Note that many Irish numbers outside Dublin were changed to seven-digit numbers (excluding the area code) in August 1999 and others in October 2000 (principally Cork numbers, which are now prefixed by 4 or 7).

When making an international call to Ireland, dial your international access code (e.g 00) followed by 353 for Ireland, then the area code minus the initial 0, then the subscriber's number. A call to Dublin, for example, might begin 00-353-1. In Ireland, you dial 10 for the operator, 114 for the international operator, and 1190 for domestic directory enquiries. The emergency number is 999.

Rental Charges: For line rental Eircom charge IR£11.87 per month and for rental of a standard telephone IR£1.33 per month; both charges are payable bi-monthly.

Call Charges: On 24th October 2000, Eircom announced new tariffs for calls from private phones based on the duration of the call (to the nearest second), subject to a minimum charge on each call, instead of the previous system of 'units'. In some cases, the minimum charge means that you pay the same for a five minute call as for a five second call (no more excuses for cutting short the mother-in-law!). The charge per second varies according to the time of day a call is made and the destination. There are three different 'time bands' for calls made during the day (between 8am and 6pm Mondays to Fridays), in the evening (6pm to 8am Mondays to Fridays) and at the weekend (all day Saturdays and Sundays and on public holidays). There are then various 'distance bands' for calls within Ireland (local, up to 56km and over 56km, as well as calls to 1891 numbers and mobile phones). Details of current call charges can be found in the telephone book.

Payphones: Payphones are widespread in Ireland, where there are more than 7,000. In some countries, it's hard to find a public phone which hasn't been vandalised, but Eircom claim that some 95 per cent of their payphones are working at any given time. Card phones are at least as common as coin-operated phones (in fact they usually appear in pairs) and it's slightly cheaper to use a card phone.

Charges for payphones are still based on a system of 'units'. The minimum charge for all calls (whether local or international) is 1 unit, which costs 20 pence from a coin phone and between 16 and 20 pence from a card phone, depending on the value of the card you use. Phone cards (known as CallCards) are sold in four denominations: an

IR£2 card buys you ten units (20p per unit), an IR£3.50 card 20 units (17.5p per unit), an IR£8 card 50 units (16p per unit) and an IR£16 card 100 units (16p per unit). CallCards are sold at most post offices and petrol stations and at many shops. Credit card phones accept CallCards as well as the four major international credit cards (Visa, Mastercard, Eurocard and American Express). Note that credit card calls are much more expensive than CallCard calls and you're charged an additional fee of 70p for the first unit plus an extra 20p for subsequent units. In competition with Eircom, the ITG Group have now set up payphones throughout Ireland, but its charges are the same as Eircom's.

Eircom offers customers a Charge Card, which can be used in payphones instead of cash or a credit card; the cost of the call is simply added to your home phone bill (but you'll pay a premium for the convenience!). You can buy Global Telecards at post offices, but note that these can be used only for phoning abroad (or phoning Ireland from abroad). Ireland Direct Prepaid Calling Cards are also available for IR£5 or IR£10 for phoning Ireland from abroad. They can be used in 21 countries and offer substantial savings on standard international charges (see below).

International Calls: International Direct Dialling (IDD) calls can be made from Ireland to most countries, from both private and public telephones. A full list of IDD country codes is shown in the information pages of your local white pages directory, plus area codes for main cities and tariffs. The international access code is 00, which must also be used for calling the UK (country code 44, followed by the STD code without its initial 0; for example, to call the Birmingham number 0121-123-4567 from Ireland you would dial 00-44-121-123-4567). To dial a Northern Ireland number, however, you use the prefix 048 followed by the area code (minus the initial 0).

Eircom Directory Enquiries are on 11811 (for Northern Ireland numbers) and 11818 (for other UK numbers); calls cost 38p + VAT for up to three enquiries on 11811 and 76p + VAT per minute (with a minimum charge of 38p + VAT) on 11818. To make a call to a country where there isn't international direct dialling (IDD), you must dial 114 for the international operator.

Internet 'Telephone' Services: The success of the Internet is built on the facility to gather information from computers around the world by connecting to a nearby service for the cost of a local telephone call. If you have relatives, friends or business contacts who are connected to the Internet, you can make international 'calls' for the price of a local telephone call to an Internet service provider (ISP). Once on the Internet, you usually have a choice between paying for the time you spend 'on-line' and paying a set fee for unlimited use. The fee varies according to the provider you use. Most ISPs offer a free trial period, usually a month, with so many free hours of Internet access. Internet users can buy software that effectively turns their personal computer into a voice-based telephone (both parties must have compatible computer software). You also need a sound card, speakers and a microphone. While the quality of communication isn't as good as using a telephone (it's similar to using a CB radio) and you need to arrange call times in advance, making international 'calls' costs virtually nothing.

Mobile Phones: As in most countries, the use of mobile phones has increased dramatically in Ireland and there are now 1.7 million mobile phone users (almost half the population and more than the number of fixed phone lines in Ireland). You may bring your mobile phone to Ireland, although the older analogue phones may not work

(American analogue phones, for example, aren't compatible with the Irish network). Cellular mobile communications in Ireland are regulated by the Office of the Director of Telecommunications Regulation (ODTR), the national regulatory authority established in 1996. There are three GSM mobile networks, Eircell (a subsidiary of Eircom), ESAT Digifone and Meteor (both private companies). All three use the international standard 900/1,800Mhz system.

Fax: Fax machines can be purchased (but not rented) from TEIS, a division of Eircom, and purchased or rented from private companies and stores. Shop around for the best price. Before taking a fax machine to Ireland, check that it will work there (i.e. is compatible) or that it can be modified. Usually, foreign fax machines will send but not receive messages in Ireland. Note also that getting a fax machine repaired in Ireland may be impossible unless the same machine is sold there.

Post Office Services

There's a post office most towns, main railway stations, major airports and ports in Ireland. In addition to the usual post office services, main post offices provide a range of facilities, including domestic and international money orders (postal orders can be purchased at any post office). Business hours at most post offices are usually from 9am until 1pm and from 2 until 5.30pm Mondays to Fridays, and from 9am to 1pm on Saturdays. Main post offices in major towns don't close for lunch and may also provide limited services outside normal business hours. The General Post Office in O'Connell Street, Dublin, is open from 8am to 8pm Mondays to Saturdays and 10am to 6.30pm on Sundays and public holidays, when only stamps and foreign exchange are available. There are also post offices at international airports that are generally open during normal office hours. Sub-post offices in small towns and villages usually close one day per week at 1pm.

The Irish postal service is operated by the state-controlled *An Post*, but the impending liberalisation of the postal market means that around a quarter of postal services will be privatised by the year 2003. International courier companies such as TNT and UPS are likely to be among the first to offer letter post services as soon as it's permitted. In the meantime, *An Post*'s service is as efficient, reliable and inexpensive as any in Europe.

Domestic post is known as 'first class' mail (there's no second class mail in Ireland!) and 90 per cent is delivered the next day, provided it's posted before the specified latest posting time (which varies from area to area). Letters weighing up to 25g cost 30p. There's no longer a cheaper rate for open letters, but here are reduced rates for newspapers and magazines.

Swiftpost is a guaranteed next day service (before 12.30pm in town centres and industrial estates), which is also subject to latest posting times, costing IR£2 for letters up to 100g. Registered post is tracked and you're compensated for loss or damage. You pay a surcharge on the normal first class letter rate according to how much compensation you require: IR£2 for up to IR£250, IR£2.50 for up to IR£750, and IR£3 for up to IR£1,250.

An Post provides numerous other services including Private Box (your mail is addressed to a PO Box and held until collected), Private Posting Box (*An Post* collects from you for an annual fee), Collection Service (you pay for each collection), Private

Bag (your post is delivered in a locked bag), Callers Service (you collect from your nearest post office), Retention (your post is held for collection), Redirection (if you have recently moved), Diversion (to another address in the same area), Poste Restante (non-residents' post can be held for up to three months free of charge), and Freepost.

International Parcel & Courier Services: International parcels are handled by a branch of *An Post* called Special Delivery Services (SDS), which also provides express mail and courier services, as do Irish railways and airlines, and international (e.g. DHL and UPS) and domestic courier companies.

GETTING THERE

Although it isn't so important if you're planning to live permanently in Ireland and stay put, one of the major considerations when buying a holiday home there is the cost of getting to it from your home abroad. How long will it take, including journeys to and from airports, ports and railway stations? How frequent are flights or ferries at the time(s) of year when you plan to travel? Are direct flights available from an airport near you? Is it feasible to travel by car, bearing in mind the high cost of ferries? What's the cost of travel from your home country to the region where you're planning to buy a home in Ireland? Are off-season discounts or inexpensive charter flights available? Are costs likely to rise or fall in the future? If a long journey is involved, you should bear in mind that it may take you a day or two to recover, e.g. from jet-lag. Obviously, the time and cost of traveling to a home in Ireland will be more important if you're planning to spend frequent long weekends there, rather than a few long stays each year.

Airline Services: There are nine airports in the Republic of Ireland: Donegal in the north; Sligo, Knock (also called Connaught or Connacht), Galway (or Connemara), Shannon, and Kerry in the west; Cork and Waterford in the south; and Dublin in the east. Dublin and Shannon are the main international 'gateway' airports and are served by scheduled flights from most European capitals and major cities. These are operated by Alitalia, British Airways, British Midland, City Jet, Crossair, Air France, Iberia, Jersey European, Lufthansa, Manx Airlines, Romanian Airlines, Ryanair, SAS (Scandinavian Air Systems), Swissair, TAP Air Portugal, and Viva Air. Aer Lingus, Ireland's national airline, also operates a large number of flights to and from Europe and, with its hostesses' lilting Irish accents and emerald green uniforms, will give you a taste of Ireland even before you arrive. You can fly direct to Dublin from Alicante, Amsterdam, Barcelona, Berlin, Bonn, Brussels, Copenhagen, Dusseldorf, Faro, Frankfurt, Hamburg, Helsinki, Lisbon, Madrid, Malaga, Milan, Moscow, Munich, Nice, Palma, Paris, Rome, Stockholm, Stuttgart, Valetta and Zurich.

There are also direct flights to Dublin from the five main London airports (including City Airport) as well as from most regional British airports. Shannon is served direct from Heathrow, Gatwick, Belfast, Birmingham and Manchester, as well as Bucharest, Dusseldorf, Jeddah, Minsk, Paris, Stuttgart, Zurich and, of course, Dublin. Cork has direct flights from Belfast, Birmingham, Bristol, Exeter, Isle of Man, Jersey, Heathrow, Gatwick, Stansted, Manchester, Newquay and Plymouth, in addition to Amsterdam, Frankfurt, Paris, Rennes and Rotterdam. There are flights to Kerry from Luton and Manchester, and to Knock and Waterford from Stansted and Manchester. Donegal, Galway and Sligo have flights from Dublin only.

Dublin and Shannon are the only airports handling flights from North America. Direct scheduled services operate from Boston, Chicago, Los Angeles, Newark and New York into both airports. Apart from Aer Lingus, which now operates in partnership with American Airlines, the major carriers are Delta Air Lines and Continental, who operate direct services from New York and Newark into Shannon and Dublin. Perhaps the most unlikely service is from Miami to Shannon with the Russian airline Aeroflot. Many other airlines fly to major European cities (such as London) from where numerous connecting flights to Ireland are available. There's a wide range of promotional air fares to Ireland. Super Apex fares can be had from London for as little as GB£69 return, and Aer Lingus, British Midland and Ryanair all offer advance booking discounts. Conversely, many airlines operate a late booking service, but this isn't recommended if you want to be sure of a seat. There are weekend return fares from most London airports to Dublin or Cork costing between IR£70 and IR£90 with most airlines. Some people even 'commute' to London from homes in Ireland in preference to buying property in the London suburbs, which would cost two or three times as much! Students with an International Student Identity Card (ISIC) can obtain discounts on certain flights, e.g. between Britain and Ireland, as well as on transatlantic flights.

Charter Flights: A number of companies in North America offer inexpensive charter flights to Ireland, such as American Holidays, American Trans Air, JWT, Keytours, Pleasure Break Vacations, Sceptre Charters, Tour America, and Translift Leisure from the USA, and Air Transat Holidays, Canada 3000, CIÉ Tours, Regent Holidays, and Sunquest Vacations from Canada. However, make sure that you read the small print, as there are often drawbacks such as heavy cancellation charges and restrictions on changing the dates of your flights. Sometimes charter companies will reserve the right to cancel your flight or change the dates and times of travel, or even add 'fuel surcharges' after you've paid the standard fare. If you're flying on to other destinations, it's usually cheaper to pay for your onward travel at the same time as your transatlantic flight. Seasonal charter flights are also available from various parts of Europe: CIÉ Tours operate from a number of German airports; Euralair, Falcon/JWT from Spain; GO Holidays, Star Europe, and TAT from France; Maersk Air from Denmark; Transwede from Stockholm; TAP from Faro in Portugal; and Crossair from Zurich. There are also special charter flights to Knock from Amsterdam, Dusseldorf, Frankfurt, Munich and Zurich during the summer (for those wanting to visit the Marian shrine). If you arrive in Ireland on a one-way ticket and need to buy your flight home in Ireland, must pay a departure tax (IR£10 for North America and IR£5 for Europe), which is usually included in the ticket price.

The shop at Shannon Airport, 26km (16mi) west of Limerick, although no longer strictly 'duty-free' (since the abolition of the duty-free system in mid-1999), still offers a wide variety of goods, including traditional Irish products such as Donegal tweed, Waterford crystal, Connemara rugs and marble. If you don't want to be weighed down by all your purchases during your stay in Ireland, you can buy them as you leave, in which case everything will be loaded straight onto the plane without you even having to pay surplus baggage charges. And, of course, if you're returning to a non-EU country, you can save 20 per cent VAT (see **Shopping** on page 62).

Ferries: Sadly, the days of leisurely transatlantic crossings by liner are gone, and the only regular scheduled sea-crossings to Ireland are from France and Britain. From various parts of Wales, there's a choice of four routes and three operators: Fishguard to Rosslare (Stena Line), Pembroke to Rosslare (Irish Ferries or Stena Line), Swansea to Cork (Swansea-Cork Ferries), and Holyhead to Dublin (Irish Ferries or Stena Line) or Dun Laoghaire (pronounced 'leary') near Dublin (Stena Line). There's also a Liverpool/Dublin service and a seasonal service to Dublin from the Isle of Man, both operated by the Isle of Man Steam Packet Company (aka Superseacat). If you're travelling from Scotland or northern England, it's easier to cross to Northern Ireland. Stena offer a Stranraer/Belfast service and Irish Ferries a Cairnryan/Larne link (slightly further north). These are the shortest crossings to Ireland from mainland Britain, with Irish Ferries' Jetliner taking just one hour.

Crossing times from the Welsh ports vary from 99 minutes on Stena Line's HSS (High-speed Sea Service) from Holyhead to Dun Laoghaire and their Lynx service from Fishguard to Rosslare (near Wexford), to ten hours on the Swansea-Cork route, allowing you sleep your way to the Emerald Isle. All ferries, including catamarans, take cars and there are between one and six crossings daily in each direction, depending on the route and the time of year. There's little to choose between the different operators for comfort and standard of service, but fares vary considerably depending on the time of year and the amount of time you want to spend on the Irish Sea. Some mid-summer fares are more than double those for winter crossings and you pay a premium for the faster services. Stena's HSS, for example, costs more than twice as much as their three-and-a-half hour ferry crossing at peak times. Where previously the standard fare was for a car, driver and up to four passengers, the ferry companies have now introduced lower fares for car-plus-driver. The comparisons below, however, are of fares for a car, driver and up to four passengers.

Stena's fares are from GB£134 (low season) to GB£169 (high season) for a five-day return on the Holyhead/Dublin Port ferry and from GB£169 to GB£408 return on the HSS into Dun Laoghaire. There are special deals to be had, such as a Wednesday Special and Two-Day Return, which can cost as little as GB£129. On the Fishguard/Rosslare route, ther's a choice between a standard ferry and a faster Lynx service. Prices range from GB£129 to GB£298 for the ferry and from GB£169 to GB£438 for the Lynx. The Lynx Summer Return or Summer Sunday Return costs from GB£269.

Irish Ferries' standard fares start at GB£139 return for their Pembroke/Rosslare ferry (a 3fl hour crossing), rising to GB£298 in the summer. The slightly faster (3/ hours) Holyhead/Dublin route costs from GB£159 to GB£339 return. Again there are deals such as a Wednesday Special, 48-hour Special and Summer Sunday Special from just GB£105 return. Swansea-Cork's overnight service costs from GB£150 to GB£378 if you're prepared to sleep in a chair (cabins are extra). Their special offers include a Weekend Return, Sunday Saver and a Midweek Special starting at GB£129 return. Ferries leave Swansea at 9pm and arrive in Cork at 7am. They run approximately every two days in each direction in low season (mid-March to mid-June and mid-September to mid-January) and daily in high season (mid-June to mid-September). There are no sailings between mid-January and mid-March. The Superseacat service from Liverpool to Dublin runs daily and takes 3fl hours. A standard six-day return fare for four people and a car starts at GB£192 in low season, rising to GB£332 in mid-summer. Again there are reduced fares such as a Day Return, Two-Day Return and Wednesday Special Return.

Irish Ferries' services from France operate from Cherbourg and Roscoff to Rosslare, while Brittany Ferries sail from Roscoff to Cork. Crossings take around 15 hours from Roscoff and around 17 hours from Cherbourg. Brittany's weekly Roscoff/Cork service costs from IR£189 (low season) to IR£509 (high season) return for a car, driver and one passenger. Irish Ferries operate approximately every other day (throughout the year on the Cherbourg route, between April and November only on the Roscoff route), with fares between IR£189 (low season) and IR£548 (high season) for a car and two people. Cabins are extra.

Those who prefer to leave their car at home can let the train take the strain. All ferry services from the UK are scheduled to link with InterCity trains serving Fishguard, Holyhead, Swansea and Stranraer, and some Irish train services connect with incoming ferries. Inclusive train/ferry tickets are available from as little as IR£42 return from Manchester or Liverpool to Dublin. Irish Ferries offer their own train/ferry service with fares from London to Dublin via Holyhead as low as GB£39 (low season) and GB£59 (high season) return per person. As well as being a good deal cheaper than taking the car, the rail route can save you time. For example, London (Euston) to Dublin via Holyhead/Dun Laoghaire takes around 11 hours and London (Paddington) to Wexford via Fishguard/Rosslare around 12 hours 30 minutes.

Irish Ferries also offer a coach/ferry service via Holyhead or Pembroke which is even cheaper, London/Dublin fares starting at just GB£29 return per person. Eurolines, a National Express company, operate daily coach/ferry services from major UK cities to Cork, Dublin, Limerick, Tralee, Waterford and other main towns, with onward connections to more than 100 destinations throughout Ireland. There's a choice of single, return (valid for six months) and open-dated return tickets. Prices for the London/Dublin route are similar to those of Irish Ferries. Other bus services are provided by Irish Bus and numerous small companies that can be found on the back pages of Irish newspapers (available in Britain). The disadvantages of coach travel (slowness and relative discomfort) are offset by the advantage of being able to reach parts of Ireland other services cannot.

GETTING AROUND BY PUBLIC TRANSPORT

Public transport in Ireland is provided by CIÉ (*Coras Iopair Éireann*), the state-subsidised national transport company, in addition to various private operators. CIÉ has three subsidiaries, Irish Rail (*Iarnród Éireann*), Irish Bus (*Bus Éireann*), and Dublin Bus (*Bus Átha Cliath*), which together carry more than 300 million passengers per year, the highest number since the late '70s. As part of the government's commitment to ease the increasing urban grid-lock caused by cars and commercial vehicles, CIÉ is to invest IR£25 million a year in the bus network (over half of which will be swallowed by Dublin Bus), and a massive IR£700 million in the railway system between 1999 and 2007.

Public transport is generally good in Ireland, although rail services are sparse or non-existent in many areas and buses are sometimes infrequent. Irish railways provide an efficient and reasonably fast rail service and there are comprehensive intercity bus and domestic airline services. Taxis are common in main towns and cities, although they aren't a cheap form of transport. Public transport in major cities, particularly in Dublin, is inexpensive and efficient, and includes comprehensive bus and suburban rail networks. Around Dublin, systems are integrated so that the same ticket can be used for all services and a range of commuter and visitor tickets are also available. There are travel agencies in all major cities and large towns, and specialist agencies, such as USIT (☎ 01-679 8833) for young travellers.

Bus: The efficient national bus service in Ireland is operated by Irish Bus (*Bus Éireann*), which is part of CIÉ. Buses are generally cheaper than trains and reach even the most remote corners of the country. A return fare from Dublin to Cork, for example, costs less than IR£20. Irish Bus also operates services in the cities of Cork, Galway, Limerick and Waterford, and has links between Cork airport and Cork city, and between Shannon airport and Limerick town. Alternative services are provided by Expressway (which covers the main routes), Nestor Bus (which operates a Galway/Dublin service) and Suirway Bus Service in Waterford, among others. You can obtain timetables for Expressway and other provincial services from the CIÉ and from tourist offices and some newsagents.

Dublin Bus (*Bus Átha Cliath*), another branch of CIÉ, is a virtual monopoly operating all public bus services in the greater Dublin area (which includes parts of the counties of Wicklow, Kildare and Meath). Dublin Bus has invested heavily in new buses and infrastructure and has had a 15 per cent increase in passengers over the last ten years. It has also increased its number of routes and introduced new services such as City Imp (high-frequency minibuses operating on six routes), Nitelink (a Thursday to Saturday night service operating hourly between 0.30 and 4.30am on 15 routes), Cityswift (operating along ten 'quality corridors' every six minutes at peak times), Cityspeed (a special commuter service with few stops), Airlink (connecting Dublin Airport to the city centre and bus and rail stations and running every 20 minutes from early in the morning to 11pm, seven days a week), and Railink (between the three main stations: Heuston, Connolly and Tara Street).

An 'autofare' system operates on around half the routes, which means that you need to have the exact fare as drivers don't handle cash. Alternatively you can buy '2 EASY' cards, which are pre-paid for two journeys at the same fare (e.g. 55p or IR£1) and must be used within a month. There's a wide range of other discounted pre-paid tickets, from day returns to monthly seasons, which can be purchased at the CIÉ Desk at Dublin Airport, the head office of Dublin Bus at 59 O'Connell Street, and at any of the 200 plus bus ticket agencies throughout the city and its suburbs. Dublin is divided into 'hop' zones for buses and trains: short, medium, long and giant, with fares varying accordingly. There are other regional bus companies (in addition to Dublin Bus) such as Suirway, which operates in the Waterford area.

Note that destinations shown on the front of buses are often in Irish (Dublin, for example, may be shown as *Átha Cliath*) so a timetable comes in handy for translation purposes. But don't try to find a place called *An Lár* – it means 'town centre'! Concessionary bus tickets and Travelsave stamps are covered in the section on rail travel below.

Rail: The Irish rail network is operated by the Irish Rail (*Iarnród Éireann*) arm of CIÉ, which has 'serious' financial problems, running at an annual loss of over IR£50 million and state supported to the tune of over IR£90 million per year. Nevertheless, it has an increasing number of passengers, totalling some 30 million annually. A IR£1 billion restructuring plan, On Track 2000, has recently been given government and EU support.

Most railway lines radiate from Dublin, so the network isn't much good for travelling up and down the west coast, for example, and there are no lines at all north of Sligo. Mainline services operate between Dublin and Ballina, Ennis, Galway, Limerick, Rosslare harbour, Waterford, Sligo, Tralee and Westport, the last three routes being the object of Irish Rail's latest investment programme. Trains run frequently between the major airports and nearby city centres; services are reliable and efficient and fares reasonable. The trains themselves are fairly modern and clean and, although in some parts railwaymen still operate the signals from little signal boxes and even open level crossing gates by hand, computerisation is inexorably bringing the Irish rail system 'up to date'.

There are two categories of rail ticket: standard and super standard (there are no first and second class people in Ireland!). A standard single from Dublin to Cork costs around IR£35 (almost twice the bus fare) and a super standard single IR£5 more. The Belfast/Dublin Enterprise service is a new cross-border service (it commenced in September 1997) which is a joint Irish Rail/Northern Ireland Railways initiative supported by the EU as part of its European High Speed Railway Network. Its 90mph diesel trains currently complete the 113 mile trip in two hours at a cost of IR£19 (IR£29 for a return).

The Dublin area is served by the DART (Dublin Area Rapid Transit) suburban rail system, which connects 25 stations around the capital from Howth in the north to Bray in the south – soon to be increased to 27 with extensions to Malahide and Greystones. Daily, weekly, monthly and annual tickets are available as well as a four-day Explorer. In late 2000, the government announced a IR£14.5 billion transport plan for Dublin city, which would create a 'metro' line extending from Shanganagh near Bray in the south to Dublin airport and Swords in the north, and west as far as Quarryvale with an underground section in the city centre. The first sections of the new system, from Tallaght in the south-west to the city centre and from Sandyford to St Stephen's Green just to the south of the city, are due to be open by 2003.

Air: It's possible to fly between major towns in Ireland, although most internal flights are routed via Dublin. In any case, the distances involved are quite small: the longest possible flight, from Donegal in the north to Cork in the south (via Dublin), is only 400km (ca. 250mi). Aer Lingus, Ireland Airways and Ryanair offer services between Dublin and Knock, Cork, Donegal, Kerry, Shannon, Galway and Sligo. Aer Árann provides flights to the Aran Islands from Galway airport. Private aeroplanes and helicopters can be rented from Dublin and Shannon airports. Airlink Airways (☎ 094-23349) and West Air (☎ 061-475166) have small planes for hire and Celtic Helicopters (☎ 01-890 1349) provide helicopters. Note that private aircraft heading for Dublin must land at Dublin airport, as there are no private airfields near the capital.

Boat: Most of the islands off the west coast of Ireland can be reached by boat (the type of vessel varies from a modern hydrofoil to a converted Second World War landing craft), although some only in the summer months. The Irish Tourist Board publishes details of the various island boat services.

Taxi: Telephone numbers of local taxi companies are listed under 'Taxis & Taxicabs' in the Golden Pages. In Dublin and Cork, all taxis have meters (the minimum fare in Dublin is IR£1.90 – lower than in most other major European cities). Elsewhere, standard fares generally apply but, as in most countries, it pays to confirm the fare before setting off. On the whole, Irish taxis wait at ranks and outside airports, railway stations and larger hotels, but they can also be stopped in the street. The number of taxis in Dublin has been increased (a recent government proposal to deregulate taxi services caused nationwide blockades) and waiting times correspondingly reduced – except on Friday and Saturday nights, when it's almost impossible to get one! Irish taxi drivers usually expect a tip of around 10 per cent of the fare, but are probably unique in occasionally rounding the fare *down* to the nearest punt!

DRIVING IN IRELAND

Motoring in most parts of Ireland contrasts strongly with almost everywhere else in Europe. There's only some 60km (40mi) of motorway (all of it near Dublin) and barely more than twice as much dual carriageway in the whole country. All other roads have just a single lane in each direction (although there's sometimes an extra lane on long hills for slow vehicles). A peculiarity of these roads is their so-called hard shoulder, which is indicated by broken yellow lines – so-called because it's used in rather a different way from hard shoulders in most other countries. Instead of being reserved for breakdowns or other emergencies, it's also used for overtaking. This doesn't mean that the Irish overtake on the inside, but that when you see a vehicle approaching rapidly from behind with the intention of overtaking, you're expected to pull over onto the hard shoulder to let it pass. Even more disconcerting is to find an oncoming vehicle heading straight towards you on your side of the road, forcing you to veer onto the hard shoulder to avoid a head-on collision. The Irish won't thank you for doing so – not because they're inconsiderate, but because to them it's a completely normal manoeuvre.

Another feature of Irish roads is their unevenness. Although much resurfacing work is being done, most roads are positively bumpy and you need to keep a weather eye out for pot holes; it's a great relief to come upon one of the strips of new or resurfaced road which will reassure you that your suspension is still working properly (or confirm that it isn't, as the case may be!).

Outside the cities and towns, roads are often deserted and traffic jams rare. Because there are few ring roads or bypasses, however, most towns suffer from congestion, which is particularly bad in Cork and Dublin. Although statistics state that, of the major European capitals, Dublin has one of the lowest car-to-population ratios, you're no better advised to take your car into the city centre than to drive into the middle of London, Paris or Rome. The current growth in Ireland's population and economy, however, is expected to lead to an increase of more than 50 per cent in the number of cars on the roads to 1.6 million (or one car for every 2.75 people) by the year 2006. Despite the government's efforts to persuade more people to use public transport, Irish car registrations in January/February 2000 were almost 50 per cent up on the same period the year before.

There's currently only one place in Ireland where you'll be charged a toll (less than IR£1 per car) for using a road: on the M50 and the R131 when crossing the Liffey near the capital. However, the government has recently announced plans to introduce a nationwide network of toll roads, starting with a 35km (22mi) stretch linking the towns of Kilcock and Kinnegad in Co. Westmeath and with a new

Waterford bypass. Other planned toll roads are the Portlaoise/Castletown stretch of the N8, the Nenagh/Limerick part of the N7, the Clonee/Kells section of the N3 and a Fermoy bypass, as well as the long-awaited completion of Dublin's ring-road by western and eastern bypasses (up to 6km of which will run through a tunnel under Dublin Bay). These will mean that drivers commuting into and out of Dublin on most of the main 'corridors' could face daily charges of up to IR£8 (or IR£2,000 per year!).

The speed limit on motorways is 70mph (113kph), on other main roads 60mph (97kph) and in built-up areas 30mph (48kph), unless otherwise indicated (the speed limit signs are in miles per hour). 'Traffic calming' schemes have been introduced in many parts of the country in an attempt to slow traffic as it approaches built-up areas. You can be fined up to IR£150 for a first offence and up to IR£350 for a second if you exceed these limits. If you're foolish enough to be caught a third time within a year of your second offence, you can be imprisoned for up to three months. As in Britain, cars drive on the left side of the road (when not in the middle) and the wearing of seat belts is compulsory for both front and rear passengers. The legal limit of alcohol in the blood is 0.08 per cent and it's a law which is strictly enforced: contravention can lead to fines of IR£1,000, a year's disqualification and even a jail sentence.

Road signs, like all signs, are generally in both English and Gaelic, although in some of the more remote western areas (where Irish is in everyday use) English may be dispensed with. Further confusion can be caused by the use of both miles and kilometres on road signs to indicate distances. The newer green and white signs are in kilometres, whereas the traditional black-on-white signs (which are now seen only occasionally) are in miles. Roads are in the process of being renumbered and what used to be T (trunk) and L (link) roads are being converted to N (national) and R (regional) roads – you'll encounter both old and new numbers on road signs, although again the old system is gradually disappearing.

Petrol stations usually stay open until around 8pm and in villages they open after Sunday Mass. If you've run out of petrol or are about to and cannot find a station open, a knock on the door and a polite request will generally get the pumps going. All grades of petrol and diesel are widely available in Ireland, where prices tend to be a little lower than in Britain.

Yellow lines along the road indicate parking or waiting restrictions. In Dublin you'll need to park at a meter or in a multi-storey car park (where the charge is around IR£1.30 per hour), whereas in the centre of Cork and most other main towns a disc system is used to control parking. Discs can be bought singly (for 50 pence of IR£1) or in books of ten at shops and garages near town centres.

Those with vehicles registered in Ireland will need to pay motor tax, which is done at the Motor Tax Office (there's one in each county), not at post offices, and is levied on a sliding scale according to a vehicle's engine capacity, from IR£98 for engines of less than 1,000cc up to IR£849 for engines over 3,000cc. It's possible to pay motor tax half-yearly or even quarterly, but of course you'll pay more per year if you do.

The introduction of the National Car Test system in January 2000 means that from the year 2002 all vehicles more than four years old will have to be tested for roadworthiness every two years.

Because of the relative scarcity of traffic in most parts of Ireland, motorists tend to be less aggressive than those found in many other countries. That isn't to say that they're necessarily good or even patient drivers. Although a booklet entitled *The*

Rules of the Road is obtainable from post offices for just IR£1, few drivers seem to have assimilated its contents. In fact, Irish drivers tend to fall into two categories: fast or very slow. Nevertheless, outside the main cities you'll rarely hear a horn sounded in anger and, if raised fingers are a common sight, they invariably indicate thanks rather than rudeness. It's common also to encounter animals on the road, particularly sheep, which will happily graze at the roadside inches from passing traffic. Quite often you'll find yourself following tractors or other farm machinery or one of those very slow drivers (usually wearing tweed caps), who may pull onto and off the road without warning or signals at that unhurried pace which is the norm in rural Ireland. Foreigners are advised to pick up a free leaflet entitled *Traffic Rules*, which explains (in English, French and German) the most common road signs.

If your car breaks down there's no need to worry or feel embarrassed as you might at home. You're unlikely to be left standing at the side of the road for long and the next vehicle will probably stop to find out what's wrong and help you to a garage or at least seek out a mechanic to get you back on the road. Breakdown services are available from AIT (☎ 01-800 667788) and FIA (☎ 01-800 535005) and are included with membership of the AA (☎ 01-697 9977) and RAC (☎ 01-676 0113).

If you're unfortunate enough to be involved in a road accident, you're required by law to stop immediately and to remain at the scene of the accident long enough to inform the *Gardaí* (police) and give your name, address (and those of the vehicle's owner if it isn't yours), registration number and insurance details to anyone else involved in the accident. You should also, of course, obtain the same information from them as well as the particulars of any witnesses. Before leaving the scene of the accident, you should take photographs or make drawings of the scene and note any relevant information, such as the date, time and location of the accident, the weather and road conditions, the speed of the vehicles involved, any road signs or markings, and, if relevant, details of any injuries sustained.

Driving Licences

The minimum age for driving in Ireland is 17 for a motor car or a motorcycle with an engine capacity over 125cc and 16 for a motorcycle up to 125cc (note also that motorcyclists are restricted to machines of less than 350cc for two years after passing their test). There's no maximum age for obtaining your first licence and it has been known for people in their late 70s to take driving lessons for the first time. Anyone can drive in Ireland on a foreign or international driving licence for up to 12 months, even in an Irish-registered vehicle. Drivers of EU-registered vehicles don't require a green card, although it's recommended (see below). Those living permanently in Ireland, on the other hand, must obtain an Irish driving licence within one year of taking up residence. Citizens of Australia, Iceland, Japan, Liechtenstein, South Africa and Switzerland can exchange their national licences for an Irish one (this is no longer necessary for EU nationals). All other foreigners must apply for a provisional Irish driving licence (valid for two years) and take a driving test in Ireland.

Presently, the Irish driving test consists of a practical test only, but a written test similar to the British one is likely to be introduced in the near future. The cost of a driving test is IR£30. No medical examination is necessary unless you wish to obtain a truck or bus licence or suffer from a specified illness (e.g. epilepsy) or disability. If it's your first driving test, however, you'll need to produce an eyesight report. Driving licences aren't issued for life, but must be renewed every ten years at a cost of IR£20. This isn't simply because they wear out, but so that you can be recognised more easily from your photograph, which must be replaced at the same time.

Car Insurance

Under Irish law, all motor vehicles, trailers and semi-trailers must be insured when entering Ireland. However, it isn't mandatory for cars insured in most European countries to have an international insurance 'green card' (see below) in Ireland. Motorists insured in an EU country, the Czech Republic, Hungary, Liechtenstein, Norway, Slovakia and Switzerland are automatically covered for third-party liability in Ireland. There are essentially two categories of car insurance available in Ireland: third-party and comprehensive.

Third-Party: Third-party insurance is compulsory and is the minimum required by law. A third party is anyone apart from the driver, including your own passengers, and you must be insured against third-party claims for personal injury and damage to property. There's no limit to your liability if you have third-party insurance, although it won't usually cover you against natural hazards such as rocks falling on your car. Additional cover can be purchased to protect against personal accidents as well as fire, theft (of the car or its contents), windscreen damage, roadside assistance, etc. Personal accident cover, for example, costs an additional IR£10 to IR£20 per year.

Comprehensive: Comprehensive insurance usually covers all the risks listed above and includes damage to your own vehicle irrespective of how it's caused. It usually includes theft of factory-fitted stereo systems and may also cover legal expenses in the event of a court case. Comprehensive cover is usually available on all vehicles irrespective of age, but cars more over four years old may need to be inspected before insurance is granted. Note that comprehensive cover may be compulsory for lease and credit purchase contracts. Irish insurance doesn't always pay for a replacement car when yours is being repaired after an accident, although this is becoming more common.

Premiums: Insurance premiums in Ireland vary enormously according to numerous factors including the kind of insurance, the type and make of car, your age and sex, your accident record, and the area where you live. A policy which costs IR£200 for a middle-aged female with a good driving record living in the country may cost a young Dublin man with a poor record IR£3,000. There are some 25 companies providing car insurance in Ireland, each offering different packages and rates. Some companies separate cars into insurance brackets or groups, although most vary their rates according to the value, age and engine size of a car. Some won't insure high performance vehicles, while others offer low-cost policies for older drivers, e.g. those aged over 50 or 55, with a good safety record. Your annual mileage, on the other hand, won't usually affect the price you pay. Most companies in Ireland charge men and women different rates (women generally pay less). If you've been driving for a year or more without an insurance claim, you may be entitled to a 'no-claims bonus', which is usually transferable from one insurance company to another provided that you furnish evidence of no claims. You should therefore shop around or, better still, use an insurance broker.

Car insurance is also available from a number of foreign insurance companies registered in Ireland. In general, the Irish car insurance market is quite stable and there are few 'cowboy' operators to be avoided. Policies for periods of less than one year are available for a small premium from a few companies in Ireland. There's no VAT on insurance premiums, but there's a government levy of 2 per cent, which goes into a fund to pay for injuries caused by uninsured drivers.

Green Cards: All Irish insurance companies and most other insurance companies in western Europe provide an automatic 'green card', which extends your existing insurance cover (e.g. comprehensive) to most other European countries. This is available on request and is usually free. The exception is Britain, where insurance companies usually provide only third-party cover in other EU countries and charge for a green card which is issued for short periods only (i.e. 30 to 45 days) and for a maximum number of days per year, e.g. 90. However, you should shop around, as some companies allow drivers a green card for up to six months per year. If you're British and have comprehensive insurance, it's wise to have a green card when visiting Ireland.

If you drive a British-registered car and spend more than six months per year in other EU countries, you may need to take out a special (i.e. expensive) European insurance policy or obtain insurance with a European company. Another alternative is to insure your car with a British insurance company in Ireland. Note that from 1995, EU rules have required that all vehicles be insured in their country of registration. For example, if you keep a British-registered car in Ireland, you can insure it through an insurance agent in Ireland, but it must be with a UK-based insurance company. If you want to insure your car with an Irish company, you'll need to re-register it in Ireland. Similarly, if you have an Irish-registered car, it must be insured with an Irish insurance company (or a foreign insurance company registered in Ireland). Irish residents are obliged to display a valid insurance disc on their cars and failure to do so can result in a fine of IR£50.

Car Crime

All European countries have a problem with car crime, i.e. thefts of and from cars, but happily Ireland's is less severe than most, except perhaps in Dublin, where quite a few cars are stolen (often by young joyriders). It goes without saying that you should always lock your car and never leave any valuables inside. If you drive anything other than a worthless heap, you should have theft insurance, which includes your car stereo and belongings. If you drive a new or valuable car, it's wise to have it fitted with an alarm, an engine immobiliser (the best system) or another anti-theft device, plus a visible deterrent such as a steering or gear-stick lock. It's particularly important to protect your car if you own a model that's desirable to professional car thieves, e.g. most new sports and executive models, which are often stolen by crooks to order.

Few cars are fitted with deadlocks and most can be broken into in seconds by a competent thief. Even the best security system won't prevent someone from breaking into your car (which usually takes expert thieves a matter of seconds) and may not stop your car being stolen, but it will at least make it more difficult and may persuade a thief to look for an easier target.

Thieves often smash windows to steal stereo systems and articles from cars, even things of little value such as sunglasses or cigarettes. When leaving your car unattended, don't forget to remove your mobile phone and store any valuables (including clothes) in the boot (trunk). Note, however, that storing valuables in the boot isn't foolproof, as an empty car may tempt a thief to force open the boot with a crowbar. Some people leave the boot of their car unlocked (and empty) to avoid having it broken open, as repairs can be expensive. It's never wise to leave your original car papers in your car (which will help a thief dispose of it). When parking overnight or when it's dark, you should use a secure overnight car park or garage, or at least in a well-lit area. If possible, avoid parking in insecure long-term car parks, as these are favourite hunting grounds for car thieves. Foreign-registered cars, particularly camper vans and mobile homes, are popular targets, especially when parked in ferry ports.

If your car (or any of its contents) is stolen, report it to the police in the area where it occurred. You can report it by telephone but must go to the police station to complete a report. Don't, however, expect the police to find the car or stolen items or even to take any interest in your loss. Report a theft to your insurance company as soon as possible.

Car Rental

Renting (hiring) a car Ireland isn't cheap. Although there's considerable competition among rental companies, demand for rental cars has increased over the last few years as more and more people visit Ireland. At best the rates are comparable with those in France and the UK, but high by US standards. A small saloon car (group A), for example, costs from around IR£135 per week compared with IR£95 in Spain, IR£140 in France, and IR£145 in the UK. Seasonal variations, on the other hand, are smaller than in some countries. If you're paying IR£135 for a week's rental of a small car in the low season, you should expect to pay only an extra IR£20 or IR£30 in the summer. International companies such as Avis, Hertz and Budget have offices at major airports and in main towns, as do Irish companies such as Murrays Europcar (☎ 01-614 2888). Car rental companies are listed in the Golden Pages under 'Car Hire'.

While smaller companies may offer cheaper rates, they usually charge extra for leaving the car anywhere other than where you rented it (particularly if it's in the middle of nowhere), whereas the multi-nationals allow you to do so free, at least on a week's rental or longer (you'll need to pay around IR£30 extra for the same facility on a day's hire). You can sometimes save money by booking in advance (which is advisable at peak times, although you'll still have to stand around when you arrive while the paperwork is completed), particularly if you take a fly-drive or sail-drive package through an airline, ferry company or tour operator. If you're coming from America and have credit card insurance (though not with American Express), you can save as much as IR£60 on a week's car rental.

You need to be aged at least 21 to rent a car in Ireland; most companies have a minimum age limit of 23 or more – some as high as 27. Some companies charge extra for 21 to 24 year-olds and there's usually an upper age limit, which varies between 65 and 75. You also usually need to have held a driving licence for at least 12 months without endorsements. When booking in advance, you should specify an automatic model if you're unused to a manual (stick-shift) gearbox, as most rental cars are manual – but note that automatics are often more expensive (by as much as 25 per cent in some cases).

Prices generally vary considerably, so shop around. Most companies have low rates for weekend hire and for rentals of 14 days or longer. When comparing rates, check what's included in the price. Basic third-party insurance is usually included in the rental charge, but make sure you check exactly what you're covered for. In some cases you can be liable for the cost of damage to a car unless you pay an additional Collision Damage Waiver (CDW) premium of between IR£3 and IR£5 per day (although this is usually included). Personal accident insurance can usually be taken out for a similar premium and a second driver can be added for around IR£3 or IR£4 per day. Some companies don't offer unlimited mileage but provide a certain number of 'free' kilometres (or miles), after which there's a charge per kilometre, which usually works out more expensive unless you plan to drive only a relatively short distance. Theft protection is usually included, but VAT at 12.5 per cent may not be.

If required, check that you're permitted to take a car out of Ireland, e.g. to Northern Ireland, as you may need additional insurance, although there's usually no surcharge. For an extra fee you may be able to obtain extras such as baby seats and roof racks. Note also that there's usually an accident 'excess' of IR£250 but it can be as high as IR£400. In other words, if you crash the car you may need to pay that amount even if you're properly insured. Again you can pay a 'waiver' of around IR£4 per day to secure peace of mind.

Around 30 car hire companies are members of the Car Rental Council of Ireland (CRCI), which means that they have been approved by the Irish Tourist Board (a list is available from the CRCI, ☎ 01-676 1690; 💻 www.carrentalcouncil.ie).

When choosing a rental car for touring, you should ensure that you have sufficient power for mountain driving, e.g. at least a 1.6 litre engine for two people and their luggage. When parking overnight or at any time in cities, don't leave any valuables in your car (see **Car Crime** on page 40). Always check the car (e.g. for body damage and to ensure that everything works) and the contract carefully before setting out.

Drivers must produce a valid licence (a copy isn't acceptable) and some drivers require an international driving licence. If more than one person will be driving, all the drivers' names must be entered on the rental agreement. Unless you use a credit card, you'll usually need to pay a cash deposit equivalent to the excess and possibly the whole rental in advance. When paying by credit card, carefully check your bill and statement as unauthorised charges aren't unknown. It may be possible to sign a credit card authorisation slip and pay cash when you return a car. However, if you do this, make sure that you obtain (and destroy) the credit card payment slip.

2.

FURTHER CONSIDERATIONS

This chapter contains important considerations for most people planning to buy a home in Ireland, particularly those intending to live there permanently or semi-permanently. It includes information about the Irish climate, geography, health, insurance, shopping, pets, TV and radio, and learning English and Irish.

CLIMATE

Ireland's climate is hardly the overwhelming attraction for most foreigners. Ireland is one of the wettest countries in Europe, with average annual rainfall in parts of the west coast (where it rains on at least half the days of the year) as high as 20cm (8in) per month and nowhere much less than 5cm (2in) per month. The driest regions are in the east and in low-lying areas. The 'reward' for all that rain is, of course, the lush green vegetation for which Ireland is famous.

Influenced by the relatively warm water of the Gulf Stream and the prevailing south-westerly winds from the Atlantic, Ireland enjoys generally mild temperatures. Winters are cool and summers warm, although extremes of temperature are rare. July and August usually bring the highest temperatures, around 14°C to 24°C (57°F to 75°F) and most of the country enjoys an average of at least six hours of sunshine per day between May and August. Nevertheless, you're unlikely to encounter lengthy spells of dry, sunny weather, and bright intervals between showers are more common ,as are what the locals refer to as 'soft' days, when the rain is like a fine mist. The best advice is to expect constant rain; then you'll be pleasantly surprised when the sun appears, as even the wettest days often have sunny intervals. Perhaps this is why the Irish are habitually optimistic about the weather.

If summer is rarely hot, winter is seldom severe, with only occasional snow except on high ground. Spring tends to be relatively dry and autumn mild until as late as the end of November. The coldest months are January and February, when average temperatures are between 4°C and 7°C (39°F to 45°F).

The Irish are almost as obsessed by the weather as the British and frequent weather forecasts are given on TV and radio and in daily newspapers.

GEOGRAPHY

The Republic of Ireland (known in Irish as *Poblacht na hÉireann* or simply as *Éire*, after a goddess of Irish mythology called *ériu*) forms the greater part of the island of Ireland in the Atlantic Ocean to the west of Britain (encompassing England, Scotland and Wales), lying between 51fi° and 55fi° north latitude and between 5fi° and 10fi° west longitude. The island, which is one of the British Isles, also includes Northern Ireland, part of the United Kingdom. The Republic is sometimes referred to as Southern Ireland, although that's a misnomer as the most northerly point on the island, Malin Head in Co. Donegal, is within the Republic. The island is separated from the British mainland by the Irish Sea. While Northern Ireland is only some 30km (19mi) from the coast of Scotland and is easily visible on a clear day, the nearest point to the Irish Republic in southern Britain is St David's Head in South Wales, which is some 80km (50mi) away across St George's Channel. The Republic of Ireland covers an area of 70,282km^2 (27,136mi^2) and measures 486km (303mi) from north to south and 303km (189mi) from east to west.

Overall, Ireland resembles a shallow bowl with hills and mountains forming a rim around the coast, where often dramatic cliffs are interspersed with sandy beaches (called *strands*). Ireland's highest mountain, Carrantuohill, rises to 1,041m (3,414ft) in a range called MacGillicuddy's Reeks in Co. Kerry in the south-west. Other mountain ranges are to be found further up the west coast in the counties of Donegal and Galway. The most spectacular cliffs are also in the west, the highest plunging nearly 650m (2,000ft) into the sea at Slieve League in Co. Donegal.

The central part of Ireland consists of a flat or gently rolling limestone plain, occasionally interrupted by low hills (*drumlins*) and liberally scattered with lakes (*loughs*) and bogs where the land is below the water table. This is where Ireland's famous peat comes from, while its equally famous lush grass grows on the higher ground, which is covered with rich, light soil. The gently winding River Shannon is Ireland's longest river, almost dividing the country in half. Other major rivers include the Erne in the north, and the Slaney, Barrow, Sluir and Blackwater in the south. There are literally thousands of lakes on the island – almost 1,500km^2 (5,800 mi^2) of the country is covered by water. The most attractive, Lough Corrib, Lough Mask and Lough Conn, are in the west of Ireland, not forgetting Loughs Allen, Derg and Ree, through which the River Shannon flows on its leisurely way to Limerick and the sea. There are also numerous tiny islands just off the west coast of Ireland, the best known being the Aran Islands in Galway Bay (not to be confused with the Isle of Arran off Scotland's west coast). Over 80 per cent of Ireland is pasture or arable land, woods and forests accounting for a mere 7 per cent.

Ireland is divided into four provinces of roughly equal size: Munster (south), Connacht (west), Ulster (north) and Leinster (east). These derive from pre-Christian times (roughly corresponding to the divisions made by the Fir Bolg invaders) and have no political significance. Part of Ulster, for example, is in Northern Ireland and part in the Republic. They are, however, socially and culturally important: Ulster is supposedly the land of battle, Munster the land of music, Leinster of prosperity, and Connacht of learning (how true this is today is debatable). The capital, Dublin (*Baile Átha Cliath*), lies on the east coast and has a population of just under one million. It's the only really large city in Ireland, the next biggest being Cork with a population of around 180,000, Limerick with 80,000, Galway with 57,000 and Waterford with 44,000. No other town exceeds 30,000 and more than half the population lives in rural areas.

Like Britain, Ireland is on GMT (i.e. five hours ahead of US eastern time and one hour behind standard European time) from late March until late October. For the other half of the year Ireland is on GMT plus one hour, i.e. six hours ahead of US eastern time.

HEALTH

One of the most important aspects of living in Ireland (or anywhere for that matter) is maintaining good health. The quality of health care and health care facilities in Ireland is generally excellent, although facilities are limited in some rural areas. There are around 1,650 general practitioners (GPs) and the number of people per doctor (approximately 680 on average) is about the same as in the UK, although higher than in most of the rest of Europe. However, the number of public hospitals is limited. Irish medical staff are highly trained and major hospitals have all the latest equipment. Since 1970, Ireland's public health system has been administered by eight Regional Health Boards, which come under the jurisdiction of the Department of Health and Children. In 1995, the Department produced a five-year plan called 'Shaping a Healthier Future', which aimed to promote good health in a positive way rather than merely as an avoidance of illness and disease, and investigated attitudes to health among children and adults, culminating in the formulation of national strategies relating to nutrition, alcohol consumption, heart disease, women's health, health in the workplace, health of children and old people, and suicide, which has increased significantly in recent years. The Department's latest five-year plan, the National Health Promotion Strategy, which began in 2000, is more general in aiming to promote health in various ways to all sectors of the population (a copy of the Strategy can be obtained from Government Publications, ☎ 01-647 6834, price IR£5).

Ireland and the UK are the only EU countries where you can obtain public health care without having to make social security contributions. In Ireland, your entitlement to benefits is determined solely by your residence status. The Health (Amendment) Act 1991 introduced the concept of 'ordinary residence', which is the minimum requirement for eligibility. In order to be 'ordinarily resident' in Ireland, non-EU nationals must be able to show that they intend to remain in Ireland for a minimum of one year. This means producing an Alien's Registration Book or residence/work permit, proof of property purchase or rental (including evidence that it's your principal residence), confirmation of registration with a school or college, or details of an Irish bank account. Note that if you establish ordinary residence, your dependants won't necessarily be eligible for public health care unless they're also ordinarily resident. EU citizens who are resident in Ireland but insured in another EU or EEA country are automatically eligible for health care, as are their dependants, although if you're self-employed you'll receive few benefits. If you're ordinarily resident in Ireland and receiving a social security pension from another EU country, you're entitled to public health care, provided you don't also have an Irish Department of Social Welfare pension and aren't earning more than IR£2,500 per year from employment or self-employment in Ireland.

Short-term visitors to Ireland (i.e. those who aren't ordinarily resident) from EU countries are entitled to free urgent medical treatment. Unless you're a UK national, you need to produce form E111 (which you should obtain from your own health authority before travelling). Non-EU visitors are entitled to nothing free!

In general, the Irish are as healthy as most other Europeans, although their life expectancy of 73 for men and 79 for women is slightly below the EU average (life expectancy figures at the age of 40 are particularly poor). On the other hand, the infant mortality rate of eight deaths before the age of five for every 1,000 births is comparable with the rest of Europe.

Cardiovascular disease is the major cause of death in Ireland, which has the highest death rate for heart disease in the EU (almost double the EU average), although it has been steadily declining since the mid-'70s, as has the rate of other cerebrovascular diseases (e.g. strokes and thromboses). Deaths from cancer, the second most frequent cause of death, are also above the EU average among women, but below it among men and the rate has remained constant for the past 30 years. The next most common cause of death, traffic accidents, is also well below the EU average and the rate is declining gradually. The suicide rate, on the other hand, has steadily increased and is now higher than that for road accidents and above the EU average. The annual number of deaths from AIDS, which peaked at 45 in 1995, fell to 7 in 1997, with rates of 21 and 17 in 1998 and '99. This equates to around one in every 200,000 people.

From a psychological point of view, Ireland's slower pace of life is beneficial to those who are prone to stress (it's difficult to remain uptight while gazing out over green fields listening to the bleating of sheep), although it takes some foreigners time to adjust. The climate and lifestyle in any country have a noticeable effect on mental health and this should be taken into account when considering buying a home in Ireland.

Health & Retirement

Maintaining good health is important for anyone retiring to Ireland. Many people are ill-prepared for old age and the possibility of health problems, although you're better provided for in Ireland than in many other countries. All retirees over 65, whether or not they have a Medical Card, are entitled to regular visits by a public health nurse and, if required, occupational therapy. Meals on wheels and a home help service are provided by voluntary organisations on behalf of the Health Board, usually for a small fee. A few hospitals are 'day hospitals', where services such as physiotherapy are available for a lower fee than at in-patient departments. A number of public hospitals have specialised geriatric departments, although these aren't intended for long-term care. For this you'll need to be admitted to either a geriatric hospital or a welfare home. In both cases you'll be expected to make a means-related contribution towards your keep – known as 'extended-stay maintenance charges', which are determined by Regional Health Boards. If you need to be admitted to a nursing home and there's no space at a state home (e.g. there are only eight in the Dublin area), the Health Board will pay a subvention of up to IR£120 per week towards the cost of accommodation in a private home (of which there are more than 100 in Dublin).

There are also grants for security devices for elderly people living alone, although these aren't usually paid directly to individuals. Other schemes offer home improvement grants, free draught proofing and insulation (in some parts of the country), and house alterations for disabled people. The only universal benefit for elderly people is free travel, for which everyone over 66 qualifies, but even that has various conditions attached. Note that, in general, to obtain any benefits in Ireland you must apply for them. No one is going to come along and offer them to you! On the other hand, a number of private establishments such as cinemas, theatres and other places of entertainment, as well as hairdressers, dry-cleaners and certain shops, offer reductions to pensioners, and anyone over 55 can take advantage of 'Golden Holidays' (contact the Tourist Board for details).

Ireland's provision for handicapped travellers is improving as awareness of the need for such facilities increases. New building regulations introduced in 1991 require all public buildings to be wheelchair accessible, so all modern hotels and restaurants (etc.) have good access. The Irish Wheelchair Association (☎ 01-833 8241) has a database of accessible buildings and will provide a list on request.

Pre-Departure Check: If you're planning to take up residence in Ireland, even for just part of the year, it's prudent to have a health check before your arrival, particularly if you have a record of poor health or are elderly. If you're already taking regular medication, you should note that the brand names of drugs and medicines vary from country to country and should ask your doctor for the generic name. If you wish to match medication prescribed abroad, you'll need a current prescription with the medication's trade name, the manufacturer's name, the chemical name and the dosage. Most drugs have an equivalent in other countries, although particular brands may be difficult or impossible to obtain in Ireland. It's possible to have medication sent from abroad, when no import duty or value added tax is usually payable. If you're visiting a holiday home in Ireland for a short period, you should take sufficient medication to cover your stay. In an emergency, a local doctor will write a prescription which can be filled at a local pharmacy. You should also take some of your favourite non-prescription drugs (e.g. pain killers, cold and flu remedies, lotions) with you, as they may be difficult or impossible to obtain in Ireland or may be much more expensive. If applicable, take a spare pair of spectacles, contact lenses, dentures or a hearing aid with you.

There are no special health risks in Ireland and no immunisations are required. However, although you're unlikely to get sunburnt, you can suffer badly from midge bites on warm summer evenings, particularly on the west coast, so it's as well to stock up with insect repellent. Wasps, hornets and horseflies can also be quite persistent in the summer months. You can safely drink the water anywhere in Ireland (but the stout tastes *much* better!). Note that the telephone number to dial in emergencies is 999.

INSURANCE

An important aspect of owning a home in Ireland (or anywhere else) is insurance, not only for your home and its contents, but also for your family when visiting Ireland. If you live in Ireland permanently, you'll require additional insurance. It's unnecessary to spend half your income insuring yourself against every eventuality from the common cold to being sued for your last penny, although it's important to insure against any event that could precipitate a major financial disaster, such as a serious accident or your house being demolished by a storm. The cost of being uninsured or under-insured can be astronomical!

As with anything connected with finance, it's important to shop around when buying insurance. Simply collecting a few brochures from insurance agents or making a few telephone calls can save you a lot of money. Note, however, that not all insurance companies are equally reliable or have the same financial stability, and it may be better to insure with a large international company with a good reputation than with a small local company, even if this means paying a higher premium. Read all insurance contracts carefully and make sure you understand the terms and the cover provided before signing them. Some insurance companies will do almost anything to avoid honouring claims and will use any available legal loophole, so it pays to deal only with reputable companies (not that this provides a guarantee). Note that Irish insurance companies can compel you to renew your insurance for a further year if you don't give adequate written notice (e.g. up to three months) of your intention to terminate it, although most companies allow policy holders to cancel on renewal. Check in advance.

In all matters regarding insurance, you're responsible for ensuring that you and your family are legally insured in Ireland. Regrettably you cannot insure yourself against being uninsured or sue your insurance agent for giving you bad advice! Bear in mind that if you wish to make a claim on an insurance policy, you may be required to report an incident to the local police within 24 hours (this may also be a legal requirement). The law in Ireland may differ considerably from that in your home country or your previous country of residence and you should never assume that it's the same. If you're unsure of your rights, you're advised to obtain legal advice for anything other than a minor claim. Under EU rules, an insurance company registered in an EU member country can sell its policies in any other EU country.

The following pages contain information about health, household, third-party liability and travel insurance. See also **Car Insurance** on page 39.

Health Insurance

If you're visiting, living or working in Ireland and aren't entitled to free public health care (see page 49), it's extremely risky not to have private health insurance for your family, because if you're uninsured or under-insured you could be faced with some *very* high medical bills. When deciding on the kind and extent of health insurance, make sure that it covers *all* your family's present and future health requirements in Ireland. A health insurance policy should cover you for *all* essential treatment whatever the reason, including accidents and injuries, whether they occur in your home, at your place of work or while travelling. Don't take anything for granted but check in advance. Note, for example, that BUPA's health insurance covers car accidents whereas VHI's doesn't, although it's available for a small premium (see below).

Even if you're eligible for free health care, it's wise (if you can afford it) to take out private health insurance, which provides a wider choice of medical practitioners and hospitals, and more importantly, frees you from public health waiting lists. Under the state system, you may need to wait six months for a routine (non-urgent) operation, whereas with private insurance you can expect to be treated within two or three weeks. In many areas there are also long waiting lists for dental treatment. Some 40 per cent of Irish people have private health insurance, mainly to bypass waiting lists.

Proof of health insurance must usually be provided when applying for a visa or permission to establish a business in Ireland, so that the authorities can be sure you won't be a burden on the state if you require medical treatment. Visitors to Ireland should have holiday health insurance (see page **Holiday & Travel Insurance** on page 57). Short-stay visitors may be covered by a reciprocal agreement between their home country and Ireland (see page 52); long-stay visitors should have travel or long-stay health insurance or an international health policy (see page 53). Note that some foreign insurance companies don't provide sufficient cover to satisfy Irish regulations, so you should check the minimum cover necessary with an Irish consulate or embassy in your country of residence. When travelling in Ireland, you should carry proof of your health insurance at all times.

Health Insurance for Residents

There are only two private health insurers in Ireland: the Voluntary Health Insurance (VHI) board and the British-based BUPA. If you're already covered by private health insurance abroad, you may be able to transfer to VHI or BUPA in Ireland (both companies have reciprocal agreements with foreign insurance companies including Blue Shield, Blue Cross and PPP). EU legislation requires insurers to allow members to transfer to another provider without penalty. Both VHI and BUPA premiums are calculated on the basis of 'community rating', which means that all members pay the same amount and premiums don't increase with age. This means that younger people generally pay more than they would under a risk-based system, but there's a lower rate for those aged under 21 with BUPA or under 18 with VHI.

You must be under 65 to join either BUPA or VHI and neither organisation requires new policy holders to have a medical examination, although both impose a 'waiting period' of 26 weeks for those under 55 and 52 weeks if you're over 55, during which you're unable to make claims. If you become pregnant within 52 weeks of joining, you won't be entitled to maternity benefit. If you have a 'pre-existing' medical condition, you'll need to have been a member for at least five years (seven years if you're aged over 55 but under 60, ten years if you're over 60) before being able to claim for treatment for that condition – in which case you may be better off insured with a foreign company registered in Ireland (see page 54). These conditions are standard among all private health insurance companies in Ireland, but they're also 'transferable'; e.g. if you've been a member of VHI for 26 weeks and transfer to BUPA (or vice versa), you'll be entitled to claim immediately.

VHI is a non-profit organisation established in 1957 with some 1.5 million members. BUPA, also a 'not-for-profit' organisation, was established in 1947 and its services became available in 1996 in Ireland, where it now claims a membership of 170,000. BUPA offers a choice of three plans (Essential, Essential Plus and Gold), whereas VHI has no fewer than ten to choose from (A to E with 'options' on each). Although VHI claims 50 per cent lower running costs than UK health insurers, its premiums are higher than BUPA's. BUPA's lowest child rate, for example, is around IR£65 per year compared with VHI's Plan A rate of around IR£80 and adult charges start at IR£202 per year with BUPA and IR£240 with VHI. VHI charges an annual excess of up to IR£250 on claims for doctors' visits, X-rays, consultant and hospital out-patient fees, and certain other costs. BUPA charges an excess of IR£50 for certain kinds of hospital accommodation on its Essential Plus scheme, but there's no excess on the Gold or new HealthManager schemes. This scheme, which was introduced by BUPA in August 2000, offers comprehensive cover without any excess charges for just under IR£400 per year (adult). Both companies operate group schemes (six or more members) for companies and organisations, providing a 10 per cent discount off individual rates. Private health insurance is provided by many employers in Ireland, although in most cases employees are required to make a contribution. Note that tax relief at the standard rate (22 per cent) is available to those paying private health insurance.

The conditions and benefits offered by BUPA and VHI are similar. Both companies provide full hospital cover in most of their designated hospitals (VHI lists 97 hospitals compared with BUPA's 83) but only partial cover in the remainder (in

BUPA's case patients must pay the first IR£100 of costs). Both companies provide help towards maternity costs (up to IR£300), as well as offering an allowance for mothers who choose to give birth at home. BUPA also provides the option of certain 'approved' alternative therapies such as acupuncture. Both VHI and BUPA operate a world-wide emergency medical assistance scheme (VHI call theirs 'VHI Assist'), which is included in the normal cover. Note that the rules applicable to both VHI and BUPA can change at any time, so you should check the current situation. BUPA Ireland is based at Mill Island, Fermoy, Co. Cork (☎ 025-42121; www.bupa ireland.ie) and VHI has offices in Dublin, Cork, Dun Laoghaire, Galway and Limerick (Dublin office ☎ 01-872 4499; 💻 www.vhi.ie).

Changing Employers or Insurance Companies: When changing employers or leaving Ireland, you should ensure that you have continuous health insurance. If you and your family are covered by a company health plan, your insurance will probably cease after your last official day of employment. If you're planning to change your health insurance company, you should ensure that important benefits aren't lost; existing medical conditions, for example, won't usually be covered by a new insurer. Before changing health insurance companies, check that your old company has settled all bills for which it's liable.

Health Insurance for Visitors

Visitors spending short periods in Ireland (e.g. up to a month) should have a travel health insurance policy (see **Holiday & Travel Insurance** on page 57), particularly if they aren't covered by an international health policy. If you plan to spend up to six months in Ireland, you should take out a travel, long-stay or international health policy (which should cover you in your home country and when travelling in other countries). Note that premiums vary considerably and it's important to shop around. Most international health policies include repatriation or evacuation, which may also include shipment (by air) of the body of a person who dies abroad to his home country for burial. An international policy also allows you to decide to have non-urgent medical treatment in the country of your choice.

Most international insurance companies offer health policies for different areas, e.g. Europe, the world excluding North America, and the world including North America. Most companies also offer different levels of cover – e.g. basic, standard, comprehensive and prestige. There's always a limit on the total annual medical costs covered, which should be at least IR£250,000 (although many provide cover of up to IR£1 million) and some companies limit costs for specific treatment or care such as specialists' fees, operations and hospital accommodation. A medical examination isn't usually required for international health policies, although existing health problems are excluded for a period, e.g. one or two years. Claims are usually settled in all major currencies; large claims are normally settled directly by the insurance company , although your choice of hospitals may be limited. Always check whether an insurance company will settle large medical bills directly, because if you're required to pay bills and claim reimbursement from an insurance company, it can take several months before you receive payment. Most international health insurance companies provide emergency telephone assistance.

The cost of international health insurance varies considerably according to your age and the extent of cover. Note that with most international insurance policies, you must enrol before you reach a certain age, e.g. between 60 and 80 depending on the company, in order to be guaranteed continuous cover in your old age. Premiums can sometimes be paid monthly, quarterly or annually (some companies insist on payment annually in advance). When comparing policies, carefully check the extent of cover and exactly what's included and excluded from a policy (often indicated only in the very small print), in addition to premiums and excess charges. In some countries, premium increases are limited by law, although this may apply only to residents in the country where a company is registered and not to overseas policy holders. Although there may be significant differences in premiums, generally you get what you pay for and can tailor premiums to your requirements.

The most important questions to ask yourself are: does the policy provide the cover required and is it good value for money? If you're in good health and are able to pay for your own out-patient treatment, such as visits to a family doctor and prescriptions, the best value is a policy covering only specialist and hospital treatment.

Reciprocal Health Agreements: If you're entitled to social security health benefits in another EU country or in a country with a reciprocal health agreement with Ireland, you'll receive free or reduced cost medical treatment in Ireland. For emergency treatment, EU residents (excluding UK citizens) should apply for a certificate of entitlement to treatment (form E111) from their local social security office before they travel to Ireland. The E111 form can officially be used for a stay of up to three months only (although many people use them for much longer periods). If you use the E111 in Ireland, you must apply for reimbursement to Irish social security (instructions are provided with the form), which can take a number of months. Note, however, that you can still receive a large bill from an Irish hospital, as your local health authority assumes only a percentage of the cost. For example, although serious illnesses and accidents are totally reimbursed, minor ailments and injuries are reimbursed at only 20 per cent for out-patient treatment and 35 per cent for ambulance costs. Participating countries include all EU member states and most other European countries, except Albania, Switzerland and Turkey.

Ireland also has a reciprocal arrangement with Australia, but not with the USA, so Americans who aren't covered by Irish social welfare must have private health insurance in Ireland.

UK citizens planning to visit or live and work in Ireland don't require form E111 but need to show evidence of UK residence (e.g. a passport or driving licence). Further information about reciprocal health treatment for UK residents can be obtained from the Inland Revenue, National Insurance Contributions Office, International Services, Longbenton, Newcastle-upon-Tyne, NE98 1ZZ, UK (☎ 0645-154811).

Household Insurance

Household insurance in Ireland generally includes the building, its contents and third-party liability, all of which are contained in a multi-risk household insurance policy. Policies are offered by both Irish and foreign insurance companies, and premiums are similar, although foreign companies may provide more comprehensive cover.

Buildings: Although it isn't compulsory, it's wise for owners to take out property insurance (usually referred to as buildings insurance) that covers damage to a building due to fire, smoke, lightning, water, explosion, storm, freezing, snow, theft, vandalism, malicious damage, acts of terrorism, impact, broken windows and natural catastrophes (such as falling trees). Insurance should include glass, external buildings, aerials and satellite dishes, gardens and garden ornaments. Note that, if a claim is the result of a defect in building or design (e.g. the roof is too heavy and collapses), the insurance company won't pay up – another reason why it's wise to have a survey before buying a home (see page 151). If you're taking out a mortgage on a property, most lenders will insist on your having buildings insurance.

Buildings insurance is based on the cost of rebuilding your home and should be increased annually in line with inflation. Make sure that you insure your property for the true cost of rebuilding. It's commonly thought that a property should be insured for its market value (i.e. the price it would fetch if sold), but in fact the market value of a property often bears little relationship to the cost of rebuilding. The Society of Chartered Surveyors in Ireland (☎ 01-676 5500) publishes a *Guide to House Rebuilding Insurance*, according to which the minimum rebuilding cost of properties in and around the main cities in July 2000 was between IR£854 and IR£960 per m² in Galway, between IR£908 and IR£1,016 in Cork and IR£1,030 to IR£1,129 in Dublin (note that these costs don't include patios, outbuildings or boundary walls, nor carpets or furnishings). It's particularly important to have insurance for storm damage in Ireland, which can be severe in some areas. If floods are one of your concerns, make sure you're covered for water coming in from ground level, not just for water seeping in through the roof. Always read the small print of contracts. Note that if you own a home in an area that has been hit by a chain of natural disasters (such as floods), your household insurance may be cancelled or premiums increased dramatically.

Contents: Contents are usually insured for the same risks as a building (see above) and are insured for their replacement value (new for old), with a reduction for wear and tear for clothes and linen. Valuable objects are covered for their declared (and authenticated) value. Most policies include automatic indexation of the insured sum in line with inflation. Contents insurance may include accidental damage to sanitary installations, theft of money, credit cards, bicycles, garden furniture, satellite dishes, replacement of locks following damage or loss of keys, frozen food, alternative accommodation, and property belonging to third parties stored in your home. Some items are usually optional, e.g. contact lenses, caravan and camping equipment, musical instruments, emergency assistance (plumber, glazier, electrician, etc.), redecoration, garaged cars, replacement pipes, loss of rent, and the cost of emergency travel to Ireland for holiday homeowners. Many policies include personal third-party liability, e.g. up to IR£250,000, although this may be an option. Items of high value (e.g. over IR£1,500) must usually be itemised and documentation (i.e. a valuation) provided. A photograph may be required of anything worth more than IR£5,000. Some companies even recommend or insist on a video film of belongings.

When claiming for contents, you should produce the original bills if possible (always keep bills for expensive items) and bear in mind that replacing imported items in Ireland may be more expensive than buying them abroad. Contents policies always contain security clauses and if you don't adhere to them a claim won't be considered. If you're planning to let a property, you may be required to inform your insurer. Note that a building must be secure with key operated locks on ground-floor windows and patio doors. Most companies give a discount if properties have high security locks and alarms (particularly alarms connected to a monitoring station), but only if they're installed to certain recognised standards. An insurance company may send someone to inspect your property and advise on security measures. Policies pay out for theft only when there are signs of forced entry; you aren't covered for thefts by a tenant, but may be covered for thefts by domestic personnel. All-risks policies offering a world-wide extension to a household policy covering jewellery, cameras and other items aren't usually available from Irish insurance companies, but are offered by a number of foreign companies.

Leasehold Properties: If you own a leasehold property, such as an apartment or flat, buildings insurance will be arranged by your landlord or the management company (it's worth checking that it's adequate), so you'll be responsible only for insuring the contents of the property. Household insurance policies in Ireland usually include third-party liability up to around IR£250,000.

Holiday Homes: Premiums are generally higher for holiday homes because of their high vulnerability, particularly to burglaries. Most policies include restrictions if a property is unoccupied for more than 30 days at a time. Premiums are usually based on the number of days a year a property is inhabited and the interval between periods of occupancy. Cover for theft, storm, flood and malicious damage may be suspended when a property is left empty for an extended period. Note that you're generally required to turn off the water supply at the mains when vacating a building for more than 72 hours. It's possible to negotiate cover for periods of absence for a hefty surcharge, although valuable items are usually excluded (unless you have a safe). If you're absent from your property for long periods, e.g. more than 30 days a year, you may be required to pay an excess on a claim arising from an occurrence that takes place during your absence (and theft may be excluded). Note that it's important to ensure that a policy specifies a holiday home and not a principal home. In areas with a high risk of theft (e.g. Dublin), an insurance company may insist on extra security measures. It's unwise to leave valuable or irreplaceable items in a holiday home or a property that will be vacant for long periods. Note that some insurance companies will do their utmost to find a loophole making you negligent and relieving them of liability. You should ensure that the details listed on a policy are correct, or your policy could be void.

Rented Property: A lease requires you to insure against 'tenant risks', including damage you may make to the rental property and to other properties, e.g. due to flood, fire or explosion. Your landlord will usually insist that you also have third-party liability insurance. You can choose your own insurance company and aren't required to use one recommended by your landlord.

Premiums: Premiums are usually calculated on the size of a property, its age and type of construction, but the amount you pay may vary considerably according to a property's location and the measures you take to protect it from accidental damage and burglary. Smoke detectors, window locks and security alarms, for example, can reduce your insurance bill by as much as 15 per cent, and participation in a local Community Alert scheme by a further 5 per cent. If you're aged over 50 or 55, you may qualify for an extra discount of 10 per cent. Some companies also offer 'no-claims' bonuses of up to 20 per cent. Several companies offer a combined buildings and contents insurance with the contents automatically insured for 50 per cent of the value of the building. Some companies offer discounts (for alarms, Community Alert, etc.) only if you take out a combined policy, while others offer an extra 30 per cent discount on buildings and/or contents insurance if they also insure your car. A typical three-bedroom house fitted with smoke detectors and security alarms in a Dublin suburb valued at IR£100,000 with IR£30,000 worth of contents would cost around IR£275 a year to insure. For a similar property outside Dublin you may pay up to 30 per cent less. There's usually an excess of between IR£50 and IR£100 (which may be reduced on payment of an additional premium). All insurance premiums are subject to a government levy of 2 per cent.

As policies and prices vary, it pays to shop around or to use a broker to do so on your behalf. The 600 members of the Irish Brokers Association (IBA) offer an independent service and are bound by a code of conduct (they must meet a minimum standard of 'competence') as well as being required to offer compensation of up to IR£70,000 should you suffer financial loss as a result of their negligence or bankruptcy. Further details of the IBA and its members can be obtained on ☎ 01-661 3061; 🖳 www.irishbrokers.com.

Claims: If you wish to make a claim, you must usually inform your insurance company in writing (by registered letter) within two to seven days of an incident or 24 hours in the case of theft. Thefts should also be reported to the local *Gardaí* (police) within 24 hours, as the police report, of which you receive a copy for your insurance company, constitutes irrefutable evidence of your claim. Check whether you're covered for damage or thefts that occur while you're away from your home and are therefore unable to inform the insurance company immediately.

Take care that you don't under-insure your contents and that you periodically reassess their value and adjust your insurance premium accordingly. You can arrange with your insurance company to have your insurance cover automatically increased annually by a fixed percentage or amount. If you make a claim and the assessor discovers that you're under-insured, the amount due will be reduced by the percentage by which you're under-insured. For example, if you're insured for IR£20,000 and you're found to be under-insured by 50 per cent, a claim for IR£5,000 will be reduced by 50 per cent and you'll lose IR£2,500.

Insuring Abroad: It's possible and legal to take out buildings and contents insurance in another country for a property in Ireland (some foreign insurance companies offer special policies for holiday homeowners), although you must ensure that a policy is valid under Irish law. This may seem like a good option for a holiday home in Ireland, although it can be more expensive than insuring with an Irish company and can lead to conflicts if, for example, the building is insured with an Irish-registered company and the contents with a foreign based company. Most experts advise that you insure an Irish home and its contents with an Irish insurance company through a local agent.

Holiday & Travel Insurance

Holiday and travel insurance is recommended for all who don't wish to risk having their holiday or travel ruined by financial problems or to arrive home broke. As you probably know, anything can and often does go wrong with a holiday, sometimes before you even get started (particularly when you *don't* have insurance). The following information applies equally to residents and non-residents, whether they're travelling to or from Ireland or within Ireland. Nobody should visit Ireland without travel (and health) insurance!

Travel insurance is available from many sources including travel agents, insurance companies and agents, banks, motoring organisations and transport companies (airline, rail and bus). Package holiday companies and tour operators also offer insurance policies, some of which are too expensive and don't provide adequate cover. You can also buy 24-hour accident and flight insurance at major airports, although it's expensive and doesn't offer the best cover. Before taking out travel insurance, carefully consider the range and level of cover you require and compare policies. Short-term holiday and travel insurance policies should include cover for holiday cancellation or interruption, missed flights, departure delay at both the start *and* end of a holiday (a common occurrence), delayed, lost or damaged baggage, personal effects and money, medical expenses and accidents (including evacuation), flight insurance, personal liability and legal expenses, and default or bankruptcy insurance, e.g. against a tour operator or airline going bust.

Health Cover: Medical expenses are an important aspect of travel insurance and you shouldn't rely on insurance provided by reciprocal health arrangements (see page 54), charge and credit card companies, household policies, or on private medical insurance (unless it's an international policy), none of which usually provide adequate cover (although you should take advantage of what they offer). The minimum medical insurance recommended by experts is IR£250,000 in Ireland and most of the rest of Europe, and IR£1 million for the rest of the world (many policies have limits of between IR£1 million and IR£2 million). If applicable, check whether pregnancy related claims are covered and whether there are any restrictions for those over a certain age, e.g. 65 or 70 (travel insurance is becoming increasingly expensive for those aged over 65, although they don't usually need to worry about pregnancy!).

Always check any exclusion clauses in contracts by obtaining a copy of the full policy document, as not all relevant information will be included in an insurance leaflet. High risk sports and pursuits should be specifically covered and *listed* in a policy (there's usually an additional premium and 'dangerous' sports are excluded from most standard policies). Third-party liability cover should be IR£2 million in North America and IR£1 million in the rest of the world. Note that this doesn't cover you when you're using a car or other mechanically propelled vehicle.

Cost: The cost of travel insurance varies considerably, depending on where you buy it, how long you intend to stay in Ireland and your age. Generally, the longer the period covered, the cheaper the daily cost, although the maximum period covered is usually around six months. With some policies an excess must be paid for each claim; with others the excess applies only to certain items such as luggage, money and medical expenses. As a rough guide, travel insurance for Ireland (and most other European countries) costs from around IR£20 for one week, IR£30 for two weeks and IR£45 for a month for a family of four (two adults and two children under 16). Premiums may be higher for those aged over 65 or 70.

Annual Policies: For those who travel abroad frequently, whether on business or pleasure, an annual travel policy usually provides the best value, but always carefully check exactly what it includes. Many insurance companies offer annual travel policies for a premium of around IR£100 to IR£150 for an individual (the equivalent of around three months' insurance with a standard travel insurance policy), which are excellent value for frequent travellers. Some insurance companies also offer an 'emergency travel policy' for holiday homeowners who need to travel abroad at short notice to inspect a property, e.g. after a severe storm. The cost of an annual policy may depend on the area covered, e.g. Europe, although it doesn't usually cover travel within your country of residence. There's also a limit on the number of trips per year and the duration of each trip, e.g. 90 or 120 days. An annual policy is usually a good choice for owners of a holiday home in Ireland who travel there frequently for relatively short periods. Again, check exactly what's covered (or omitted), as an annual policy may not provide adequate cover.

Claims: If you need to make a claim, you should provide as much documentary evidence as possible to support it. Travel insurance companies gladly take your money, but they aren't always so keen to pay claims and you may need to persevere before they pay up. Always be persistent and make a claim *irrespective* of any small print, as this may be unreasonable and therefore invalid in law. Insurance companies usually require you to obtain a written report and declare a loss (or any incident for which you intend to make a claim) to the local police or carriers within 24 hours. Failure to do so may mean that a claim won't be considered.

SHOPPING

Shopping in Ireland is unusually pleasurable because you're never made to feel as if you need to buy something, so you can browse as much as you like. Shop assistants won't stand over you or watch your every move, but politely ignore you until you're ready to buy or need help. Generally prices are comparable with other European countries and similar to the UK, apart from a few items such as books, which are significantly more expensive. As in many other countries, there was a huge downturn in consumption during the recession in the early '90s. In recent years, however, there has been a strong recovery (retail sales have risen by an average of 7.5 per cent per annum since 1994) and the cost of living (see page 99) has risen considerably.

Small family-run stores still constitute the bulk of Irish retailers and the invasion of shopping centres and hypermarkets has, for the most part, been resisted. They are, however, more common than they were a few years ago, particularly on the outskirts of the four major cities (Dublin, Cork, Limerick and Galway). Recently, there has also been an influx of British and other foreign supermarket chains into Ireland. Marks & Spencer, for example, now challenges the Irish-owned Dunne's, Penny's and Roches stores, which have outlets in all the main towns. Tesco is making inroads on the food front, while US stores like Gymboree children's wear have recently opened attractive outlets. Chains such as Benetton and the Body Shop are a familiar sight and high street shopping in Ireland is quite a different experience from ten years ago. On the other hand, the Irish value quality and are far less 'discount mad' than many other Europeans.

It's worth shopping around and comparing prices in Ireland as they can vary considerably, not only between small shops and supermarkets, but also among supermarkets in the same town. Note, however, that price differences often reflect different quality, so ensure that you're comparing similar products. The best time to have a shopping spree is during the winter and summer sales in January/February and July/August respectively. You won't, however, find shops advertising sales all year round as in the UK. Among the best buys in Ireland are the diverse handicrafts which include lace, linen, tweed, knitwear, pottery, glass, and silverware, all of which are well made, although not cheap. Handicrafts can be found in most towns as well as in the many craft centres that have been set up recently by the Craft Council of Ireland (mostly in Industrial Development Authority parks).

You'll invariably be warmly received in small shops where you're a regular customer and many shopkeepers will even allow you to pay another day if you don't have enough money with you. In major cities, particularly Dublin, and tourist areas you must be wary of pickpockets and bag-snatchers, particularly in markets and other crowded places. *Never* tempt fate with an exposed wallet or purse, or by flashing your money around.

Irish shops are usually open from 9am to 5.30pm, Monday to Saturday, although newsagents and 'all-purpose' shops are often open for longer hours and even on Sundays. Craft shops generally also open on Sundays. Many towns have late night shopping (until 8 or 9pm) on Thursdays or Fridays (or both days). In small towns and villages there's generally an early closing day (usually Wednesday) when shops close at 1pm. A number of supermarkets in the larger urban areas are now open on Sundays from noon to 6pm and large shopping centres (which have sprung up on the outskirts of towns such as Cork and Galway) usually open from 9am to 6pm each day.

Ireland has officially 'gone metric' (see conversion tables in **Appendix D**), but many shops still display imperial measures, e.g. pounds, and the beer still comes in pints!

Furniture & Furnishings

The kind of furniture you buy for your Irish home will depend on a number of factors including its style and size, whether it's a permanent or holiday home, your budget and, not least, your taste. Properties are occasionally sold furnished (for example, if they were previously rented or if the vendors are intending to buy new furniture for a new home) or you may be able to persuade the vendors to part with some or all of their furniture if you make a suitable offer. Ex-rental furniture used to be cheap and nasty, but now it often tends to be of reasonable or even good quality, so buying a furnished property can represent a bargain as the cost of the furnishings usually isn't reflected in the price. In the case of new properties, agents and developers won't normally get involved in furnishing them (as in some other countries), so you'll need to either buy or import your own furniture.

If you plan to furnish a holiday home with antiques or expensive modern furniture, bear in mind that you'll need adequate security and insurance. If you own a holiday home in Ireland, it may be worthwhile shipping surplus items of furniture you have in your home abroad (but not if you live in Australia!). If you intend to live permanently in Ireland in the future and already have a house full of good furniture abroad, there's little point in buying expensive furniture in Ireland. Nevertheless, many foreigners who decide to live permanently in Ireland find that it's better to sell their furniture abroad and buy furniture locally.

A wide range of modern and traditional furniture is available in Ireland, although it tends to be of good quality and therefore isn't cheap. The best time to buy furniture and furnishings (and all expensive items) is during sales, when prices of certain items are reduced. It's possible for residents to pay for furniture (and large household appliances) over a period of up to 12 months. Payment over three months is usually interest-free, but you'll be charged interest on a 12-month payment period and may need to pay a 25 per cent deposit. It may also be worthwhile comparing the cost of furniture in Northern Ireland or Wales with that in Ireland.

If you're looking for antique or mock-antique furniture, there's no shortage of genuine and reproduction antique furniture shops in Ireland. There are also a number of second-hand furniture dealers for those on a tight budget (look under 'Furniture – Used' in the Golden Pages). Note that do-it-yourself hypermarkets such as are common in other European countries aren't easy to find in Ireland, where most things must be purchased in smaller specialist shops.

Household Goods

Household goods in Ireland are generally of high quality and the choice is as wide as in most other European countries. Bear in mind, when importing household goods that aren't sold in Ireland, that it may be difficult or impossible to get them repaired or serviced locally. If you import appliances, don't forget to bring a supply of spares and consumables such as bulbs for a refrigerator or sewing machine and spare bags for a vacuum cleaner (unless you have a bagless machine!). Note that the standard size of kitchen appliances and cupboard units in Ireland may not be the same as in your own country and it may be difficult to fit an imported dishwasher or washing machine into an Irish fitted kitchen. Check the size and the latest Irish safety regulations before shipping these items to Ireland or buying them abroad, as they may need expensive modifications.

If you already own small household appliances, it's worthwhile bringing them to Ireland, as usually all that's required is a change of plug. However, if you're coming from a country with a 110/115V electricity supply such as the USA, you'll need a lot of expensive transformers (see **Electricity** on page 163) and it's usually better to buy new appliances in Ireland. Small appliances such as vacuum cleaners, toasters and irons aren't expensive in Ireland and are of good quality. Don't bring a TV or video recorder without checking its compatibility first, as TVs made for other countries often don't work in Ireland without modification (see **TV & Radio** on page 64). You won't usually be able to hire electrical goods in Ireland, with the exception of TVs and video recorders. Tools and do-it-yourself equipment can, however, be rented in most towns. If you need kitchen measuring equipment and cannot cope with decimal measures, you'll need to bring your own measuring scales, jugs, cups and thermometers, etc.

Shopping Abroad

Shopping 'abroad', i.e. outside Ireland, is generally limited to Northern Ireland, although shopping excursions to mainland Britain and France are possible. A day trip across the border makes an interesting day out for the family and can save you money, depending on what and where you buy and the exchange rate between punts (or euros) and pounds. Most shops in towns near the border (such as Newry) will accept Irish punts and may even give you a better exchange rate than the banks. Whatever you're looking for, always compare prices and quality before buying. Bear in mind that, if you buy goods that are faulty or need repairing, you may need to return them to the place of purchase.

Since 1st January 1993, there have been no cross-border shopping restrictions within the European Union for goods purchased duty and tax paid, provided that all goods are for personal consumption or use and not for resale. Although there are no official restrictions, there are 'indicative levels' for items such as spirits, wine, beer and tobacco products, above which goods may be classified as commercial quantities.

Never attempt to import illegal goods into Ireland and don't agree to bring a parcel into Ireland or deliver one to another country without knowing exactly what it contains. A popular confidence trick is to ask someone to post a parcel abroad (usually to a poste restante address) or to leave a parcel at a railway station or restaurant abroad. THE PARCEL USUALLY CONTAINS DRUGS! Many truck drivers are languishing in foreign jails having been the unwitting victims of drug traffickers (who conceal drugs in shipments of goods).

VAT Free Shopping

Your local customs regulations apply to the goods you take home from Ireland. US residents may take goods up to the value of US$400, including their tobacco and alcohol allowance, without having to pay duty. Canadians can take home up to C$300 worth of goods, excluding tobacco and alcohol, in a year. Britons should note that they aren't allowed to bring fresh meat, vegetables or plants into the UK.

Non-EU residents can reclaim VAT (at up to 20 per cent) on goods purchased in Ireland provided that they're taken out of the EU within three months of purchase and that their total value exceeds IR£50. You need a Global Refund Tax Free Shopping Cheque (also known as a 'cashback' voucher), which needs to be stamped by the retailer and by customs before you leave Ireland. If you're planning to leave Ireland within two months of the date of purchase, you can have the VAT deducted on the spot and simply present the voucher at your point of departure. Alternatively, you can pay the full amount including VAT and then present your vouchers at the Global Refund desk at the airport or port for an instant refund (less a service charge of around 4 per cent) or send them to Customs and Excise on your return home (refunds will take a further six to eight weeks to reach you). For more information on VAT refunds contact the Global Refund Head Office (☎ 091-553258; 🖥 www.globalrefund.ie).

With certain purchases, particularly large items, it's better to have them shipped directly abroad, when VAT won't be added. Remember also that the prices of some items (e.g. books and children's clothes) don't contain any VAT.

PETS

There have recently been minor changes to Irish quarantine regulations, which are due to be revised again ly in 2001, so you're advised to check with your local embassy or consulate or directly with the Department of Agriculture's quarantine section in

County Dublin (☎ 01-607 2862) before making any decisions regarding the import of pets into Ireland. In any case, you should contact the Department of Agriculture (DoA) at least four months in advance of your move in order to ensure you obtain the necessary paperwork in time.

The recent changes are a response to new UK quarantine regulations introduced in February 2000. Under the Pets Pilot Project, pet dogs and cats from all EEA member states are allowed to enter the UK without needing to be quarantined according to certain criteria. In order to maintain 'free movement' of pets between the UK (including the Channel Islands and the Isle of Man) and Ireland, the Irish authorities now allow dogs and cats entering the UK from qualifying countries to travel on to Ireland without the need for quarantine, again provided that they meet certain requirements. Details of the Pets Pilot Project may be obtained from the Ministry of Agriculture Fisheries and Food's 'Pets Helpline' (UK ☎ 0870-2411710; ✉ pets@ahvg.maff.gsi.gov.uk).

Dogs and cats imported from all non-qualifying countries must, however, spend at least six months in quarantine, during which time they must be given an anti-rabies vaccination. Quarantine space won't usually be made available for animals imported on a temporary basis, so you should only consider importing pets if you intend to stay in Ireland permanently or at least for an extended period. You should bear in mind not only the expense of quarantining an animal, but also the distress it can cause (to you as well as your pet!). There's only one approved public quarantine centre, which is in Dublin (Lissenhall Quarantine Kennels and Catteries, ☎ 01-840 1776). Pets arriving from certain countries may be permitted to be quarantined privately, provided that they have a current rabies vaccination certificate. They will still need to spend a minimum of one month at Lissenhall, but may then be transferred to your own (permanent) residence for a further five months' 'private quarantine'. This is subject to a satisfactory blood test on the pet and to the DoA's inspection and approval of the quarters in which it will be quarantined (you must submit a detailed plan to the DoA at least three months in advance of importation – the conditions for approval are available from the DoA on request). Transport from the port of arrival to Lissenhall (and, if appropriate, to your home for private quarantine) must be undertaken by Irish Rail's Road Freight Section (☎ 01-703 4262), which is the only authorised carrier.

Public quarantine fees for dogs vary according to size and breed, but are in the region of IR£1,400 for the statutory 26 weeks for the average dog. There's a fixed fee for cats of IR£1,052.70. These fees don't include transport to Ireland or to and from the quarantine centre, which must be arranged by owners. There's also a mandatory charge of around IR£135 for vaccinations, irrespective of your pet's vaccination history. You must obtain an import licence; if your local embassy doesn't have the necessary forms, write to the Department of Agriculture, Veterinary Division, Kildare Street, Dublin 2. You'll also need a Form of Declaration and Health (Form PQB), which must be completed by your vet and a magistrate, notary public or commissioner for oaths. Note that an import licence won't be granted until the necessary bookings have been made with both the public quarantine centre and Irish Rail. The import licence must accompany your pet in transit to Ireland and be presented to Customs and Excise on arrival. Animals must be sent by air as 'manifested freight' and arrive at Dublin, Cork or Shannon airports (if they're sent to Cork or Shannon, they'll need to be air-freighted to Dublin for quarantine).

Similar regulations apply to the import of other kinds of pets. Animals such as gerbils, guinea pigs, chinchillas and mice require an import licence and must be quarantined for at least six months unless imported from the UK. All birds imported into Ireland must have a health certificate in accordance with EU directives. In general, whatever kind of pet you plan to take to Ireland, it's important to check the latest regulations and to ensure that you have the correct papers, not only for Ireland, but for any countries you'll pass through to reach Ireland.

If you're transporting a pet to Ireland by air or sea, you should obtain a certificate from your vet that the pet is fit to travel, as this may be required by the airline or shipping company. If you're travelling by sea, you should notify the shipping company as some insist that pets are left in vehicles (if applicable), while others allow pets to be kept in cabins. If your pet is of a nervous disposition or unused to travelling, it's best to tranquillise it on a long sea crossing.

If you intend to live permanently in Ireland, most vets recommend that you have pets vaccinated against rabies before you leave home, which saves you having to get them vaccinated on arrival in Ireland. It's also advisable to have them vaccinated against the most common contagious diseases, particularly if they're likely to spend some time in a cattery or kennels. You should obtain advice from your vet as to the best way to protect your pets. Note that there are no animal diseases which are peculiar to Ireland.

All dogs kept in Ireland must have a licence, which is available from any post office for IR£10 (you can be fined IR£100 for not having one). Dogs (with the exception of guide dogs) are prohibited from entering certain public places, particularly restaurants and cafés. Some breeds must be muzzled and kept on a strong lead or chain (not more than a metre long) in any public place and accompanied by a person aged over 16, in addition to wearing a collar bearing the name and address of the owner. These include bulldogs and bull mastiffs, bull terriers and pitbull terriers, rottweilers, doberman pinschers, German shepherds (alsations), Rhodesian ridgebacks, and Japanese akitas, bandogs and tosas. Note also that there may be discrimination against pets when renting accommodation, particularly if it's furnished. Many hotels accept pets such as cats and dogs, and the Irish Tourist Board's guides to hotels and bed & breakfast accommodation indicate whether pets are allowed.

TELEVISION & RADIO

Television

Irish television (TV) services are operated by RTÉ (*Radio Telefís Éireann*), the public broadcasting company, which transmits nationally on three channels: RTÉ 1, Network 2 and *Teilifís na Gaeilge* (the Irish Gaelic station), known as TG4. It also runs a local TV station in Cork city, imaginatively called 'The Local Channel'. The country's first independent national TV station, TV3, was launched in late 1998. The publicity material described TV3's target audience as the 15 to 44 age group with a "psychographical make-up of affluent acquirers, liberal sophisticates, young aspirers and comfy full nesters" (!?) and it offers a highly original mix of... news, sport, movies and imported soaps. In fact the station recently pulled off a major coup in pinching Coronation Street from RTÉ when it was part-bought by the UK network Granada. British radio and TV (including Ulster TV) are also widely available, as are satellite and cable services (see pages 66 and 68).

RTÉ 1 provides European news each day between 5 and 7.30am and shows several of the same 'soaps' broadcast on British TV in addition to programmes originating in Northern Ireland. Network 2 shows sport and also a number of British programmes. Irish broadcasting and the local taste in programmes is similar to most other countries, the most popular inevitably including soaps such as Coronation Street and Home & Away, each of which is screened no fewer than four times a week. An annoying tendency in Ireland is for TVs and radios to be blaring away in public places such as pubs and hotels, where they're even more intrusive than the usual background music.

Although RTÉ is a partly commercial network (i.e. programmes are interspersed with advertising), it's a public service broadcaster and a major part of its revenue derives from licensing. A TV licence currently costs IR£70 per year (it's due to be increased) and can be purchased at post offices. TV programmes are listed in Irish newspapers and in TV guides such as the *RTE Guide* (the best-selling publication in Ireland).

Standards: The standards for TV reception in Ireland aren't the same as in some other countries. Ireland, like Britain, uses the PAL I standard, so TVs and video recorders (VCRs) operating on the French (SECAM) or North American (NTSC) systems won't work. Machines operating on the European PAL B/G system can be converted for between IR£50 and IR£70. It's also possible to buy a multi-standard European TV (and VCR) containing automatic circuitry that switches between different systems. Some multi-standard TVs also include the North American NTSC system and have an NTSC-in jack plug connection allowing you to play back American videos. Grundig is the only make generally available in Ireland and prices are high – almost twice as much as standard TVs/VCRs. Some people opt for two TVs, one to receive Irish TV programmes and another (e.g. SECAM or NTSC) to play back their favourite videos.

British-made TVs need a 'televerter' so that they can receive VHF as well as UHF signals (most cable transmissions are in VHF, as are RTÉ's broadcasts in certain areas). This is an external, mains-powered unit costing around IR£80. If you decide to buy a TV in Ireland, you'll find it advantageous to buy one with Aertel Teletext, which, apart from allowing you to display programme schedules, also provides a wealth of useful and interesting information. In fact, most new TVs (apart from very basic ones) come with Aertel Teletext. A small portable colour TV can be purchased in Ireland for as little as IR£140. A 55cm (21in) TV costs between IR£250 and IR£300 depending on the make and features, and one with Nicam stereo about an extra IR£30. Interest-free credit for up to 12 months can be obtained on some makes of TV and VCR.

It's possible to rent TVs, VCRs and video cameras in Ireland. The cost of renting a standard 55cm (21in) TV is around IR£12 to IR£14 a month (to which an insurance premium of around IR£3 per month may be added) for an eight-month or longer period. The same TV plus VCR costs around IR£20 per month and a 65cm (25in) TV and VCR around IR£25. Note, however, that it's cheaper to buy a TV over the long term as you can buy a small portable set for around IR£140 and could sell it for half this amount or more if it was no longer required. If you need a TV for a short period only, some companies rent them by the month, but obviously the charges are higher. Usually, no deposit is required when renting, but you must pay a month in advance and non-residents are required to give the name and address of their employer or some other guarantor. VAT at 20 per cent is included in all rental rates.

Satellite TV: Some 25 geostationary satellites are positioned over Europe, carrying more than 200 TV channels in a variety of languages. All the European satellite TV services can be received throughout Ireland; the Astra and Eutelsat satellites provide a particularly strong signal which requires only a small dish.

Astra: Although it wasn't the first in Europe (which was Eutelsat), the European satellite revolution really took off with the launch of the Astra 1A satellite in 1988 (operated by the Luxembourg-based *Société Européenne des Satellites* or SES), positioned 36,000km (22,300mi) above the earth. TV addicts (easily recognised by their antennae and square eyes) are offered a huge choice of English and foreign-language stations which can be received throughout most of Ireland with a 60cm (or smaller) dish and receiver. Since 1988, a number of additional Astra satellites have been launched, increasing the number of available channels to 64. A bonus is the availability of foreign radio stations via satellite, including all the popular British Broadcasting Corporation (BBC) stations (see **Cable & Satellite Radio** on page 69).

Among the many English-language stations available on Astra are Sky One, Movimax, Sky Premier, Sky Cinema, Film Four, Sky News, Sky Sports (three channels), UK Gold, Channel 5, Granada Plus, TNT, Eurosport, CNN, CNBC, UK Horizons, The Disney Channel and the Discovery Channel. Other stations broadcast in Dutch, German, Japanese, Swedish and various Indian languages. The signal from many stations is scrambled (the decoder is usually built into the receiver) and viewers must pay a monthly subscription fee to receive programmes (you can buy pirate decoders for some channels). The best served by clear (unscrambled) stations are German-speakers (most German stations on Astra are clear).

Eutelsat: Eutelsat (owned by a consortium of national telephone operators) was the first company to introduce satellite TV to Europe (in 1983) and it now runs a fleet of communications satellites carrying TV stations to more than 50 million homes. Until 1995, they had broadcast primarily advertising-based, clear-access cable channels. Following the launch in March 1995 of their Hot Bird satellite, Eutelsat hoped to become a major competitor to Astra, although its programmes are mostly non-English. The English-language stations on Eutelsat include Eurosport, Euronews, BBC World, European Business News, CNBC and Worldnet. Other networks broadcast in Arabic, French, German, Hungarian, Italian, Polish, Portuguese, Spanish and Turkish. The Eutelsat satellite also links with digital TV and radio broadcasts from Europe (see below and page 69).

Sky Television: You must buy a Videocrypt decoder (an integral part of the receiver in most models) and pay a monthly subscription to receive all Sky stations except Sky News (which isn't scrambled). Various packages are available costing from around IR£12 for a basic package to IR£30 a month for the premium package offering all movie channels plus Sky Sports. When you sign your contract (for a minimum of one year), you'll be sent a satellite viewing card (similar to a credit card), which must be inserted in the decoder to switch it on (cards are frequently updated to thwart counterfeiters). Sky have an office in Ireland, so you won't need a friend or relative in Britain to subscribe for you.

Digital Television: Digital TV, which was launched by Sky Television in 1998, offers a superior picture, better (CD) quality sound and widescreen cinema format. To watch Sky Digital in Ireland you require a decoder, which is presently being offered free with a Sky Digital contract. This will cost you between IR£9 and IR£36 per month depending on whether you want the basic five-station package (plus ten audio stations) or the all-singing, all-dancing 72-station package. Customers must take out a 12-month subscription and agree to have the connection via a phone line (to allow for future interactive services). Sky Digital are currently the only digital TV provider in Ireland, but both NTL and Cablelink are expected to be offering digital services soon. A Broadcasting Bill presented in April 2001 is expected to accelerate the introduction of digital terrestrial TV, which is scheduled to be separated into six 'multiplexes' (one for RTÉ, one for TV3 and TG4, the other four for UK channels, subscription services and possibly Internet and other services) and will use the existing nationwide transmission system. It's likely that digital TV will also be available via cable in the near future. Further information on digital TV can be found on the Internet (💻 www.digitag.org).

Widescreen digital TVs cost from around IR£600, but will inevitably become cheaper as more models become available and the demand increases. Digital TV will also be available via cable and terrestrial aerials in the near future. NICAM digital stereo sound is available on most TV programmes.

BBC Worldwide Television: The BBC's commercial subsidiary, BBC Worldwide Television, broadcasts two 24-hour channels: BBC Prime (general entertainment) and BBC World (24-hour news and information). BBC World is free-to-air and is transmitted via the Eutelsat II F1 satellite. No subscription fee or decoder is needed. BBC Prime, on the other hand, is a subscription channel (GB£75 plus VAT per year). It's available in analogue or digital format and the analogue signal can be received from Telenor Satellite Services satellite position Intelsat 707. The signal is encrypted and you'll need a D2-MAC decoder and a smartcard costing GB£12, which will be sent to you when you register. Note, however, that BBC Prime is available in digital format from Telenor and from the Eutelsat II F1 satellite, so that both Prime and World can be received using the same source. One or both channels may also be available via cable and you should contact your local cable operator to check. For more information and a programming guide contact BBC Worldwide Television, Woodlands, 80 Wood Lane, London W12 0TT, UK (☎ 020-8576 2555).

The BBC publishes a monthly magazine, ***BBC On Air***, giving comprehensive information about BBC Worldwide Television programmes. A programme guide is also listed on the Internet (💻 www.bbc.co.uk/whatson) and both BBC World and BBC Prime have their own websites (💻 www.bbcworld.com and www.bbc prime.com). When accessing them, you need to enter the name of the country (e.g. Ireland) so that the schedules appear in local time.

Equipment: A satellite receiver should have a built-in Videocrypt decoder (and others such as Eurocrypt, if required) and be capable of receiving stereo radio. In most parts of Ireland, you'll need a 1.2m or 1.5m dish to receive satellite broadcasts from outside Europe. A basic fixed satellite dish (which will receive programmes from one satellite only) costs around IR£275; a motorised dish (which will automatically adjust its orientation so that you can receive programmes from all satellites) will set you back around IR£1,200. If you wish to receive satellite TV on two or more TVs, you can buy a satellite system with two or more receivers. To receive stations from two or more satellites simultaneously, you need a motorised dish or a dish with a double feed antenna (dual LNBs). There are numerous satellite sales and installation companies in Ireland (listed under 'Television' in the Golden Pages). Shop around and compare prices. Alternatively, you can import your own satellite dish and receiver and install it yourself. Before buying a system, ensure that it can receive programmes from all existing and planned satellites.

Location: To receive programmes from any satellite, there must be no obstacles (e.g. trees, buildings, mountains) between the satellite and your dish, so check before renting or buying a home. Before buying or erecting a satellite dish, check whether you need permission from your landlord or a local authority. In general, dishes of up to 1m in diameter don't require planning permission provided that they aren't positioned on the front wall or roof and don't protrude above the top of the roof, and that there's only one per house. Dishes can usually be mounted in a variety of unobtrusive positions and can be painted or patterned to blend with the background. Most new apartment blocks are fitted with at least one communal satellite dish. Less expensive blocks may only have CATV, which provides seven or eight popular satellite channels, whereas the more expensive ones will often have SMATV, which allows each apartment to have its own control unit ('flave').

Programme Guides: Many satellite stations provide Teletext information and most broadcast in stereo. Sky satellite programme listings are provided in a number of British publications such as *What Satellite*, *Satellite Times* and *Satellite TV* (the best), which are available on subscription. Satellite TV programmes are also listed in some newspapers and magazines in Ireland. The *World Radio TV Handbook*, edited by David G. Bobbett (Watson-Guptill Publications) contains over 600 pages of information and the frequencies of all radio and TV stations world-wide.

Cable TV: Most households in urban areas subscribe to a cable service, which provides a range of TV (and radio) programmes from other European countries including the UK, France, Germany, Italy and Spain, as well as from North America (e.g. CNN and CNBC). Ireland is divided into eight franchise areas, each allocated to a cable company. Cablelink, for example, operates in the counties of Dublin, Galway and Waterford where it provides a choice of 17 TV channels and 17 fm radio channels for a basic monthly fee of IR£8.50. Various 'premium packages' enable you to receive Sky Sports and up to four movie channels. The minimum subscription period is six months. Those in remote areas (where cables haven't been laid) can receive the same service via a microwave signal (called MMDS), which can be received by an ordinary aerial. The only disadvantage of this method of reception is that the signal can be interrupted by obstacles such as buildings and mountains.

Radio

Irish national radio services are operated by RTÉ, which transmits in English on four channels: Radio 1 (24-hour news, current affairs, chat and 'middle-of-the-road' music), 2fm (popular music), Lyric fm (classical music), and *Raidió na Gaeltachta*, RTÉ's Irish language channel. Radio 1 and *Raidió na Gaeltachta* are also available on the Astra satellite across Europe, and a number of RTÉ programmes are available as audio files on the Internet (provided you have the appropriate audio card). Radio 1 and 2fm can also be found at 🖥 www.rte.ie and certain programmes at 🖥 www.wrn. org. RTÉ also has a local radio station called Radio Cork based in Cork city.

1998 saw the launch of a national independent radio station called Today fm (formerly Radio Ireland), which provides round-the-clock music, news and entertainment. Since the Radio and Television Licensing Act of 1988, a rash of independent regional and community radio stations has emerged throughout the country. Atlantic 252 is a commercial, popular music station which broadcasts from Ireland on long wave and is targeted at the British market. RTÉ's fm signals (as well as those of some local stations) incorporate RDS (radio data service) signals, which are particularly useful for in-car listening.

BBC: The BBC World Service is broadcast on short wave on several frequencies (e.g. 12095, 9410, 7325, 6195, 3955, 648 and 198 khz) simultaneously and you can usually receive a good signal on one of them. The signal strength varies according to where you live in Ireland, the time of day and year, the power and positioning of your receiver and atmospheric conditions. All BBC radio stations, including the World Service, are available on the Astra satellite. The BBC publishes a monthly magazine, *BBC On Air*, containing comprehensive information about BBC World Service radio and TV programmes. For a sample copy and frequency information write to BBC On Air, Room 205 NW, Bush House, Strand, London WC2B 4PH, UK (an annual subscription costs GB£24).

Cable & Satellite Radio: If you have a cable or satellite TV system, you can also receive many radio stations via your cable or satellite link. For example, BBC Radio 1, 2, 3, 4 and 5, BBC World Service, Sky Radio, Virgin 1215, and many foreign-language stations are broadcast via the Astra satellites. Satellite radio stations are listed in British satellite TV magazines such as *Satellite Times*. If you're interested in receiving radio stations from further afield, you should obtain a copy of the *World Radio TV Handbook*, edited by David G. Bobbett (Watson-Guptill Publications).

Digital Radio: Also known as DAB (digital audio broadcasting) digital radio was pioneered in Britain and Sweden in 1995. RTÉ began broadcasting in November 1999 on its new Lyric fm station and is planning to extend the service to other channels. DAB offers improved (CD quality) sound with (theoretically) no interference and 'printed' data services such as information about the music being broadcast, sports results and stock prices. For in-car listening, DAB also offers the considerable advantage of a 'single frequency network', which means that you don't have to keep re-tuning as you move from place to place. For this reason, most receivers currently on the market are in-car models, but 'PC Card' and hi-fi units are also available. PC Cards cost around IR£300, car receivers around IR£500 and hi-fi units from IR£800

LEARNING ENGLISH & IRISH

Although Irish is Ireland's 'first official language' (see below), the second official language and *lingua franca* of Ireland is English, which is spoken by almost everyone. If you want to make the most of the Irish way of life and your time in Ireland, it's absolutely essential to learn (or improve your) English as soon as possible, preferably before your arrival. For those living in Ireland permanently, learning English isn't an option, but a necessity. Although it isn't always easy, even the most non-linguistic person can acquire a working knowledge of English. All that's required is a little hard work, some help and perseverance. **Note that your business and social enjoyment and success in Ireland will be directly related to the degree to which you master English.**

Most people can learn a great deal through the use of language teaching books, tapes, CDs and videos. However, even the best students require some help. Teaching English is a thriving business in Ireland, with classes offered by language schools, colleges and universities, private and international schools, foreign and international organisations, local associations and clubs, and private teachers. Tuition ranges from language courses for complete beginners through specialised business and cultural courses to university-level courses leading to recognised diplomas (there are even courses that combine English lessons with studies in disciplines such as holistic therapy or with golf lessons!).

Most Irish universities provide language courses and many organisations offer residential holiday courses all year round, particularly for children and young adults (it's best to stay with a local Irish family). If you already speak English but need conversational practice, you may prefer to enrol in an art or craft course at a local institute or club. For information about language schools in Ireland contact an Irish embassy or tourist office or MEI-RELSA, who publish a brochure entitled *Ireland, the Quality Location for Learning English*, giving details of all schools recognised by the Irish Department of Education (☎ 01-475 3122; 💻 www.mei.ie).

Irish: The first official language of Ireland is Irish Gaelic, one of the most ancient languages in Europe. It's closely related to Scottish Gaelic, Welsh and Breton, and is claimed to be the purest of the Celtic tongues. Until the early 19th century, Irish Gaelic was spoken by the vast majority of the population, but within 100 years over 85 per cent of people were speaking English. The establishment of an independent Irish State in 1921 led to a cultural revival and an attempt to revive the Gaelic language. However, although civil servants and the police are required to know at least some Irish, the majority of the population don't speak it at all. A recent survey found that only around a third of adults have any knowledge of the language. On the other hand, virtually everyone speaks English (with a distinctive, lilting Irish accent).

In a bid to prevent the extinction of Irish Gaelic, the government provides grants to encourage people to live in the few areas where it's still a living language. These are known collectively as the *Gaeltacht* and are mainly in the west, in Counties Donegal, Mayo, Galway and Kerry. They tend to be pretty and unspoiled areas – or poor and isolated, depending on your point of view. A state authority, *Údarás na Gaeltachta*, promotes industrial development in these areas, while another state agency, *Bord na Gaeilge* (the Irish Language Board) ensures that at least some Irish Gaelic is learnt by all children by making it a core school subject. There's also a growing number of all-Irish schools (*Gaelscoileanna*) and an increase in the number of people enrolling in Irish language courses. *Raidió na Gaeltachta* broadcasts nationally in Irish and an Irish language TV channel, *Telefís na Gaelige*, was launched in 1996. The most conspicuous evidence of official support for Irish Gaelic is that all signposts are in both languages, which will help you to pick up a few words of Irish, although as Irish spelling is far from standardised you may encounter different versions of certain words and place names.

As an English speaker, you'll already be familiar with a large number of Irish words, probably without realising it, e.g. cranky, dither, skidaddle, galore, lashings, smidgen, hooligan, brogue and bog, which all have their origins in Irish Gaelic, as well as more obvious borrowings such as leprechaun and shamrock. The English word smashing, meaning good, derives from Irish *is maith é sin* (that's good) and there's even a theory that the word sure, as used to mean yes (particularly in North America), derives from the Irish *is sa* (it is). However, the strangest derivation is surely that of the word Tory (as used to describe the British Conservative Party), which comes from the Irish *toraidhe* meaning bandit – not so strange after all perhaps!

There are also one or two other words and phrases deriving from Gaelic with which you'll need to be familiar. Most important perhaps is the word *garda* (pronounced 'gorda'), which is what a policeman is called (the police are collectively called the *Garda Síochána*, usually shortened to *Garda*, and the plural of *garda* is *gardaí*, pronounced 'gordee'). Then there are words such as *ben* for mountain, *caher* (or *cahir*) for fort, *currach* (or *curragh*) for either a grassy plain or a leather boat, *inis* (or *ennis*) for island, *glen* for valley, *knock* (or *cnoc*) for hill, *lough* for lake or inlet, and *strand* for beach. *Mór* (or *more*) means big, *wee* is little, a country lane is a *boreen*, *doley* means lovely, a *mullarkey* is a man, a *wean* (pronounced 'wain') is a child, and if it's *mizzlin* (as it often is in Ireland) it's raining gently.

Other words that sound familiar are used in strange contexts: a temple (or *teampull*) is a church; a chick isn't a young woman but a child; if something is clever ,it fits well; if someone is brave, he's a worthy sort but, if he's a caution, he's a devil-may-care fellow; to be cut is to be insulted, to be destroyed is to be exhausted, and to be scalded is to be vexed; fairly means excellently; fierce and terrible mean extremely; a skiff is a shower of rain; and if it's soft – you've guessed it – it's raining! As a *fern* (foreign) homeowner, you'll be known as a blow-in. If you're in fiddler's green, you're in a mess, and if an Irishman says to you, "I'm after meeting your wife," he doesn't mean he would like to meet her – he already has!

But if the Irish language is struggling for survival, the Irish way with the words of their adopted tongue is famously vigorous. You'll encounter that legendary loquacity wherever you choose to travel, stay or live in Ireland and one word you'll undoubtedly come across is *craic*. *Craic* is in fact derived from the English word crack and means simply a good time: a pleasant atmosphere, agreeable company and something to drink – all of which are in plentiful supply in Ireland!

3.

FINANCE

One of the most important aspects of buying a home in Ireland and living there (even for relatively brief periods) is finance, which includes everything from transferring and changing money to mortgages and taxes. If you're planning to invest in a property or a business in Ireland financed with imported funds, it's important to consider both the present and possible future exchange rates. On the other hand, if you live and work in Ireland and are paid in Irish pounds (or euros), this may affect your financial commitments abroad. Bear in mind that, if your income is received in a foreign currency, it can be exposed to risks beyond your control when you live in Ireland, particularly regarding inflation and exchange rate fluctuations.

If you own a holiday or second home in Ireland you can employ a local accountant or tax consultant to look after your financial affairs there and to declare and pay your local taxes. You can also have your agent receive your bank statements and ensure that your bank is paying your standing orders (e.g. for utilities) and that you have sufficient funds to pay them. If you let a home in Ireland through an Irish company, the company may perform the above tasks as part of its service.

Although the Irish generally prefer to use cash rather than credit or charge cards, it's wise to have at least one credit card when visiting or living in Ireland (both Visa and Mastercard are widely accepted). Even if you don't like credit cards and shun any form of credit, they do have their advantages: no-deposit car rentals; no pre-payment of hotel bills (plus guaranteed bookings); obtaining cash 24-hours a day; simple telephone and mail-order payments; greater safety and security than cash; and above all, convenience. Note, however, that while 'plastic' is now widely accepted in shops, hotels, and restaurants, not all Irish businesses accept credit cards.

Wealth Warning: If you plan to live in Ireland, you must ensure that your income is (and will remain) sufficient to live on, bearing in mind possible devaluations (if your income is paid in a foreign currency), rises in the cost of living, and unforeseen expenses such as medical bills or anything else that may reduce your income (e.g. stock market crashes and recessions!). Foreigners, particularly retirees, shouldn't under-estimate the cost of living in Ireland, which has increased significantly in the last decade. If you're planning to live permanently in Ireland, it's important to seek expert financial advice, as it may offer the opportunity to (legally) reduce your taxes significantly.

This chapter includes information on Irish currency, importing and exporting money, banking, mortgages, taxes (income, capital gains, capital acquisition, etc.), and the cost of living.

IRISH CURRENCY

On 1st January 1999, the euro became the national currency of Ireland (as well as that of Austria, Belgium, Finland, France, Germany, Italy, Luxembourg, the Netherlands, Portugal and Spain). That's to say, the currencies of all 11 countries are now locked into a fixed exchange rate with the euro and consequently with each other. Until 31st December 2001, only 'cashless transactions' (e.g. cheques, direct debits, credit transfers) can be conducted in euros and, although all prices should appear in euros as well as Irish pounds or punts, the punt continues to be the everyday unit of currency. On 1st January 2002, euro notes and coins will be introduced, and punts and pence will be withdrawn during the following six months. Euro notes are printed in denominations of 5, 10, 20, 50, 100, 200 and 500, and coins minted in 1, 2, 5, 10 and 50 cents and 1 and 2 euro denominations (the plural of euro is officially euro!). One side of each coin will have an Irish design on it.

The punt or Irish pound is usually written as IR£ (as in this book) to distinguish it from the pound sterling. Like sterling, the punt is divided into 100 pence (p) and is minted in coins of 1, 2, 5, 10, 20 and 50p, and IR£1. Bank notes are printed in denominations of 5, 10, 20, 50, and 100 punts. Now that the punt is locked into the European exchange-rate mechanism, it has a fixed value of approximately 1.27 euro (1 euro = IR£0.787564) and is of course no longer equivalent to the pound sterling, which in March 2001 was worth around IR£1.22.

You should obtain some Irish coins and notes before arriving in Ireland and to familiarise yourself and your family with them. You should have some Irish money in cash (e.g. IR£50–IR£100 or 75–150 euro in small denominations) when you arrive, although you should avoid carrying a lot of cash. This will save you having to queue to change money on arrival at the port or airport (where exchange rates are usually poor). It's best to avoid high-value notes (unless you receive them as a gift!) as sometimes they aren't accepted, particularly for small purchases or on public transport.

IMPORTING & EXPORTING MONEY

Exchange controls have been abolished in Ireland (as in other EU countries) and, in principle, there are no restrictions on the import or export of funds. However, when you open an account, a bank must routinely inform the Central Bank of Ireland of any large account movements as required by the EU Directive regarding money laundering. Similarly, cash, notes and bearer-cheques in any currency (as well as gold coins and bars!) may be freely imported or exported by residents and non-residents without approval or declaration. However, if it's possible that you'll re-export more than IR£10,000, you should declare it, as this will certify that the foreign currency was imported legally and will allow you to convert Irish pounds, back into a foreign currency without suspicion. If you don't declare it, you may find the bank contacting you to enquire where the money came from.

International Bank Transfers: When transferring or sending money to (or from) Ireland, you should be aware of the alternatives and shop around for the best deal. A bank-to-bank transaction can be made by a normal transfer or by a SWIFT electronic transfer. A normal transfer is supposed to take three to seven days, but in reality it usually takes much longer (particularly when sent by mail), whereas a SWIFT telex transfer *should* be completed in as little as two hours. Note that it's usually faster and cheaper to transfer funds between branches of the same bank or affiliated banks than between non-affiliated banks. If you intend sending a large amount of money to Ireland for a business transaction such as buying premises, you should ensure that you receive the commercial rate of exchange rather than the tourist rate. Charges for transferring funds to Ireland vary according to the method of transfer. An electronic transfer, for example, may cost you around IR£15. If a cheque or bank draft is sent, normal bank charges apply (see page 78). The charge is usually the same, whether a transfer is made in Irish pounds or foreign currency. However, in many cases the charge is incurred by the bank sending the funds. Always check charges and rates in advance and agree them with your bank (you may be able to negotiate a lower charge or a better exchange rate).

Bank Drafts & Personal Cheques: Another way to transfer money is by bank draft, which should be sent by registered mail. Note, however, that if a draft is lost or stolen, it's impossible to stop payment and you must wait around six months before a new draft can be issued. Bank drafts are treated as cash in Ireland, so they don't need to be cleared like personal cheques, but there's usually a small charge (around IR£3.50). It's possible to pay personal cheques and cheques drawn on a foreign account, into an Irish bank account, but the money can take a number of weeks to reach your account as cheques must be cleared with the paying bank. Note that personal cheques from foreign banks aren't accepted by retailers anywhere in Ireland.

Eurogiros: Eurogiros issued by post offices in Belgium, Denmark, Finland, Germany, Luxembourg, the Netherlands, Norway, Spain and the UK (France and Italy are expected to join the list in 2001) can be cashed at main post offices in Ireland in local currency (euro from 1st January 2002) or be paid into a post office or bank account in Ireland. Charges are paid by the sender and transfers can take four days to complete. The maximum amount you can send by Eurogiro varies from country to country (the limit on Eurogiros issued in Ireland is IR£1,500).

Note that, since the advent of the ERM, Eurocheques have been virtually phased out and the postcheque system was terminated in 1998.

Telegraphic Transfers: One of the fastest (it takes around ten minutes) and safest methods of transferring cash is by telegraphic transfer, e.g. Western Union, but it's also one of the most expensive. Western Union will accept Visa or Mastercard but not American Express. Amex card holders can use Amex's Moneygram service to transmit money to the nearest American Express office in Ireland in just 15 minutes.

Obtaining Cash: One of the simplest methods of obtaining (usually relatively small amounts) of cash in Ireland is to draw on debit, credit or charge cards. Many foreigners living in Ireland (particularly retirees) keep the bulk of their money in a foreign account (perhaps in an offshore centre) and draw on it with a cash or credit card in Ireland. This is an ideal solution for holidaymakers and holiday homeowners (although homeowners will still need an Irish bank account to pay their local bills). Otherwise, most banks in major cities have foreign exchange windows where you can buy and sell foreign currencies and buy and cash traveller's cheques. Banks and building societies throughout Ireland have cash machines (automated teller machines or ATMs) and you can usually withdraw money directly from a foreign bank account using your usual debit or credit card.

Note that most banks charge around 1 per cent commission on foreign exchange with a minimum charge of IR£1 and a maximum of IR£5. There are numerous private *bureaux de change* in Ireland (including most travel agents), but you should compare exchange rates and fees with banks before changing any money. Post offices, tourist information centres and some stores also provide a *bureau de change* service. Post offices tend to charge a slightly higher commission rate than banks, e.g. 1.5 per cent. There are also exchange desks at Dublin, Shannon, Cork and Knock airports. Note that *bureaux de change* at airports and ports usually offer the worst exchange rates and charge the highest fees (e.g. a standard IR£2.50 fee at Dublin airport's Bank of Ireland *bureaux*). The Irish pound exchange rate for most European and major international currencies is listed in banks, post offices and daily newspapers, and announced on Irish radio and TV. There are now fixed conversion rates between ERM currencies, but banks will charge a commission (e.g. AIB charge 3.5 per cent on all such exchanges up to IR£500, with a minimum charge of IR£2.50 on cheques and bank drafts). If you're changing a large sum of money, you may be able to negotiate a better exchange rate. Always shop around for the best rate and the lowest commission, as they can vary considerably.

UK travellers should note that, whereas sterling is widely accepted in the Republic, you won't be able to use Irish pounds in Britain, including Northern Ireland (except perhaps in towns near the border).

Traveller's Cheques: If you're visiting Ireland, it's safer to carry traveller's cheques than cash, although they aren't as easy to cash as in some other countries. They aren't generally accepted by businesses, except hotels and some restaurants and shops, which usually offer a poor exchange rate. Bear in mind that you must show your passport when cashing traveller's cheques. Most banks charge the same commission when cashing foreign currency traveller's cheques as for exchanging foreign cash. Traveller's cheques aren't available in Irish pounds.

Always keep a separate record of the cheque numbers and note where and when they were cashed. Cheque issuers offer a replacement service for lost or stolen cheques, although the time taken to replace them varies considerably. American Express claim a free, three-hour replacement service at any of their offices worldwide, provided that you know the serial numbers of the lost cheques. Without the serial numbers, replacement can take three days or longer. Note that, for Europeans travelling within Europe, Giro postcheques are a useful alternative to traveller's cheques (see above).

Footnote: There isn't a lot of difference in cost between buying Irish currency with cash, buying traveller's cheques or using a credit or debit card to obtain cash in Ireland. However, many people simply take cash when visiting Ireland, which is asking for trouble, particularly if you have no way of obtaining more money once you're there, e.g. with a credit card or traveller's cheques. One thing to bear in mind when travelling anywhere, is not to rely on one source of funds only!

BANKS & BUILDING SOCIETIES

All towns in Ireland have at least one bank, which is generally housed in its most imposing building. Banks are usually open from 9.30 or 10am until 4pm (sometimes closing for an hour) on weekdays, with late opening until 5 or 5.30pm on one day (usually market day). In Dublin, for example, the banks close at 5pm on Thursdays and the larger branches stay open during the lunch hour. There are eight banks in Ireland, the most widespread being the Bank of Ireland (with 320 branches) and the Allied Irish Bank, known somewhat tautologically as AIB Bank (with 300 branches). These two along with Ulster Bank (114 branches) and the National Irish Bank (62 branches) are known as the Associated Banks, because they provide a clearing system for all other Irish banks. The four remaining banks are the Trustee Savings Bank (83 branches), First Active, formerly the First National Building Society, (65 branches), ACC Bank (49 branches) and ICC Bank (5 branches).

Banking in Ireland is generally fairly non-bureaucratic and branch managers have greater autonomy and authority than in many other countries (e.g. in granting or denying an overdraft facility or a loan). As elsewhere in the world, banking has become highly automated in recent years and in terms of electronic services Irish banks are at least as sophisticated as those in other European countries. All the major banks now offer 24-hour telephone banking as well as Internet banking services (there are, as yet, no drive-in banks in Ireland!).

Bank charges in Ireland generally compare favourably with those in other European countries. As elsewhere, there's a trend towards increasing 'non-interest' income by levying charges against specific services while reducing interest margins, i.e. the difference between the interest rate paid for deposits and the rate charged to borrowers. All the major banks make charges on personal as well as business accounts, although they vary significantly from bank to bank. Charges are usually waived if you maintain an average credit balance of IR£100 in your current account or IR£200 in a deposit account or make fewer than 30 transactions per quarter. There are no transaction charges with budget accounts. Full-time students are exempt from most charges and those over 60 or who are retired, widowed or blind qualify for free account transactions and reductions in other bank charges. In fact, more than 30 per cent of Irish account holders don't pay bank charges.

In addition to its eight banks, Ireland also has three building societies. These are less widespread than the banks but offer an increasing range of services and are open slightly longer hours, generally from 9.30am to 5.30pm Mondays to Fridays (and in some cases also on Saturdays) and until 7 or 8pm on at least one day per week. The Educational Building Society (EBS) has 135 branches, the Irish Permanent Bank (technically a bank but offering limited banking services) 92 branches and the ICS Building Society (part of the Bank of Ireland group) just one, in Dublin (its other branches have become 'mortgage stores'). Increasingly, building societies are offering banking services and they generally don't make charges. However, you should check exactly what kind of account you can open, as some societies offer deposit accounts only, which means that you won't be issued with a cheque book. The Irish Permanent, for example, will only consider you for a current account if you have had a deposit account for at least six months, and only issue you with a cheque book if you have at least IR£5,000 in the account!

Another kind of financial institution in Ireland is the credit union, a non-profit, community-based, co-operative organisation offering loans and savings facilities. Interest rates on loans tend to be quite low, while the rates on savings can be as high as those of a conventional bank. However, credit unions don't offer long-term loans or mortgages. Opening times vary, but all credit unions open on some evenings and some open on Saturday mornings. There are 536 credit unions in Ireland and you should enquire locally for the names and addresses of your nearest branches. Further information on credit unions can be obtained from the Irish League of Credit Unions (☎ 01-614 6700; 🖥 www.creditunion.ie).

An Post, the Irish postal service, offers a range of saving and investment options, and their savings products have the advantage of being state-guaranteed. Also in their favour is the large number of 'branches' (almost 1,900) throughout the country.

There are a number of foreign banks operating in Ireland, although fewer than in most other European countries, despite the fact that EU regulations now allow any bank trading in one EU country to trade in another. There are a dozen or so foreign banks in Dublin, although branches are rare in other cities. Most, however, offer corporate services only. The most prominent British bank is the TSB, which is the only one with a national network. Note that foreign banks in Ireland operate in exactly the same way as Irish banks, so you shouldn't expect, for example, a branch of the TSB in Ireland to operate like a branch in Britain.

When choosing a bank, you should consider the convenience factor, e.g. how many branches it has, where you can use your ATM card, and what international services are provided. All banks and most building societies in Ireland provide credit cards, most commonly Visa and Mastercard, but interest rates are steep (APRs usually *start* at 21 per cent). American Express and Diners Club charge cards are also available, as is the US credit card MBNA, which provides more competitive rates as long as you keep the amount owed under control.

Opening an Account

You can open a bank account in Ireland whether you're a resident or a non-resident. It's best to open an Irish bank account in person, rather than by correspondence from abroad. In fact most Irish banks will insist on seeing you before they'll open an account for you. Ask your friends, neighbours or colleagues for their recommendations and simply go along to the bank of your choice and introduce yourself. You must be aged at least 18 and provide two forms of identification (including one with a photograph, such as a passport) plus proof of residence in Ireland (e.g. a recent utility bill) if applicable. It's best to set up an account before moving to Ireland so that you can transfer funds in advance. It's also sensible to keep an account open in the country you're leaving to deal with final bills and unexpected expenses.

If you need to open an account with an Irish bank from abroad, you must first obtain an application form, available from foreign branches of Irish banks or direct from banks in Ireland. You should select a branch near to where you will be living in Ireland. If you open an account by correspondence, you need to provide evidence of your place of residence and, if you're depositing a large sum of money, confirmation of where the funds originated.

Credit rating is calculated differ tly in Ireland from other countries and you should supply as much information as possi e about your financial status in your present country of residence. If you're leavir a country where credit rating is important, such as the USA, and to which you m. return later, it's worth asking your bank or credit card company if you can maintain a credit card rating while resident abroad, as credit cards invoiced in Europe won't show in credit records in the USA. The Irish Credit Bureau (ICB) is a private compa y operating a credit referencing system. For a small fee (IR£5) you may have access to your own file and challenge or request clarification of any details you believe to be incorrect or potentially misleading.

Non-Residents: Since Ireland became a full member of the European Union (EU), banking regulations for both resident and non-resident EU citizens have been identical, so that even non-resident EU citizens may open an Irish pound account. Although it's possible for non-resident homeowners to do most of their banking via a foreign account using debit and credit cards, you'll still need an Irish bank account to pay your Irish utility and tax bills (which are best paid by direct debit). If you have a holiday home in Ireland, you can have all your correspondence (e.g. cheque books, statements, payment advices, etc.) sent to an address abroad. Most banks offer non-resident savings accounts in which you can deposit money in virtually any major currency without incurring handling or administrative charges.

In addition to ordinary deposit accounts, you may have the option of a term deposit account (in which you must leave your money for an agreed period of up to 12 months) or guaranteed bonds (which are for cash deposits of between 18 and 78 months with a minimum deposit of IR£2,000). Occasionally, banks come up with 'special offers' for non-residents like the Bank of Ireland's Double Option account. To open a non-resident savings account, you'll need to provide proof of identity or a reference from your current bank. Non-residents can have interest paid gross in Ireland, provided that the relevant statutory documentation has been completed. You may, however, have tax liabilities in your country of origin on income earned in Ireland (see **Liability** on page 90).

Residents: You're considered to be a resident of Ireland if you have your main centre of interest there, i.e. if you live and work there more or less permanently. The procedure for opening a bank account is no different whether you're a resident or a non-resident, but residents are subject to tax on all interest earned whereas non-residents are entitled to earn interest on deposits free of Irish tax. Note that you shouldn't close your bank accounts abroad unless you're certain you won't need them in the future. Even when you're resident in Ireland, it's cheaper to keep money in local currency in an account in a country you visit regularly than pay commission to convert Irish pounds. Many foreigners living in Ireland maintain at least two cheque (current) accounts: a foreign account for international and large transactions, and a local account with an Irish bank for day-to-day business.

Offshore Banking

If you have a sum of money to invest or wish to protect your inheritance from the tax man, it may be worthwhile looking into the accounts and services (such as pensions and trusts) provided by banks in tax havens such as the Channel Islands (Guernsey and Jersey), Gibraltar and the Isle of Man (around 50 locations world-wide are officially classified as tax havens). Offshore banking has had a good deal of media attention in recent years. The big attractions are that money can be deposited in a wide range of currencies, customers are usually guaranteed complete anonymity, there are no double taxation agreements (see page 91), no withholding tax is payable, and interest is paid tax-free. Many offshore banks also offer telephone and Internet banking services (usually seven days a week).

A large number of American, British and other European banks and financial institutions provide offshore banking facilities in one or more locations. Most institutions offer high-interest deposit accounts for long-term savings and investment portfolios, in which funds can be deposited in any major currency. Many people living abroad keep a local account for everyday business and maintain an offshore account for international transactions and investment. However, most financial experts advise investors not to rush into the expatriate life and invest their life savings in an offshore tax haven until they know what their long-term plans are.

Accounts have minimum deposit levels, which usually range from the equivalent of around IR£600 to IR£12,000, with some as high as IR£120,000. In addition to large minimum balances, accounts may also have stringent terms and conditions, such as restrictions on withdrawals or high early-withdrawal penalties. You can deposit funds on call (instant access) or for a fixed period, e.g. from 90 days to one year (usually for larger sums). Interest is usually paid monthly or annually; monthly interest payments are slightly lower than annual payments, although they have the advantage of providing a regular income. There are usually no charges, provided that a specified minimum balance is maintained. Many accounts offer a cash or credit card (e.g. Mastercard or Visa) which can be used to obtain cash from ATMs throughout the world.

When selecting a financial institution and offshore banking centre, your priority should be the safety of your money. In some offshore banking centres, all bank deposits are guaranteed under a deposit protection scheme, whereby a maximum sum (e.g. GB£20,000) is guaranteed should the financial institution go to the wall (the Isle of Man, Guernsey and Jersey all have such schemes). Unless you're planning to bank with a major international bank (which is only likely to fold the day after the end of the world!), you should check the credit rating of a financial institution before depositing any money, particularly if it doesn't provide deposit insurance. All banks have a credit rating (the highest is 'AAA') and a bank with a high rating will be happy to tell you what it is (but get it in writing). You can also check the rating of an international bank or financial organisation with Moody's Investor Service. You should be wary of institutions offering higher than average interest rates; if an offer looks too good to be true, it probably will be!

Ireland has its own 'offshore centre' in Dublin's International Financial Services Centre, where there are subsidiaries of both Irish and foreign banks offering a variety of financial services to non-residents, including foreign currency transactions such as non-resident deposits and euro loans and deposits.

There are specific tax rules relating to offshore funds in Ireland, which may negate the tax advantages. In the case of non-distributing funds, such as a foreign life assurance policy, you'll be liable to capital gains tax at 40 per cent on the redemption or sale of the fund and you won't be entitled to indexation relief or the annual capital gains tax exemption of IR£1,000 (see **Capital Gains Tax** on page 96). Any gain on a distributing fund, on the other hand, is subject to income tax at the highest rate that applies to you, as well as PRSI (see page 91) and levies.

MORTGAGES

Mortgages or home loans (for both residents and non-residents) are usually obtained from Irish banks and building societies. The Irish Mortgage and Savings Association (IMSA), which represents the Irish Permanent, First Active, EBS, ICS, Irish Nationwide and Irish Homeloans (formerly Irish Life), has almost 80 per cent of the mortgage market and funds over 50,000 mortgages every year. Mortgages are also available from foreign banks in Ireland and offshore banks.

Although there are relatively few foreign banks in Ireland, more are expected to enter the mortgage market with the change to the euro. British banks in particular will probably start offering competitive mortgages to Irish homebuyers. The euro will certainly affect lending criteria. For example, whereas there are high penalties for opting out of a short-term fixed rate (with some lenders demanding as much as five months' interest), lenders will in future be able to obtain funding from the large euro market instead of the restricted IR£ market and will be in a position to offer more flexible US-style re-mortgage options. If you raise a mortgage outside Ireland for an Irish property, you should be aware of any impact this may have on your foreign or Irish tax liabilities or allowances.

As a result of increased competition, lenders have tended to relax their criteria for borrowing in recent years. Whereas previously you needed to be a long-term saver with a building society, you can now literally walk in off the street and, provided you have the required income, take out a mortgage with more or less any institution.

Mortgages are based on the lending institution's valuation, which is usually below the market value of the property. The maximum mortgage in Ireland is 90 per cent of valuation (although there's usually a limit of 70 per cent for non-residents), subject to certain conditions – principally that the buyer can demonstrate his capacity to repay the loan over the agreed term. Note that the amount you *may* borrow isn't necessarily the same as the amount you can *afford* to borrow! Most institutions will lend up to 250 per cent of annual income in the case of sole applicants or 250 per cent of the main income plus 100 per cent of the second income in the case of joint applicants (e.g. a husband and wife). For example, if one partner is earning IR£25,000 per year and the other IR£15,000, the maximum loan will be IR£77,500. The minimum cash deposit required on agreeing to buy a property is usually 10 per cent of the purchase price, although a 5 per cent deposit is often accepted.

There's a variety of mortgages available in Ireland. The most straightforward is a repayment or 'annuity' mortgage, which is effectively a simple loan which you pay off monthly. In the early stages, a high proportion of your payments are taken up by the interest on the loan; as the amount you owe is reduced, you begin to pay off more of the capital. This type of mortgage is particularly attractive to first-time buyers because of the tax relief they can obtain on mortgage interest – a benefit which is greatest during the first few years when buyers are most likely to be short of cash. With a repayment mortgage, you usually have a choice between fixed rate repayments over a variable term and variable rate repayments over a fixed term. With the former method, the amount repaid each month remains constant regardless of fluctuations in interest rates, but the number of monthly payments varies (if interest rates go up, the term lengthens and vice versa). With the latter method, the reverse applies: the number of repayments is fixed, but the amount repaid each month varies with the prevailing interest rate.

There are advantages and disadvantages to each option. When interest rates sank to 4 per cent in mid-1999, three-quarters of homebuyers were opting for fixed rates; as they crept up again, more than half chose variable rates (currently around 5.75 per cent). Note also that it's possible to fix the interest rate for a limited period only (usually up to ten years). Some banks offer split or combination interest rates, whereby part of the loan is repayable at a fixed rate and part at a variable rate.

Another option, which is becoming more common, is a capped rate mortgage, whereby you pay a premium to guarantee that your mortgage rate won't rise above the rate originally fixed. You can, of course, always increase the amount you repay each month or year, either as a fixed percentage or by lump sum payments. Needless to say, few people do! Note that, if you opt for a fixed rate mortgage or one where the rate of increase is limited, you may incur a redemption fee if you sell the property and redeem the loan (or part of it) before the end of the term. Similarly, if you decide to switch from a fixed rate to a variable rate before the end of the fixed rate period, you may need to pay a 'funding fee'.

The vast majority of Irish homebuyers opt repayment mortgages (over 97 per cent in 1999 compared with around 60 per cent in 1992). Another option is an endowment mortgage, which combines the mortgage repayment with savings through a life assurance policy; by the end of the mortgage term, the value of the endowment policy should have grown sufficiently to repay the mortgage and may leave you with a surplus. On the other hand, there's no guarantee that the proceeds of the policy will be sufficient to repay the mortgage loan and you risk being left with a substantial deficit (as many UK homeowners are discovering to their cost!).

Banks offer other schemes from time to time, as well as more sophisticated options such as pension mortgages, which are only available to those who are self-employed or work for a company that doesn't offer an occupational pension scheme. A pension mortgage operates in essentially the same way as an endowment mortgage: your monthly repayments cover only the interest on the loan, while separate payments are made into a personal pension plan. At the end of the mortgage term the proceeds of the pension plan pay off the capital, and the surplus provides you with a retirement income (you hope!).

There are other options: a 'deferred start' mortgage, whereby you make no repayments for the first one to three months of the term, is available only with repayment mortgages; a 'flexible month', whereby you don't make a repayment for one or two months of the year but pay correspondingly more in the remaining months, is available with repayment and endowment mortgages, although the endowment element must be paid each month; a 'mortgage break' allows you to suspend your repayments for up to three months of a year (this can be done up to four times, making a total break of 12 months, but the mortgage must still be repaid within the original term). Always shop around for the best offer (or engage a mortgage broker to do it for you) and ask the effective interest rate including all commissions and fees.

If you borrow more than 70 or 80 per cent (depending on the lender) of the purchase price, you must usually pay a mortgage indemnity fee (sometimes called a mortgage indemnity bond). This is to safeguard lenders against making a loss if they need to repossess the property and sell it. The fee is usually around 3 per cent of the difference between a specified percentage of the purchase price and the amount borrowed. For example, if the purchase price is IR£100,000 and you borrow IR£80,000 from a bank which requires indemnity above 70 per cent (i.e. IR£70,000), you must pay an indemnity fee of 3 per cent of the difference between IR£70,000 and IR£80,000, i.e. IR£300. To this must be added a 2 per cent government levy, bringing the total to IR£306. Some lenders will spread the cost of the indemnity over the term of the mortgage, while others don't charge an indemnity fee, but impose a higher rate of interest for loans above 80 per cent (the Bank of Ireland recently announced that they are waiving all mortgage indemnity fees). If you're buying a property for investment, the indemnity fee is 4 per cent.

A mortgage indemnity fee isn't to be confused with a mortgage protection plan, which is insurance against losing your home if you're unable to pay the mortgage (e.g. if you lose your job or suffer a major accident or illness) or against your family losing their home in the event of your death. There are various plans available, costing around 4.5 per cent of your monthly repayment. A mortgage protection policy is usually the minimum cover required by lenders, who insist that you have life assurance before advancing you a mortgage. Note also that in purchasing a property you'll incur expenses and fees totalling at least 5 per cent of the purchase price (see **Fees** on page 131).

Commercial Property: If you're purchasing commercial premises, the mortgage procedure is essentially the same as with a normal home loan, but the lending criteria are usually slightly different and it's generally less straightforward. Whereas you may be able to borrow 90 per cent of the value of a residential property, for example, you're usually limited to 75 per cent in the case of commercial property. If you're self-employed, you must usually provide a copy or yourr accounts or, in the case of a new business, a business plan in support of a mortgage application. If you're buying a residential property for letting, you must usually take out a commercial loan unless you opt for a fixed rate for ten years.

Mortgage Term: The normal mortgage term in Ireland is 15 years, although mortgages can be repaid over as little as five years or up to 25 years or more. In his government report on house prices (published in April 1998), Dr Peter Bacon called for the introduction of longer-term loans to help young house-hunters gain a foothold on the mortgage ladder. The Irish Permanent was the first to react, introducing a 35-year mortgage in March 1998, and the TSB followed by increasing its maximum term to 30 years. Perhaps not surprisingly (th longer the term, the more interest you pay), there have been few takers for these new long-term mortgages. In any case, some institutions impose a shorter maximum repayment period on non-residents. Repayments are usually made monthly, but can be made weekly, fortnightly, quarterly or even annually.

Mortgage Application: Mortgages are usually applied for locally. If you live abroad or in a different part of Ireland from where the property you're planning to buy is situated, you must submit written confirmation that you have employment in the area where the property is located. If you're an employee on Pay As You Earn (PAYE), you'll need to provide a copy of your most recent P60 or PAYE balancing statement and a letter from your employer confirming your basic salary and your employment status. If you've been with your present employer for less than a year, you'll need a reference from your previous employer. If you're self-employed, a copy of your audited accounts for the last three years will be required, with a letter from your accountant confirming that your tax affairs are in order.

If you're buying a house which is under construction, detailed plans, specifications and a site map need to be submitted. You'll also need to produce the original National House Building Guarantee Scheme Certificate (HB47), which will be provided by the builder, or (if you're employing a builder directly) a letter from an architect confirming that he will supervise the construction and certify compliance with planning permission and building regulations.

In all cases you must also produce details of any outstanding loans, including your most recent annual bank statement showing all payments made to date, estimates for any proposed work to be done on the property (which should also be taken account of when making the valuation) and any documents relating to separation or divorce (if applicable).

Buying Through a Broker: Between 30 and 40 per cent of all new mortgages in Ireland, plus an increasing proportion of re-mortgages and investment mortgages, are arranged through mortgage brokers. From the borrower's point of view, brokers make the job of choosing a mortgage much simpler. They save you time and trouble shopping around, check the details of all loans available and in some cases even provide a form-filling service, so that all you need to do is sign on the dotted line. If you're self-employed and derive your income from various sources, you may find it easier to obtain a mortgage through a broker rather than direct from a bank or building society. Note, however, that although brokers insist that they are completely independent, there are cases where they seem reluctant to deal with certain lenders. Banks and building societies pay some brokers more than others for the business they introduce (commission rates vary from nothing to one and a half per cent) and some brokers may have special arrangements with particular lenders.

A few estate agents (such as Sherry FitzGerald) have their own brokerage service. Hooke & MacDonald owns 50 per cent of the Irish Mortgage Corporation, one of Ireland's bigger brokers, which also provides life and pensions advisory services, in addition to a tax consultancy. Such arrangements offer the advantage of a 'one-stop shop' for homebuyers and investors, and in some cases offer a better chance of obtaining mortgage approval before viewing properties, so that meaningful offers can be made on the spot (but they won't necessarily give you the best deal).

Buying Through an Offshore Company: It may be possible to avoid certain Irish taxes by purchasing a property through an offshore company located in a tax haven such as Jersey or the Isle of Man. For example, you'll still pay the purchase stamp duty, but on resale the buyer may be able to purchase the shares of the company owning the property and therefore pay stamp duty at 1 per cent instead of the normal rate, which could be as high as 9 per cent (see **Stamp Duty** on page 131). This would effectively enable to you raise the selling price by up to 8 per cent. Before undertaking any such purchase, however, you should seek expert advice.

Mortgages for Second Homes: If you have spare equity in an existing property, either in Ireland or abroad, it may be more cost-effective to re-mortgage that property (or take out a second mortgage on it) than take out a new mortgage for a second home. It involves less paperwork and therefore lower legal fees, and a plan can be tailored to your requirements. Depending on the equity in your existing property and the cost of your Irish property, this may enable you to pay cash for a second home or take out an unsecured personal loan. The disadvantage of re-mortgaging or taking out a second mortgage is that you reduce the amount of equity available in a property. If you do take out a second mortgage, you'll need to provide a recent statement from your existing mortgage lender. If you've paid off the mortgage on your existing property, you'll be able to 'cross-secure' a loan on a second home. If you let your second home, you may be able to offset the interest on your mortgage against letting income. For example, if you let an Irish property for three months of the year, the income will offset a quarter of your annual mortgage interest.

Foreign Currency Loans: It's possible to obtain a foreign (i.e. not Irish) currency mortgage, e.g. in pounds sterling, Swiss francs, US dollars or even 'exotic' currencies such as Japanese yen. This is an extremely risky way to borrow money, as interest rate gains can be wiped out overnight by currency swings. On the other hand, if the currency happens to be devalued, the rewards can be huge. Anyone who took out a yen loan a few years ago, for example, is now benefiting from its 20 per cent devaluation. Now that Ireland is a euro economy, foreign currency loans will become less attractive, as the euro zone will offer low-interest rates (only a few countries such as Japan and Switzerland may offer lower rates).

If you do decide to take out a foreign currency loan, experts advise that it's in the currency in which you're paid or in the currency of the country where a property is situated (in this case, Irish pounds or euros). In this case, if the foreign currency is devalued, you'll have the consolation of knowing that the value of your Irish property will (theoretically) have increased by the same percentage when converted back into the foreign currency. When choosing between an Irish currency loan and a foreign currency loan, make sure that you take into account all costs, fees, interest rates and possible currency fluctuations. Note that, if you have a foreign currency mortgage, you must usually pay commission charges each time you transfer foreign currency into Irish pounds or euros and remit money to Ireland, and that most banks 'load' foreign currency loans (e.g. charge high fees). **Irrespective of how you finance the purchase of a second home in Ireland, you should always obtain professional advice**.

Payment Problems & Changing Lenders: If you're unable to meet your mortgage payments, lenders are usually willing to re-schedule your mortgage so that it extends over a longer period, thus allowing you to make lower payments. Note that, if you simply stop paying your mortgage, your lender will embargo your property and could eventually repossess it and sell it at auction. If you want to change lenders, you may be offered an incentive to do so by an institution that's keen to have your business, although this isn't common in Ireland. Also bear in mind that, if you make a change, you'll usually incur solicitor's fees, and no lender will offer to pay those for you! Finally, note that when a mortgage is taken out on an Irish property, it's based on the property and not on the individual, so it isn't possible to take over (assume) an existing mortgage from a previous owner or pass your mortgage on when you sell a property.

TAXATION

They say there are only two disadvantages to living in Ireland: the weather and the taxes. Nothing can be done about the weather, but taxes – or at least some of them – can be avoided. The Irish have always believed that they are the most highly-taxed people in Europe. In fact, thanks to the biggest tax reduction package in the history of the state in 1997 and further cuts in 1998, 1999 and 2000, Irish taxes are slightly below the EU average. Belgians, Dutch and Scandinavians will find Irish income tax low, while most other Europeans will pay around the same or less. Those in the UK, the USA and Canada, on the other hand, will find Irish taxes high.

This section explains the general tax situation in Ireland, although before deciding to settle in Ireland permanently you should obtain expert advice regarding Irish taxes. This will (with luck) ensure not only that you don't make any mistakes you'll regret later, but also that you take optimum advantage of your current tax status. There are usually a number of things you can do in advance to reduce your tax liability, both in Ireland and abroad. Be sure to consult a tax adviser who's familiar with both the Irish tax system and that of your present country of residence. For example, you may be able to avoid paying tax on a business abroad if you establish both residence and domicile in Ireland before you sell. On the other hand, if you sell a foreign home after establishing your principal residence in Ireland, it becomes a second home and you may then be liable to capital gains tax.

Tax evasion in Ireland is a criminal offence, for which you can be heavily fined or even receive a prison sentence. On the other hand, tax avoidance, i.e. legally paying as little tax as possible (if necessary by finding and exploiting loopholes in the tax laws) isn't only legal but highly recommended!

FINANCIAL REPRESENTATION

If you're a non-resident with property in Ireland, you should appoint someone locally to look after your financial affairs and to declare and pay taxes on your behalf. This person is normally an accountant or tax consultant, to whom all communications are automatically sent by the Irish tax authorities. You can also have your representative check your bank statements and ensure that your bank is paying your regular bills by standing order (such as electricity, gas and telephone) and that you have sufficient funds in your account to pay them.

Note that, if you're a non-resident and are collecting rent on a property in Ireland, you must appoint a 'collecting agent', or your tenants will be obliged to deduct tax at the standard rate from their rental payments. A collecting agent doesn't need to be an auctioneer, accountant or tax consultant, but can be anyone who's resident (and therefore paying tax) in Ireland.

An Irish accountant or tax consultant will charge around IR£400 per year to keep your tax affairs in order and complete an annual return on your behalf, depending on the complexity of your finances.

INCOME TAX

Ireland has a Pay As You Earn (PAYE) system of income tax, which applies to all paid employees. Under this system, you receive a personal allowance of IR£4,700 (i.e. you pay no income tax on the first IR£4,700 of your earnings)and are taxed at 22 per cent on your net earnings between IR£4,700 and IR£17,000 (if you're single) or IR£28,000 (for married couples with one income) or IR£34,000 (for married couples with two incomes). Earnings above these levels are taxed at 44 per cent.

Note that in the short transitional tax 'year' 6th April–31st December 2001 (see page 93) all exemption limits, allowances, credits, etc. are adjusted to 74 per cent of the normal annual amounts.

Exemption & Marginal Relief

If you aren't on PAYE and/or are on a low income, you may qualify for tax exemption or what is called 'marginal relief'. If you earn less than IR£4,100 (or IR£7,500 if you're over 65 or double these amounts if you're married), you're exempt from income tax. These exemption limits are increased if you have dependent children: by IR£450 for each of the first two children and by IR£650 for each additional child. Even if your earnings are above these limits, you may benefit from marginal relief, which is a tax at 40 per cent on your total income less exemption.

Royalties: There's a special dispensation under Irish income tax for artists, writers and sports stars, who don't pay tax on their royalties.

Termination Payments: If your employment is terminated (e.g. by redundancy) and a payment is made to you, this may be exempt from tax. For example, statutory redundancy payments are exempt, as are ex-gratia payments of up to IR£8,000 (plus IR£600 for each complete year of service) and immediate or deferred lump sums from a Revenue-approved pension scheme. Ex-gratia payments made in connection with the death or injury of an employee are also tax exempt, as are certain compensation payments for salary reductions resulting from company restructuring schemes. However, the taxable element of ex-gratia payments is subject to PRSI at 2 per cent (see page 91).

Rent-a-Room Scheme: If you let a room in your home, the first IR£6,000 rental income is exempt from tax.

Taxable Income

Even if you don't fall into one of the above categories, there are various ways to reduce your income tax liability, and there are more allowances for some people than there are in many other countries. If you're able to choose the country where you're taxed, you should obtain advice from an international tax expert. Employees' income tax is deducted at source by employers and individuals aren't responsible for paying their own income tax, unless they have other sources of income. Self-employed people are liable to tax in the same way as employees, but it's collected differently and there are different rules regarding allowable expenses. If you're self-employed, you must pay a lump sum before 1st November each year and then make a detailed tax return by the end of the following January.

Irish income tax is payable on both earned and unearned income. Taxable income includes salaries, pensions, capital gains, property and investment income (dividends and interest), and income from professional or business activities. It also includes employee perks such as overseas and cost-of-living allowances, contributions to profit sharing plans; bonuses (annual, performance, etc.), benefits-in-kind (such as a company car, preferential loan, health insurance, club subscriptions, free accommodation or meals), stock options, home leave or holidays (paid by your employer); children's private education, and storage and relocation allowances. Note that, if you're returning to Ireland and your employer is paying your relocation expenses, you'll need a tax exemption for these payments from the Inspector of Taxes.

If you set up a business in Ireland and hire employees, you must obtain their P45 or tax-free allowance certificate and notify your local tax office that you've employed them. If neither a P45 nor a current year's tax-free allowance certificate is available (e.g. with a first-time employee), you'll need to complete form P46 and operate PAYE on an 'emergency' basis until a tax-free allowance certificate is received. This means you're given the equivalent of a single person's allowance (IR£4,700 a year) for the first four weeks only (i.e. approximately IR£90 a week) and taxed at 20 per cent on the rest of your earnings. For the next four weeks, you're taxed at 20 per cent on all your earnings and thereafter at 42 per cent on all earnings. You'll receive a rebate (as appropriate) once you've obtained a PPSN number (see page 23) and a tax-free allowance certificate, depending on your residence status.

Note that, if you lose your P45, a copy may not be made and the necessary information must be sent by your employer to the Revenue Commissioners. If you're a director of a limited company, you must submit a P45 or P46 to the tax office yourself. As a company director you may make lower PRSI contributions (see **Pay Related Social Insurance** on page 91), but are subject to the same PAYE as other employees.

If you're self-employed, you won't need to pay income tax until after your first year of trading. Two months before your 'year end', you'll be sent a preliminary tax notice informing you when your first payment is due. As a sole trader you pay income tax at the same rates as PAYE employees but based on your net annual profit (i.e. after the deduction of legitimate expenses). If you're operating as a limited company, however, you could be paying tax at only 10 per cent (see **Corporation Tax** below). This means that there can be a considerable tax advantage in operating a business through a company instead of as an individual.

There are also various tax incentives and reliefs for companies, such as the Business Expansion Scheme (BES) relief, research and development incentives, and film investment relief (see below). On the other hand, there are tax penalties for closely controlled family owned companies ('close' companies) if excess funds are allowed to build up. If your business is expected to make a loss in its early stages, it may be better to operate initially as a sole trader, because losses can be offset against income from other sources (if you have any) and you can then establish a company without immediately incurring high taxes. In terms of individual income, there's a tax advantage in taking a dividend rather than a salary from the business, but the total tax paid by the individual and the company will be greater, as salary payments are tax deductible for corporation tax purposes.

Corporation Tax: In May 1997, the Irish government announced that a single rate of corporation tax for all companies of 12.5 per cent for trading profits and 25 per cent for non-trading profits would become effective by the year 2006. In fact, this is now to be achieved by 2003 and businesses whose annual profit is less than IR£200,000 can take advantage of it already.

Since 1st January 2000, if you're operating as a company and your trading income is derived from manufacturing, manufacturing services or one of certain specified activities (e.g. software, financial services, engineering design and planning, film production, food processing, shipping and airline repairs) you pay corporation tax at 10 per cent on that trading income and at 25 per cent on non-trading income. If your business doesn't fall into any of those categories and your annual profit is over IR£200,000, you pay corporation tax at 20 per cent on trading income and 25 per cent on non-trading income.

Note that the 10 per cent corporation tax rate is due to expire at the end of 2005 for companies operating in the International Financial Services Centre in Dublin and in the Shannon region, and at the end of 2010 for all other companies.

Liability

In general, liability for Irish taxes depends on your residence status. You're considered resident in Ireland for tax purposes if you spend 183 or more days there in a tax year or 280 days in two consecutive tax years. (But if you're in Ireland for 30 days or less in either of those years, they won't count towards the 280 days.) You become 'ordinarily resident' when you have been resident for three consecutive tax years. If Ireland is considered to be your permanent home, you're said to be 'domiciled' there (this is distinct from your legal nationality and your residence status). You may choose to be treated as an Irish resident from the date of your arrival if you intend to remain in Ireland permanently and you think it will be to your tax advantage (you must satisfy the Inspector of Taxes that you'll be resident the following year). Note that the 183-day rule also applies to other EU countries and many countries (e.g. Britain) limit visits by non-residents to 182 days in any one year or an average of 90 days per tax year over a four-year period.

If you're returning to Ireland and you're both resident and domiciled in the year of your return, you'll be liable to Irish income tax on all your income. However, if you have spent fewer than 183 days in Ireland during the previous year and aren't therefore resident, your employment income earned before your return will be exempt, although your non-employment income may be taxable. Note that Irish residents are liable to tax on both Irish income and foreign income (including foreign pension income) and that the latter is also liable for taxation in the foreign country. However, Ireland has double taxation agreements with 34 countries (see below), so you will obtain relief if your country of residence is among them.

If you take up employment on your return to Ireland but have not worked there since the start of the current tax year (i.e. 6th April 2001 or 1st January 2002 – see page 93), you must complete Form 12A, which is available from tax offices and your employer. If you intend to reside in Ireland, you'll probably receive the full income tax allowance, but if you start work part way through the tax year intending only to stay a few months, you may be restricted to a temporary or emergency tax allowance (see page 89).

If you're a tax resident in two countries simultaneously, your 'tax home' may be determined by the rules applied under international treaties. Under such treaties you're considered to be resident in the country where you have a permanent home; if you have a permanent home in both countries, you're deemed to be resident in the country where your personal and economic ties are closer. If your residence cannot be determined under this rule, you're deemed to be resident in the country where you have a habitual abode. If you have a habitual abode in both or neither country, you're deemed to be resident in the country of which you're a citizen. Finally, if you're a citizen of both or neither country, the authorities of the countries concerned will decide your tax residence between them!

If you intend to live permanently in Ireland, you should notify the tax authorities in your previous country of residence. You may be entitled to a tax refund if you depart during the tax year, which usually necessitates completing a tax return. The authorities may require evidence that you're leaving the country, e.g. confirmation of employment in Ireland or of having bought or rented a property there. If you move to Ireland to take up a job or start a business, you must register with the local tax authorities soon after your arrival.

Double Taxation: Irish residents are taxed on their world-wide income, subject to certain treaty exceptions (non-residents are taxed only on income arising in Ireland). Citizens of most countries are exempt from paying taxes in their home country when they spend a minimum period abroad, e.g. one year. Ireland has double taxation treaties with many countries, designed to ensure that income that has been taxed in another treaty country isn't taxed again in Ireland. The treaty establishes a tax credit or exemption on certain kinds of income, either in the country of residence or the country where the income is earned.

Ireland has double taxation agreements with the following countries: Australia, Austria, Belgium, Canada, Cyprus, the Czech Republic, Denmark, Estonia, Finland, France, Germany, Hungary, Israel, Italy, Japan, the Republic of Korea, Latvia, Lithuania, Luxembourg, Mexico, the Netherlands, New Zealand, Norway, Pakistan, Poland, Portugal, Russia, South Africa, Spain, Sweden, Switzerland, the UK, the USA and Zambia. Some of these agreements have recently been or are in the process of being re-negotiated (e.g. with Italy), so you should check the current position before making any tax-related decisions. Ireland is also negotiating double taxation agreements with China, Egypt, Greece, India, Malaysia, Romania and the Slovak Republic. Where applicable, a double taxation treaty prevails over domestic law. For more information on double taxation agreements, ☎ 067-3353.

Even when there's no double taxation agreement between Ireland and your country of residence, you can still obtain relief from double taxation. In these cases overseas tax may be deducted as an expense, but there are certain qualifying criteria. Note that, if your tax liability in another country is lower than that in Ireland, you must pay the Irish Revenue Commissioners the difference. If you're in doubt about your tax liability in your home country, contact your nearest embassy or consulate in Ireland. The USA is the only country that taxes its non-resident citizens on income earned abroad (US citizens can obtain a copy of a brochure, *Tax Guide for Americans Abroad*, from American consulates).

Leaving Ireland: When leaving Ireland, foreigners must pay any tax due for the previous year and the year of departure. A tax return can be filed before or after departure and must include your income and deductions from the start of the tax year in the year of departure up to the date of departure. When departure is made before the start of the tax year, the previous year's taxes are applied. If this results in overpayment, a claim must be made for a refund. A tax clearance certificate isn't required before leaving Ireland.

Pay Related Social Insurance (PRSI)

Almost all people in Ireland pay Pay Related Social Insurance (PRSI) and levies for health, employment and training. If you're employed, your first IR£100 per week (IR£5,200 per year) is exempt but all earnings between IR£5,200 and IR£28,250 per year are subject to PRSI at 4 per cent and earnings above IR£28,250 at 2 per cent.

Your employer also contributes to PRSI at 12 per cent on all your earnings. These payments include a National Training Fund Levy of 0.7 per cent.

If you're self-employed, none of your salary is exempt from PRSI, but you pay only 3 per cent. On the other hand, of course, you don't benefit from an employer's contribution. If your income is below IR£11,750 per year, you aren't insured. If, however, you were previously insured (within the last year), you may become a 'voluntary contributor' by making the minimum contribution of IR£200. Once your total income from a business (and any other employment you may have) exceeds IR£11,750 per year, you become 'compulsorily insured'.

If you're a company director and your share holding is 50 per cent or more, you'll be classed as self-employed with regard to PRSI contributions. If your share holding is less than 50 per cent, your social insurance position will need to be individually assessed.

In addition to PRSI, a government levy of 2 per cent (known as a Health Contribution) is payable on your *whole* salary (there's no upper limit), unless you earn less than IR£11,750 a year (IR£14,560 if you're self-employed) or have a Medical Card. In some cases, widows and widowers are also exempt.

PRSI and levies are payable on income from all sources. The only allowable deductions are contributions to an approved employee superannuation scheme.

Tax Calculation

You should begin by listing all your income. This may include self-employment earnings, consultancy income (net of expenses), trading profits (net of expenses), employment income (including benefits-in-kind, such as a company car), investment income (including profit from rented property, dividends and deposit interest excluding interest from special savings accounts), and any other income such as pensions. From this you should deduct any capital allowances to give you your 'aggregate income'. Make your tax deductions (i.e. covenants, non-mortgage interest and pension contributions) to arrive at your 'total income'. Calculate your tax at 22 or 44 per cent and your PRSI and levies at the appropriate rate (see page 91). From your total tax deduct any tax credits and reliefs (on PAYE paid, dividends, mortgage interest, medical insurance and local authority service charges) to arrive at your net tax liability. Finally, deduct any preliminary tax already paid.

Married Couples

If you're married, you should list your and your spouse's income separately. Income which arises in joint names should be split equally between you. In the year of marriage, a couple are taxed as two single people unless the tax paid as such is greater than the tax payable by a married couple, in which case a refund can be claimed, but only from the date of your marriage. In subsequent years, married couples have a choice of joint assessment, separate assessment or single person assessment. Unless you specify that you would like separate or single person assessment, you're automatically given joint assessment (also known as aggregation), which in any case is the only option when one partner isn't earning and is usually also the best arrangement in other cases.

Joint Assessment: Under joint assessment, you must decide which partner is the 'assessable spouse' (usually the higher earner), who's responsible for making the tax return and paying the tax. You'll both qualify for tax allowances as if you were single, but you're entitled to transfer allowances between you. If one of you is employed and the other self-employed, for example, there could be a cash flow advantage in transferring all the allowances to the employed partner. As tax isn't payable under self-assessment until ten months after the end of the tax year, you'd effectively be delaying payment of the bulk of your combined tax. If one partner earns less than your combined total tax allowances, you can transfer 'unused allowances' to the other. Similarly, if one partner earns less than IR£17,000 (the maximum income taxed at the lower rate of 22 per cent), you can transfer the 'unused rate band' to the other partner. For example, if one partner earns IR£9,000 and the other IR£25,000, you can effectively be taxed at 22 per cent on all your earnings.

Separate Assessment: Under separate assessment you're still entitled to transfer allowances between spouses, but each partner's tax affairs are treated separately, so that you must each submit a tax return and pay your share of tax. Separate assessment may be chosen by couples who prefer to be financially independent, yet don't want to lose out on the tax benefits available to married couples.

Single Person Assessment: Single person assessment (or separate treatment) is similar to separate assessment in that each partner is treated separately for tax purposes. The difference is that allowances aren't transferable between partners, so you can lose out on unused allowances and rate bands. This method of assessment is really only suited to couples who are both paying tax at the higher rate of 44 per cent.

Income Tax for Property Owners

Residents: Property income earned by residents should be included in their annual income tax declaration, and tax is payable at their standard income tax rate. You're entitled to deducations for expenses such as repairs and maintenance, security, cleaning, management and letting (e.g. advertising) and insurance, but cannot claim a deduction for mortgage interest on a let property. You should seek professional advice to ensure that you're claiming everything to which you're entitled.

Non-Residents: Non-resident property owners in Ireland are liable for income tax on all income arising in Ireland, including income from letting a property (whether long-term or holiday letting). Because they aren't part of the self-assessment system, the tax must be deducted at source. This means that, where rent is paid directly to a non-resident, income tax at the standard rate (22 per cent) should be deducted by the tenant. The non-resident can reclaim tax if the amount deducted is greater than his Irish tax liability on the net profit from the rent. If you appoint an agent to collect the rent on your behalf, the agent is responsible for paying the tax rather than the tenant.

Declarations & Tax Returns

Tax returns must be submitted by both residents and non-residents with income in Ireland, unless they're on PAYE and have no other source of income. The tax year in Ireland is being changed to a calendar tax year: there will be a short 'year' from 6th

April 2001 to 31st December 2001 and thereafter the tax year will run from 1st January to 31st December. Because most taxes in Ireland are based on self-assessment, individual taxpayers are liable to report, calculate and pay any tax due within prescribed time limits. From 2002, these will be as follows:

- 30th September is the deadline for payment of 'preliminary tax' for the year beginning 1st January last and for payment of at least 90 per cent of your capital gains tax liability for the previous tax year. (Preliminary tax is an estimate of the income tax you'll be charged in the current tax year and includes PRSI and Health Contribution. To avoid interest charges you must pay 90 per cent of your liability for the current year or 100 per cent of your previous year's tax bill or 105 per cent of your bill from the year before that – this last option is available only if you pay by direct debit, whichever is the lowest amount.)
- 31st December is the last date for availing of tax deductible investments (e.g. film schemes and BES).
- 1st January is the deadline for applying to pay next year's tax bill (i.e. the year starting the following 1st January) by direct debit.
- 31st March is the last date for married couples to claim separate assessment (see page 93).
- 30th June is the deadline for submitting your tax return for the year ending 31st December last, as well as for payment of any retirement pension premium which you wish to claim against tax for the previous year, and for payment of the remaining 10 per cent of your capital gains tax liability (see page 96).

If you set up a business part way through the tax year (e.g. on 1st October), your first tax return should cover the period from 1st October to 31st December. Your second tax return will then be for the period from 1st January to 30th September, and thereafter you'll be taxed on your full accounting year (i.e. from 1st October to 30th September).

Companies liable to corporation tax must pay income tax and advance corporation tax (ACT), as well as preliminary tax on their profits, within six months of their accounting year end and make a final tax return within nine months. Close companies must account for distribution of profits within 18 months of their year end in order to avoid a close company surcharge. Claims for excess capital allowances, trading and rental losses, and group or consortium relief must be submitted within two years of the end of the relevant accounting year. Final ACT adjustments must also be made by then.

Tax forms can be obtained only from tax offices in Ireland. If you're self-employed or a company director, you should use form 11; PAYE employees and pensioners should complete form 12 and first-time workers form 12A. Form 1 is for partnerships and Form CT1 for companies.

There are three ways of paying your income tax in Ireland. You can post your payment to the Collector-General's Office using the pre-paid envelope provided with your tax form; you can pay it in person at the Collector-General's Office (at Apollo House, Tara Street, Dublin 2 or Sarsfield House, Francis Street, Limerick); or you can pay by bank Giro. The last method is obligatory for payments of preliminary tax, VAT and employer's PAYE/PRSI.

If you need any help in completing your tax return, you can contact the central information office of the Revenue Commissioners (☎ 01-878 0000) or your tax office (there are 13 provincial tax offices, listed in the green pages of the phone book). However, unless your tax affairs are simple, it's prudent to employ an accountant or tax consultant to complete your tax return and ensure that you're correctly assessed.

VALUE ADDED TAX (VAT)

You're obliged to register for value added tax (VAT) if your taxable supplies are likely to exceed IR£40,000 (in the case of goods) or IR£20,000 (in the case of services) except in special cases (e.g. if you're operating a mail order business). You may register voluntarily before your turnover reaches those limits, e.g. if you're supplying goods or services to other VAT registered traders or if you're supplying zero-rated goods, but it's worth taking advice first.

The standard rate of VAT in Ireland was reduced from 21 per cent to 20 per cent in January 2001 and further cuts are expected in the next few years. A reduced rate of 12.5 per cent applies to certain types of fuel, the letting of property, electricity, repairs and maintenance of cars, hotel and restaurant meals, cinema, theatre and concert tickets, sporting activities, waste disposal, veterinary services, agricultural services, newspapers and periodicals, tour guide services, short-term car hire, works of art and antiques, hairdressing, photographic prints and services, truck driving lessons, and non-basic foods. A 10 per cent rate has now been introduced for the letting of property (and the hiring of vehicles) where the letting contract was drawn up before 25th February 1993. Basic foods, seeds for producing food, animal feed, fertilisers, oral medicine, books and booklets, children's clothing, education and training, passenger transport, and medical equipment are zero rated, as are items for export outside the EU or to VAT registered companies within the EU. Various financial, medical and educational services; certain types of entertainment; funeral services; and the supply of services to non-profit making organisations are exempt from VAT. If you're in doubt as to the VAT rate you should be applying to your goods or services, there's a list of 2,500 VAT ratings on the Revenue website at 🖳 www.revenue.ie.

The difference between zero rated and exempt supplies is that you can claim a VAT refund on your taxable business expenses if you make zero rated supplies, but not if you make exempt supplies. VAT is usually payable (or redeemable) every two months, but it's possible to set up a monthly direct debit and submit a VAT return once a year only. There's a new form BP1 (Business Profile) on which you can present simplified accounts for revenue inspection. All records relating to VAT calculation must be kept for a minimum of six years.

Property transactions are generally exempt from VAT. Commercial property transactions, however, may be subject to VAT at 12.5 per cent if the property was developed after 31st October 1972. The rules concerning VAT on property are complicated and you should take expert advice before completing any commercial property transaction, particularly as there can be serious implications if you make a mistake. Booklets entitled *Guide to Value-Added Tax, Property Transactions* and *VAT on Property, Finance Act, 1997 Changes* as well as leaflets *VAT on Property, Information Leaflet No.3* and *Information Leaflet No.4* are available from the Revenue Commissioners (☎ 01-874 6821).

PROPERTY TAX

There's no longer a residential property tax, 'rates' or 'poll tax' in Ireland, although an anti-speculative property tax was introduced in June 2000, which applies only to investment property. The only charge homeowners may incur is for refuse collection, which varies between nothing and more than IR£500 per year according to the location of the property. Note, however, that when selling a property you may be required to provide evidence that any property tax due before its abolition has been paid (e.g. by obtaining a clearance certificate).

CAPITAL GAINS TAX (CGT)

Capital gains tax (CGT) is levied on the profit realised on the sale of certain assets. Gains made on the sale of your principal residence (and up to one acre of land) are exempt, as are transfers of land (up to a value of IR£200,000) from a parent to a child for the purpose of building the child's principal residence. In the case of a secondary residence, allowances are made for inflation and capital expenditure, so it's important to keep records of everything you spend on a property. Note that, if you let your family home in Ireland before leaving the country, you must reoccupy it on your return in order to preserve the 'principal private residence exemption' from CGT on the future sale of the property. You're also entitled to an annual CGT exemption of IR£1,000, which you should take advantage of by, for example, selling any shares which have risen in value. It's no longer possible to transfer your CGT exemption to your spouse and disposals between spouses or relatives (known as 'connected persons') are treated as if they were made at the open market value, with CGT payable in the usual way.

In December 1997, the rate of CGT was halved from 40 to 20 per cent on all disposals except development land and in 2000 the reduced rate was also applied to development land. These reductions have been effective in encouraging investors who had tied up large amounts in stocks and shares for the last 20 or 30 years to dispose of them and re-invest – in other words, more land has become available for housing and other development (a side-effect of all this re-investment is that Irish share prices are rising, in some cases to record levels). To qualify for the reduced rate of CGT, serviced land must be released for development before 2002, after which it will be subject to CGT at 60 per cent.

If you're resident and domiciled in Ireland (see page 90), you'll be subject to CGT on the disposal of assets anywhere in the world. If you're a non-resident, your CGT liability is confined to certain Irish assets (mainly land and buildings). If you've been absent from Ireland for a period which includes three consecutive tax years, you may dispose of certain Irish assets free of CGT before your return, but you may incur tax in your present country of residence. If you elect to be resident in the year of your entry into Ireland, you'll be liable to CGT on gains in the whole tax year, even if you took up residence at the end of the year (although you'll be eligible for relief on any foreign tax paid on disposals of assets).

When calculating the gain that's subject to CGT, you may deduct the incidental costs of buying a property, any expenditure which enhances its value, costs incurred in establishing, preserving or defending title or rights to a property, and the incidental costs of disposing of a property (e.g. legal and professional costs, advertising and stamp duty). Note that all these expenses can be 'indexed' (i.e. increased to current values to compensate for inflation) except in the case of development land.

In the case of leasehold property, rent from the grant of a lease is liable to income tax, but if you receive a lump sum on granting the lease this is liable to CGT (provided that the lease is for more than 50 years – if it's for less than 50 years the lump sum is liable partly to income tax and partly to CGT).

If you sell a property for more than IR£150,000, you must obtain a clearance certificate from the Revenue Commissioners that CGT has been paid; otherwise the buyer is obliged to withhold 15 per cent of the purchase price against the possibility of CGT being unpaid.

CGT must be paid by 31st October following the tax year in which the gain was made. Note that the period of ownership (for capital gains tax purposes) starts when 'beneficial ownership' of a property is acquired.

CAPITAL ACQUISITION TAX & PROBATE TAX

Ireland imposes a tax on gifts and inheritances called capital acquisition tax (CAT), which is currently 20 per cent. For CAT to be payable, either the donor or the beneficiary of the gift or inheritance (or both) must be resident or ordinarily resident in Ireland. Probate tax (or death tax) was abolished in Ireland on 6th December 2000.

CAT (often referred to as gift tax) is payable if you receive a gift or inheritance above a certain value unless it's a transfer between spouses, which is exempt. If you're the parent or child (or, in some cases where there are no children, a nephew or niece) of the donor, you may receive gifts or inheritance worth up to IR£300,000 free of CAT. If you're a brother or sister, a niece or nephew, or a lineal ancestor or descendant, you're allowed to receive up to IR£30,000 free of CAT. Any other person may receive up to IR£15,500. (Note that these amounts include all gifts received after 2nd December 1988.) Above these thresholds, CAT is payable at 20 per cent.

If you inherit a home from a brother or sister, its taxable value is reduced by 80 per cent or IR£150,000, whichever is lower. Note also that if the donor has previously paid CGT on a gift (e.g. a property), the amount of CGT paid may be deductible from the CAT liability of the recipient.

There are various exemptions and reliefs from CAT. To begin with, the home of the deceased is normally exempt. You're also entitled to receive gifts worth up to IR£1,000 annually from any person free of CAT, so large donations can be 'broken down' into smaller annual gifts to avoid CAT. If a gift or inheritance is a business asset, you're entitled to business relief, which reduces the taxable value of the asset by 90 per cent. The asset must have been held by the donor for at least five years in the case of a gift and for at least two years in the case of an inheritance. The recipient must in turn retain the asset for a minimum of ten years or the tax relief may need to be 're-paid'. Agricultural property (including land, machinery, livestock and buildings) is also reduced in value by 90 per cent for CAT purposes. Charitable gifts are exempt from CAT, as are items of cultural, scientific or artistic interest, such as paintings, books or historic buildings, provided that the recipient allows reasonable public access to them for at least six years after the transfer. The proceeds of certain life assurance policies may also be exempt from CAT if they're used to pay taxes due on the insured person's death. So, for example, if the beneficiary is liable for taxes of IR£10,000 and a policy is worth IR£15,000, he will have to pay CAT only on the balance of IR£5,000.

If you want to spare your beneficiaries from CAT, there are certain measures you can take. For example, if your spouse is of pension age and you have no children, you should think about putting your property into a company, in which case no inheritance tax applies on your death. If you have children, you can set up a trust by which you and they jointly own the property (a trust is a concept of the common law system which may be unfamiliar to mainland Europeans). There are certain charges involved in setting up and maintaining a trust, but these are negligible (as long as your net worth is under IR£500,000). If a transfer is a 'lifetime gift' (i.e. given while you're alive rather than inherited after you're dead), the amount of CAT due is reduced by 25 per cent and the first IR£500 is exempt. However, if you die within two years of making such a gift, the remaining 25 per cent of the tax becomes due. Note that the same taxes apply to intestacy (i.e. if you have no will) as to disposition by will (see below).

It's important for both residents and non-residents with property in Ireland to decide in advance how they wish to dispose of their Irish property. Ideally, this should be decided even before buying property. Property can be registered in a single name, both names of a couple or joint buyers, the names of children, giving the parents sole use during their lifetime, or in the name of an Irish or foreign company or trust. It's advisable for a couple not only to register joint ownership of a property, but to share their other assets and have separate bank accounts, which will help reduce their dependants' liability for inheritance tax. Note that Irish law doesn't recognise the rights to inheritance of a non-married partner, although there are a number of solutions to this problem, e.g. an insurance policy used to fund payment of tax. You should obtain professional advice regarding the registration of an Irish property.

One way to reduce your liability for inheritance tax is to transfer legal ownership of property to a relative as a gift during your lifetime (see above). However, this is treated as a sale (at the current market price) and therefore incurs capital gains tax as well as any fees involved in the sale, which need to be compared with your anticipated inheritance tax liability. Whether you should will or 'sell' a property to someone depends on the value of the property and the relationship, and it may be cheaper for a beneficiary to pay CAT. Take, for example, a couple jointly owning a property in Ireland who wish to leave it to a child. When one of the parents dies, the child inherits half of the property and pays CAT on its value above IR£300,000. Inheritance tax on the other half of the property is paid when the other parent dies. In this way no tax is paid on a property with a value of less than IR£600,000.

Inheritance law is a complicated subject and professional advice should be sought from an experienced solicitor who understands both Irish inheritance law and the law of any other countries involved. Your will is also a vital component in reducing Irish inheritance tax to the minimum or deferring its payment.

WILLS

It's an unfortunate fact of life, but you're unable to take your worldly goods with you when you take your final bow (even if you have plans to return!). Once you've accepted that you're mortal (the one statistic you can confidently rely on is that 100 per cent of human beings eventually die), you should make a will, especially if you want your estate left to anyone other than those who would be entitled to it if you didn't make one. Many people in Ireland die intestate, i.e. without making a will, in which case their property is subject to Irish intestacy law (i.e. the Succession Act), which divides your estate between your spouse and children in the proportion two-thirds:one-third. In fact, all adults should make a will, irrespective of how much (or how little) they think they're 'worth'.

If you die in Ireland without making a will and aren't resident there, the intestacy laws of your home country will apply to the disposal of your estate. If you're a foreign national and don't want your estate to be subject to Irish law, you may be eligible to state in your will that it's to be interpreted under the law of another country. If you don't specify in your will that the law of another country applies to your estate, then Irish law will apply.

It isn't a legal requirement in Ireland to use a lawyer to prepare your will, although the relatively small fee (around IR£40) may save you considerable difficulties (the Irish Probate Office has dormant files going back years relating to personal applicants who've been put off by the work involved). If you want to make your own will, you must sign it in the presence of two witnesses who aren't beneficiaries. If your circumstances change, you may amend your will or make a new one. You should check your will every few years to make sure it still fulfils your wishes and matches your circumstances (your assets may increase or decrease in value). A will can be revoked simply by tearing it up. You and your spouse should make separate wills and, if you have children, set up a trust in case you both die at the same time. You should also make sure that you have a joint account; in some cases, the surviving spouse is unable to gain access to the deceased's bank account!

You must appoint someone to act as the executor of your estate. This can be your solicitor or another professional. If you appoint a professional as executor of your estate, check his fees in advance (and whether they could increase in future). It's best to make your beneficiaries the executors; they can then instruct a solicitor after your death if they need legal assistance. If you don't appoint an executor, your estate will be 'administered' by your spouse, children, grandchildren, parents, or other relatives (in that order of priority), who will need to apply to the Probate Office for a 'grant of administration'. Note that, when someone dies, his assets are 'frozen' until capital acquisition tax (see page 97) has been paid and probate (the official proving of a will) has been granted.

Keep a copy of your will in a safe place (e.g. a bank) and another copy with your solicitor or the executor of your estate. It's useful to leave an updated list of your assets with your will to assist the executor in distributing your estate. You should keep information regarding bank accounts and insurance policies with your will, but don't forget to tell someone where they are! For a small fee (around IR£10) you can register your will with the National Register of Wills and Testaments in Galway.

COST OF LIVING

No doubt you would like to try to estimate how far your punts (or euro) will stretch and how much money (if any) you'll have left after paying your bills. Unfortunately, the cost of living in Ireland is high, especially in relation to salaries. Cars, books, alcohol, tobacco and luxury items are particularly expensive. The standard rate of VAT is also high at 20 per cent (although it was reduced by 1 per cent in January 2001), but there are reduced rates for certain goods (see **VAT** on page 95). However, there's some compensation in the form of benefits to pensioners, which include free travel, healthcare, TV licences, telephone rental (plus a number of free calls), as well as allowances for clothing, fuel, electricity and gas. This makes Ireland an attractive place for retirement, as an increasing number of foreigners have discovered.

It's difficult to calculate an average cost of living in Ireland, as it depends on each individual's circumstances and lifestyle. Your food bill, for example, will depend on what sort of food you're used to eating. A list of the approximate minimum monthly major expenses for an average single person, couple, and a couple with two children are shown in the table below, although many people live on less (most people will argue that the figures are either too high or too low). When comparing costs of living, remember to allow for differences in income tax and PRSI contributions. The numbers in brackets refer to the notes following the table.

ITEM	MONTHLY COST (IR£)		
	Single person	Couple	Couple with two children
Housing (1)	260	400	600
Food (2)	110	220	330
Utilities (3)	80	110	140
Leisure (4)	110	165	220
Transport (5)	80	100	110
Insurance (6)	65	110	140
Clothing (7)	45	65	110
TOTAL	750	1,170	1,650

1. Rent or mortgage payments for a modern or modernised apartment or house in an average small town or suburb, excluding Dublin and other high-cost areas. The properties envisaged are a studio or one-bedroom apartment for a single person, a two-bedroom property for a couple, and a three-bedroom property for a couple with two children.
2. Doesn't include luxuries or alcohol.
3. Includes electricity, gas, telephone and cable or satellite TV.
4. Includes entertainment, dining out, sports and holiday expenses, plus newspapers and magazines.
5. Includes running costs for an average family car (i.e. third-party insurance, motor tax, petrol, servicing and repairs), but excludes depreciation and credit costs.
6. Includes 'voluntary' insurance such as health, household (building and contents), third-party liability, travel, vehicle breakdown and life insurance. Expensive private health insurance isn't included.
7. Includes 'essential' clothing for work and play, but not extravagant shopping sprees.

4.

FINDING YOUR DREAM HOME

After having decided to buy a home in Ireland, your first tasks will be to choose the region and what sort of home to buy. If you're unsure where and what to buy, the best course of action is usually to rent for a period. The secret of successfully buying a home in Ireland (or anywhere else for that matter) is research, research and more research, preferably before you even set foot there. You may be fortunate and buy the first property you see without doing any homework and live happily ever after. However, a successful purchase is much more likely if you thoroughly investigate the areas you're interested in, compare the range of properties available and their prices and relative values, and study the procedure for buying property. It's a lucky person who gets his choice absolutely right first time, but there's a much better chance if you do your homework thoroughly.

For centuries, Ireland's principal export was people, with the result that millions of people the world over can claim Irish ancestry. Now the tables are turning and many of these, as well as others without a drop of Irish blood in their veins, are being attracted to Ireland by its new-found prosperity. Whereas a few years ago the only foreign property buyers in Ireland were American 'showbiz' stars and business tycoons, Europeans now predominate, accounting for some 80 per cent of purchases in the early '90s. At first, the Germans and Dutch were the keenest buyers, but the recent decline of the Irish pound against sterling as well as easier and cheaper travel have brought the British back in force. They currently account for around 60 per cent of property buyers, other Europeans 15 per cent, and Americans around 10 per cent, while Irish *émigrés* constitute around 15 per cent of buyers. (After centuries of British occupation, the Irish take it as a compliment that so many Britons are 'returning' to Ireland now that they no longer own it!) In particular, Ireland is attracting artists (musicians, painters and writers), largely because their royalties are exempt from income tax. Tourism is also on the increase: the number of visitors to Ireland rose by an annual average of 12 per cent between 1994 and 1998, compared with a European average of around 3 per cent. In fact, Ireland is very much the place to be, whether temporarily or permanently.

This chapter is designed to help you decide what sort of home to buy and, most importantly, its location. It will also help you to avoid problems and contains information about the different regions of Ireland, the importance of research, the choice of location, renting as a prelude to buying, the cost of property and the fees involved in house purchase, buying new and resale, leasehold properties, timesharing and other part-ownership schemes, estate agents (known as auctioneers in Ireland), inspections and surveys, conveyance, purchase contracts and completion, renovation and restoration, moving house, security, utilities and heating, property income, and selling a home.

REGIONS

Ireland comprises 26 counties divided between four provinces (or regions), Connacht, Leinster, Munster and Ulster, each of which has a distinct identity forged in history and proclaimed in local laws, customs and values. The regions and provinces are described below and shown on the map in **Appendix C** on page 200.

Connacht

In the north-west of Ireland is the province of Connacht (or Connaught), encompassing 21 per cent of the Republic and comprising Counties Galway, Leitrim, Mayo, Roscommon and Sligo. Once regarded as a wilderness and the scene of the worst suffering during the potato famine of the 1840s, the west of Connacht is a get-away-from-it-all wilderness of rugged mountains, craggy cliffs, lakes and valleys, where little seems to have changed in centuries. The inland part of the province, bounded by the ubiquitous Shannon, is less striking, consisting of tidy fields and stone walls.

Galway: County Galway, the second-largest county in Ireland, is full of contrasts – flat in the south, alternately mountainous and boggy in the north. Irish Nationalists have traditionally referred to this area as the 'real Ireland', because its population is the least anglicised (half of its inhabitants still speak Gaelic as their first language). Galway is the centre of the *Gaeltacht* (Irish-speaking area), where people are encouraged by government grants to go and live. The Industrial Development Authority (IDA) has even managed to attract industrial businesses to the area. Efforts to preserve the language are supported by Galway-based *Raidió na Gaeltachta* and the new national Irish-language newspaper, *Foinse*, as well as by summer colleges where students from all parts of Ireland (and abroad) study Gaelic and learn traditional *céilí* dancing.

Connacht's capital, Galway city, is a busy place that has benefited from tourism and EU subsidies to such an extent that it's now one of Europe's fastest growing cities. Ireland's fourth-largest city, with a population of some 57,000, Galway has its origins in the 13th century. In mediaeval times, the city had strong commercial ties with Spain (the so-called Spanish Arch remains to this day) and tradition has it that Christopher Columbus said a prayer at St Nicholas's Collegiate Church before setting out to discover America. In the 16th and 17th centuries, the city's 'fat cats' traded skins for Spanish wine. Today its young population, combined with 10,000 or more students from University College and Galway's many other educational establishments, make the city a lively, cosmopolitan place. It's famous for its festivals, notably the Galway Races and Oyster Festival, and manages to retain a friendly, intimate atmosphere. Galway city is also the business capital of the west, offering some of the best conference facilities in Ireland.

The city is the gateway to the strikingly beautiful Connemara, a wonderland of lakes and mountains now converted into a national park. Ferries provide a year-round link to the Aran islands, as does the world's shortest scheduled air service, *Aer Árann*'s daily six-minute flights from Galway airport. Surprisingly, there are airfields on all three main islands, the smallest of which, Inisheer (*Inis Oírr* in Gaelic), measures just 3km by 4km (2 by 3mi). Irish Gaelic is the first language on the islands, where ancient traditions co-exist with a more modern lifestyle. The largest island, Inishmore (*Inis Mór*) is 12km (7mi) long and has a population of 900, while the middle island of Inisheer (*Inis Meáin*) is said to be one of the most unspoilt places in the world. Apart from one of Europe's most important pre-historic monuments (the cliff fort at Dun Aengus), you'll find only one pub and no bank – except once a month, when the bank pays the island a flying visit!

The year 1999 was a good one for house building in Galway, but prices were 14 per cent up on the previous year – 20 per cent in Galway city, where the average new house costs IR£115,000 and apartments are selling for at least IR£120,000. An average three-bedroom house costs between IR£110,000 and IR£140,000 in Galway city, a little less in some suburbs and considerably more in others. Detached properties in some areas are fetching up to IR£600,000. Plots of land are relatively plentiful but cost a minimum of IR£80,000 and in some cases up to IR£300,000 per acre.

Mayo: Even wilder than Galway, although no longer remote since the opening of Knock (or Horan) International Airport in 1986, is the neighbouring county of Mayo, where towering cliffs alternate with sandy inlets and the countryside is littered with ancient monuments. It's one of Ireland's loveliest counties and today earns most of its income from tourism, although foreign companies have been encouraged to set up factories there. The so-called Barony of Erris (Mayo's *Gaeltacht* area) incorporates Europe's largest area of bogland, barely inhabited but teeming with wildlife. Mayo also boasts the earliest known land enclosure in the world, known as Ceide Fields. The county is an angler's paradise, with some of the best salmon, brown trout and sea fishing in Europe, and it boasts excellent climbing, hill-walking and golf. Ten of Mayo's beaches have been awarded EU Blue Flags for cleanliness, four of which can be found on the island of Achill (Ireland's largest), joined to the Corraun Peninsula by a bridge. Achill is 22km (14mi) long and 19km (12mi) wide with a population of 3,000, while Clare Island (just to the south) is home to just 150 people and can be reached only by ferry.

The coastal town of Westport, one of Ireland's most popular resorts, is unusual in that it's a 'planned' town. The nearby Croagh Patrick mountain (known locally as The Reek) isn't just a famous landmark but a place of pilgrimage (Saint Patrick is reputed to have spent 40 days and nights praying and fasting on its slopes in 441 AD). The Marian Shrine in the village of Knock, where in 1879 20 villagers claimed to have seen the Virgin Mary, St Joseph and St John, attracts more than 1.5 million pilgrims from throughout the world each year and has been visited by the late Mother Teresa and Pope John Paul. Ireland's largest church, the Basilica of Our Lady, Queen of Ireland, was built in 1976 to accommodate 12,000 people and in 1986 Knock International Airport was opened to handle the vast influx of visitors (there are daily scheduled flights to and from the UK as well as charter flights from Switzerland and Germany during the summer). In contrast, the resident population is sparse – little over 100,000 in the whole county.

The people of Mayo are considered by some to be the 'purest' Irish and the county claim to some celebrated inhabitants such as Michael Davitt (founder of the Land League in 1879, the biggest mass movement in modern Irish history), Mary Robinson (the first female President of Ireland) and Captain Charles Boycott, whose name has passed into the English language. Mayo's administrative capital is Castlebar, a market town of 6,000 people, which is in every way the centre of the county. Its second-largest town is Ballina in the north, with just 7,000 inhabitants.

Property is less hard to find in Mayo than in some other areas of Ireland, although prices aren't as low as may be expected, holiday homes selling for up to IR£150,000 and detached houses for IR£300,000 or more in some areas. Development land is currently selling for around IR£50,000 per acre in rural areas and as much as IR£200,000 per acre in the towns.

Leitrim: Leitrim (pronounced 'lee-trim') is a quiet county, which seems to have been forgotten by the rest of Ireland. It stretches from the sea to the island's centre, with all the varied landscapes that implies. Carrick-on-Shannon in the south-west of the county claims to be the loveliest town on the Shannon and is the principal base for cruising Ireland's most famous river. It's also an attractive and lively place with plenty of visitor attractions. Lough Allen is the first great lake on the Shannon and has recently been linked to the Shannon Navigation by the restoration of the Lough Allen Canal. Along with neighbouring Co. Cavan (in Ulster), Leitrim is an angler's paradise with literally hundreds of lakes offering unrestricted access. Both new and resale properties are available in Leitrim and prices are reasonable.

Roscommon: Inland is Co. Roscommon, the only county in Connacht without a coastline. Rich farmland in the centre gives way to bog at its edges, while lakes and rivers abound. Lough Key Forest Park near Carrick-on-Shannon is Ireland's largest public forest, where herds of deer are among the abundant wildlife. The population of just 50,000 is almost entirely rural and the small town of Roscommon is the largest in the county. Property and land is still readily available for those who are drawn to this part of Ireland, but demand is increasing and, with it, prices (by up to 20 per cent in 1999/2000) as town dwellers sell up and move to the country.

Sligo: The gentle, civilised landscape of Co. Sligo (pronounced 'sly-go'), to the north-west, is broken spectacularly by the Ben Bulben and Knocknarea mountains. Sligo is noted for its archaeological remains and its music, traditionally played on the violin or 'fiddle'. It's also W. B. Yeats' county and most of the places which inspired his poetry remain unspoilt. Colourful Sligo town, the largest town in north-west Ireland and its unofficial capital, is a busy and prosperous place famous for its Yeats Summer School.

There's considerable demand for property in Co. Sligo, although both new and resale homes are available at reasonable prices. Towns like Ballymote and Tubbercurry offer three-bedroom semis for as little as IR£75,000 and even within a few miles of Sligo town similar properties can be had for under IR£100,000.

Leinster

The province of Leinster covers the eastern and south-eastern parts of Ireland. Although it includes the greatest number of counties (Carlow, Dublin, Kildare, Kilkenny, Laois, Longford, Louth, Meath, Offaly, Westmeath, Wexford and Wicklow), it's only the third-largest province comprising around 23 per cent of the Republic. With slightly more sunshine and less rain than the rest of Ireland, although just as green, Leinster is a pleasant place to live. It's an area of tranquil rivers and soft hills contrasting with boglands and mountains. Outside Co. Dublin (with its one million inhabitants) the province is largely rural and has many attractions. The coastline boasts long, sandy beaches and picturesque towns such as Wexford and Kilkenny. Leinster also has more than its fair share of castles, monasteries, mansions and ancient monuments, and has always enjoyed a reputation for wealth thanks to its fertile soil.

Carlow: Carlow is the second-smallest county in Ireland and is mostly flat, although it borders mountains to the south-east and north-east. It's particularly unspoilt, being far enough from Dublin to escape the notice of commuters and having also managed to avoid the indiscriminate construction of bungalows ('bungalow blight'), which are so often a blot on the landscape of the western counties. The rivers Barrow and Slaney are excellent angling waters and the county is a good place for pony-trekking and golf. Carlow is known as the Celtic Centre of Ireland and contains many Druid and early Christian as well as Celtic relics. Most of its few inhabitants are farmers or workers at the sugar-beet factory in historic Carlow town, though multi-nationals like Braun have also established factories nearby.

Property prices here are among the most reasonable in Leinster, three-bedroom semis selling for as little as IR£85,000 and four-bedroom houses from IR£100,000.

Dublin: County Dublin is dominated by the city of Dublin (*Baile Átha Cliath* in Irish, meaning 'the town at the ford of the hurdles'), whose rapid growth over the last 20 years or so has affected the whole county. It's divided into four regions: Finghal to the north of the city, Dun Laoghaire Rathdown to the south-east, South Dublin to the south-west and Dublin city itself.

Covering an area of 448km≈ (173mi≈), Finghal is the fastest growing region in Co. Dublin and includes several burgeoning city suburbs as well as Dublin airport and the industrial area of Balbriggan. On the other hand, Finghal boasts some magnificent coastline with picturesque seaside villages such as Loughshinny, Rush and Skerries, Finghal's 'jewel'. Inland there are tranquil river valleys and unspoilt villages such as Ballyboughal, Naul, Oldtown and Garristown, as well as some 30 golf courses. The Howth peninsula (just a few minutes from the capital) is a popular centre for sailing and other watersports, and provides spectacular views of Dublin Bay. Just to the north are the two-mile long 'Velvet Strand' of Portmarnock and the heritage town of Malahide with its marina and 14th century castle. One of the newest and largest shopping centres in the Dublin region is located at Blanchardstown, just to the west of the city.

On the opposite side of Dublin city, Dun Laoghaire Rathdown also has a beautiful stretch of coastline and some attractive seaside resorts. One of these is Dun Laoghaire itself (pronounced 'dun leary'), one of the main ports for ferries from Britain and the site of a vast new shopping centre. Nearby Blackrock is known for its traditional weekend market. Dalkey and Killiney, just south of Dun Laoghaire, have become favourite locations for the rich and famous, reputedly including such luminaries as Chris de Burgh, Nigel Mansell, Damon Hill, Lisa Stansfield, Gloria Hunniford, Neil Jordan and Enya – so much so that the area has recently earned the nickname 'Bel Eire'. Inland among the foothills of the Wicklow Mountains (also referred to as the Dublin Mountains) are several scenic areas such as Marlay Park, the starting point for walks along the Wicklow Way. Ireland's highest pub, Johnnie Fox's, renowned for its seafood and unique atmosphere, is here (if you can find it!).

South Dublin boasts 1,400 hectares (3,360 acres) of fine parks, where there are facilities for golf, riding, angling and watersports. King John's Bridge in Lucan's Griffeen Valley Park is claimed to be Ireland's oldest. The Griffeen River is a tributary of the better known Liffey, which holds a special place in the hearts of Dubliners. The Liffey Valley, which separates South Dublin from Finghal, has recently been developed into an 'amenity' offering a variety of recreational facilities. South Dublin also has a vast, modern shopping centre (The Square in Tallaght) as well as a wealth of more traditional shops in villages such as Clondalkin, Lucan, Rathfarnham, Saggart, Rathcoole, Newcastle and Tallaght itself. South Dublin's position, on the main road and rail routes westward out of the capital and equidistant from Dublin airport and the sea ports of Dun Laoghaire and Dublin itself, has made it an important centre for conferences and business meetings. The number of hotels in the area, particularly at the cheaper end of the market, is constantly increasing.

Property prices in county Dublin rose by 20 per cent in 1999 (the year in which the first IR£1 million houses were built) and a further 18 per cent in 2000, although the rate of increase has since slowed. The same year saw 55 new home schemes launched, compared with 38 in 1998. The average price of a new four-bedroom semi is around IR£180,000 but, in a suburb like Cabinteely, these can cost IR£250,000 or more. Three-bedroom semis, which average IR£145,000 across the county, might cost as much as IR£170,000 there. But the smartest suburbs are Donnybrook, Ballsbridge and Sandymount, where multi-million pound properties are now common. Prices of resale homes rose by an average of 25 per cent in 1999, family homes in the suburbs selling for between IR£300,000 and IR£500,000. The apartment market also continues to prosper, a recent development of two-bedroom apartments at Dun Laoghaire fetching prices of IR£275,000 per unit, with car parking spaces costing between IR£14,000 and IR£30,000 extra!

Ireland's capital, Dublin city is more than twice the size of any other city in the country and is generally regarded as a separate province in itself. Sometimes referred to as 'dear dirty Dublin' by the Irish themselves, the city is certainly no Paris or Prague and suffered particularly in the '70s from careless town planning. Its Millennium Celebrations (not to be confused with those for the year 2000) in 1988 prompted a good deal of renovation, as did its selection as European City of Culture three years later. Unfortunately, there are still thoughtless developments such as the recent construction of a 'virtual' motorway through the city centre. However, Dublin isn't about architecture but atmosphere and there's no shortage of that, although the relaxed reputation of the many bars is somewhat tempered by the conspicuous presence of bouncers at every door.

House prices in Dublin city have continued to rise rapidly, a recent development of four and five-bedroom detached houses selling for between IR£550,000 and IR£1.2 million and apartments for IR£350,000 to IR£675,000. Land for housing has in many areas reached IR£1 million plus per acre; the one-acre Chester Beatty site at Shrewsbury Road recently sold for IR£7.2 million. Prices of resale properties have similarly rocketed, the current auction record standing at IR£2.3 million compared with a mere IR£690,000 in 1995, although the number of houses sold at auction is now diminishing. On the other hand, there are still areas where property can be bought at reasonable prices. In Clontarf, for example, on the less fashionable north side of the River Liffey, there are period homes for IR£100,000 or less. The number of new apartments dropped for the first time in 1999, although a large part of the IR£1.6 billion Docklands Development, where an estimated 10,500 homes are to be created by the year 2012, is due to consist of apartment blocks. Apartment prices continue to soar: recent developments like Carnegie Court in the Swords area have attracted prices of IR£115,000 for one-bedroom apartments and, at the other end of the scale, IR£1 million apartments have been sold on the Dalkey Island site. The year 2000 saw 500 units in Milltown, Dublin 6 come on stream, priced at around IR£160,000 for one-bedroom and up to IR£280,000 for two-bedroom apartments.

Louth & Meath: Louth and Meath, the most northerly counties in Leinster, are predominantly farmland, but Louth, Ireland's smallest county, has a wild side and the Cooley Peninsula near the border with Northern Ireland is one of the most beautiful and unspoilt places in the whole country. The coastal town of Dundalk is the county capital and contains a number of fine 15th century buildings, while nearby Carlingford has even earlier remains including a castle and mint. Ancient relics are concealed in the rich pastures of Meath (the seat of the ancient kings of Ireland is said to be on Tara Hill, from where you can see seven counties), but the county also boasts the popular seaside resorts of Clogherhead, Laytown and Bettystown, all part of a 'coastal resort' scheme. Meath's principal town, Drogheda, is a colourful place with medieval origins. Dundalk in Co. Louth, on the other hand, is set for modern industrial development and will be the new location for Rank Xerox, who employ more than 2,000 people.

Both counties have experienced a huge increase in population in recent years as people with jobs in Dublin have settled there and commute to the capital. Particularly high growth has been experienced by Dunshaughlin, Ashbourne, Dunboyne, Navan, Drogheda and Dundalk, where three-bedroom semis are selling for at least IR£115,000 and detached homes for IR£185,000. Land prices have risen to IR£400,000 per acre or more in some areas and property is scarce, the 'idyllic country cottage' being virtually impossible to find.

Kildare: County Kildare is one of the most densely populated counties (relatively speaking), being within easy commuting distance of Dublin. Towns such as Naas, Newbridge and Kildare (all lying near the M7 motorway) have recently experienced growth of up to 600 new homes a year and their population is growing annually at almost 10 per cent. Villages like Celbridge and Leixlip have been all but swallowed by the rapidly expanding capital. In fact, Collinstown Industrial Park near Leixlip, where in 1990 there were stud farms and potato fields, is now Ireland's 'silicon valley', home to Intel Ireland (the European subsidiary of one of America's largest microchip producers), Rank Xerox, Hewlett Packard and IBM, among other giant corporations. None the less, there's still plenty of countryside to be enjoyed in Co. Kildare. The river Barrow, for example, provides good fishing and attractive cruising, and there are lovely drives and walks (and even barge trips) along the Grand and Royal Canals, which meet near Robertstown on their way to Dublin and the sea. Even the rather unattractive town of Kildare lies on the edge of the famous Curragh, a 2,000 hectare plain where some of the world's best race horses are bred and trained. The National Stud and Horse Museum is at Tully, adjacent to the famous Japanese Gardens.

Property prices, particularly for traditional homes in the 'commuter belt', have escalated rapidly, development land now selling for up to IR£250,000 per acre.

Kilkenny: To the west of Carlow is Kilkenny, one of the most 'English' counties of Ireland, with its neat villages and fields. It's a prosperous agricultural area noted for its craftsmen, particularly in Kilkenny city, Ireland's mediaeval capital and one of its architecturally most interesting towns. If Carlow is the Celtic Centre of Ireland, Kilkenny claims to be its 'hospitable heart': an abundance of hotels (400 bedrooms were added in 1999 alone), restaurants, pubs, festivals and warm-hearted people make Kilkenny an excellent place for relaxation and enjoyment (but then the same could be said for most of Ireland!).

Laois: The furthest south of this group of counties is Laois, a rural area divided by the N7 Dublin/Limerick road. Its only proper town, Portlaoise, has been bypassed by one of the few stretches of motorway outside the capital. The major employer in this part of Ireland is the Irish turf development authority, *Bord na Mona*, which provides work for some 5,000 people.

Longford: The counties of Longford, Westmeath, Offaly, and Laois, in the centre of Ireland, are flat and wet, being covered with lakes and bogland. They tend to be ignored by visitors passing through on their way from Dublin to the south and west, and as a result have their own unique, quiet beauty. Longford is a peaceful and picturesque county bordering Lough Ree, one of the great lakes on the Shannon. It has many pretty villages including Ardagh, Newtowncashel and Lanesborough.

Property-wise, Longford is on the point of being 'discovered' and prices, although still reasonable, are set to rise swiftly. Two-bedroom apartments and three-bedroom semis can still be had for as little as IR£80,000 and four-bedroom bungalows for IR£110,000. Development land can cost just IR£30,000 per acre.

Offaly: Offaly to the south, boasts the internationally famous monastic site at Clonmacnoise (one of Ireland's holiest places), the Slieve Bloom mountains with their cascading streams and waterfalls, the restored 18th century town of Birr (with the world's tallest box hedges!), and one of the Shannon's main boating centres at Banagher. The principal town of Tullamore is another cruising base, but on the Grand Canal rather than the River Shannon (it's also home to a famous Irish whiskey).

Westmeath: Westmeath is similarly tranquil, although watersports enthusiasts are attracted to its chain of smaller lakes (Ennel, Owel, Derravaragh and Lene). Westmeath is particularly rich in places of interest such as Edgeworthstown House, 17th century Fore Abbey and Tullynally Castle (one of the 'Seven Wonders of Fore'), Delvin Castle and Castlepollard, the largest castellated house in Ireland. Glasson, known as the village of the roses, is in the heart of 'Goldsmith Country', where Oliver Goldsmith, one of Ireland's most famous poets, lived in the 18th century. Kinnegad, in the extreme east of the county, lies at the junction of the main roads from Galway and Sligo to Dublin, and is the centre of *An Boreen Bradach*, a walker's paradise. The historic town of Athlone, once one of the few crossing points of the Shannon, is now the largest town on the river, a busy and prosperous place and a popular base for pleasure cruisers, while the county town of Mullingar ('capital of the lakes') is a thriving business and industrial centre on the Royal Canal.

Wexford: At the south-eastern tip of Ireland is Co. Wexford, the warmest and driest place in the country. In fact many Irish families spend their summer holidays there in preference to Spain! Wexford has some 200km (124mi) of coastline and numerous unspoiled sandy beaches, including the magnificent Curracloe Beach (which doubled as the scene of the Normandy landings in Steven Spielberg's film *Saving Private Ryan*). Wexford is one of the world's most important wild bird sanctuaries, visited by flocks migrating to and from the Arctic. Known as the 'model county', Wexford also offers heritage parks and museums, golf courses and race tracks (greyhounds as well as horses). The Blackstairs Mountains in the north-west of the county are a popular hiking area. Wexford is the closest point to Wales and in the past has been the landing place of many a foreign invasion, while Rosslare Harbour is a major ferry port for modern 'invaders' travelling to and from Britain and France.

Nearby Wexford town is among the most atmospheric and historically interesting places in Ireland and is internationally famous for its annual Opera Festival in October.

The county is proving particularly attractive to Dubliners, who are finding that they can sell a relatively modest property in the capital for IR£300,000 and buy a similar one in Wexford for half as much. The town of Gorey in the northern part of the county, for example, has seen 1,000 or more new houses built in the last few years and starter-home prices have risen to IR£100,000. Sites, where they can be found, are selling for IR£60,000 and more. Nearby Courtown, on the coast, has been transformed by the Seaside Resorts Scheme and a three-bedroom house here costs at least IR£90,000.

Wicklow: County Wicklow, to the north, is another quintessentially Irish county, yet it's within half an hour's drive of Dublin. City dwellers call it the 'garden of Ireland', although it may be more accurately described as the 'playground of Dublin'. Many of the growing population of 100,000 work in the capital and commute from towns such as Greystones and Blessington, where the Liffey Valley was flooded in 1940 to create the Blessington Lakes. Further south, on the other hand, farming is widespread and the Wicklow Mountains are among the most impressive in Ireland (the film *Braveheart*, supposedly set in Scotland, was filmed here). The sixth century monastic complex at Glendalough, one of Ireland's greatest national monuments, nestles in the heart of the mountains at the spectacular Wicklow Gap, and there are other fascinating places nearby such as the Devil's Glen Forest Park, wild and beautiful Glenmalure, the 'meeting of the waters' at Avoca (location for the popular British TV series *Ballykissangel*), Baltinglass Abbey and Roundwood (Ireland's highest village).

The county town of Wicklow is situated on the slopes of Ballyguile Hill, overlooking a wide curve of coastline. On the coast, the fishing port of Arklow is renowned for its pottery, Brittas Bay boasts 5km (3mi) of safe sandy beach and Bray, on the border with Co. Dublin, is one of Ireland's principal resorts. Wicklow contains no fewer than five of Ireland's finest Heritage Gardens and also claims to be one of the best golfing counties in Ireland, with more than 20 courses including the country's oldest at Woodenbridge.

Just 30 miles south of Dublin, Wicklow town is also becoming a popular commuter base – with correspondingly rising property prices: three-bedroom semis now start at IR£145,000 and four-bedroom detached houses at twice that figure. In particularly high demand in the county as a whole are period houses; even virtual ruins are selling for over IR£100,000.

Munster

Munster is Ireland's largest province, covering almost 30 per cent of the country and including the counties of Clare, Cork, Kerry, Limerick, Tipperary and Waterford. It's Ireland's most southerly region and the most popular with both holidaymakers and foreign homebuyers. The counties of Cork, Kerry and Waterford are particularly sought-after – Bantry Bay in west Cork has become something of a magnet for the international jet-set (e.g. American and British film and pop stars) and a few once parochial fishing villages now have a cosmopolitan feel. Geographically, Munster has everything that's considered typically Irish: brooding mountains, a craggy coastline with sandy bays between rocky cliffs, alternately fertile and barren plains. Cut off from the rest of Ireland by mountains, bogs and the River Shannon, Munster has become a land of myth and legend with strong musical and poetic traditions. Its people are also traditionalists: warm and relaxed but with an argumentative streak.

Cork: Munster's principal town is Cork city, the second-largest city in Ireland and capital of its biggest and most southerly county of the same name. Cork is the unofficial capital of the south of Ireland (its citizens, whom Dubliners dismiss as *culchies* or 'country folk', think it should be the capital of the country). Sophisticated and cosmopolitan with its own University, Cork is much smaller than Dublin (its population is just 180,000) and has managed to retain a friendly, small-town atmosphere. It's nevertheless a lively place full of young people and bustling with traffic. Cork county has some of the richest farming land in Ireland as well as some of the most spectacular coastal and mountain scenery, combined with gentle bays and hills and numerous marshes (the name Cork comes from the Gaelic *Corcaigh*, meaning 'marshy place'). Nearby is the port of Cobh (pronounced 'cove'), from where some two and a half million people have emigrated to America since 1848. County Cork is also home to the famous Blarney Stone, which is supposed to bestow the 'gift of the gab' upon whoever kisses it – unless you're Irish, in which case you're born with it! Ringaskiddy and Little Island near Cork city are among the few industrial areas in Ireland (the largest being at Leixlip near Dublin), where a number of large pharmaceutical companies have established major concerns.

Property prices in and around Cork city are the highest in the country after Dublin and in 1999 rose even more steeply than the capital's, partly due to the local employment boom. In towns surrounding Cork city, smarter houses that would have cost IR£85,000 in 1998 reached IR£110,000 or even IR£120,000. City apartment prices have almost reached IR£250,000 and up-market new houses are fetching up to IR£500,000. Dancer Michael Flatley (of Riverdance fame) is reported to have spent over IR£2.5 million on a house by the River Blackwater above Fermoy.

The eastern part of the county, and especially towns like Midleton which are within commuting distance of the city, is set to witness something of a housing explosion now that the Lee Tunnel is open. Land prices too have soared: satellite town land averages IR£150,000 per acre while closer to Cork city builders can expect to pay up to IR£300,000 per acre; one or two prime suburban sites have recently made IR£1 million per acre.

Clare: County Clare is one of the most barren parts of Ireland and is almost untouched by tourism despite the nearby presence of Shannon Airport. Covering an area of 160 km≈ (62mi≈), the area known as the Burren is particularly desolate and has a unique landscape (with no bogs and few pastures) strewn with limestone slabs and boulders. Legend has it that one of Oliver Cromwell's soldiers described it as 'a savage land, yielding neither water enough to drown a man, nor tree to hang him, nor soil enough to bury him'. Nevertheless, the Burren is also famous for its variety of plant and animal life, including the rarely seen pine marten and 26 of the country's 33 species of butterfly, one of which, the Burren Green, is peculiar to the area. With three-quarters of its border on the sea, Co. Clare is one of Ireland's premier holiday centres. Traditional seaside resorts such as Spanish Point, Lahinch and Kilkee, and the spectacular Cliffs of Moher plunging more than 200 metres into the Atlantic, make it popular with both foreign and Irish holidaymakers. Clare also has a fair share of historical interest, like the ancient town of Ennis and the Poulnabrone Dolmen (or Portal Tomb), one of Ireland's most photographed monuments. Ennis is of interest for another reason: in a national competition sponsored by *Telecom Éireann* in 1997, it was selected as Ireland's 'Information Age' town, where IR£15 million is being invested in cutting-edge IT development for both businesses and the local community. Nearby Shannon is Ireland's only new town to have been built for centuries, having developed as recently as the '60s to accommodate workers at the Shannon Industrial Tax Free Zone, created by an act of parliament in 1947. Today it's a thriving small town of 10,000 inhabitants. Ireland's largest hydro-electric plant, the Shannon Scheme, is also situated in County Clare.

Recent planning delays have restricted the building of new houses in Clare, so that prices, already soaring, rocketed by as much as 40 per cent in 1999. In Ennis, three-bedroom terraced houses have broken the IR£100,000 barrier. A luxury development just outside Ennis saw buyers paying as much as IR£400,000 for properties on one-acre sites. The average price of land in Clare is IR£150,000 per acre.

Kerry: The archetypal Ireland is to be found in Co. Kerry, which contains three of the country's most visited places: the rather commercialised town of Killarney with its magnificent lake, the Iveragh Peninsula (better known as the Ring of Kerry) and the Dingle Peninsula – not to mention its grandest and highest range of mountains, MacGillycuddy's Reeks. Ballybunion is one of Ireland's premier seaside resorts and Kinsale is popular for yachting as well as laying claim to be Ireland's gourmet capital (it has hosted the International Gourmet Festival in October since 1987). Tralee is home to the internationally famous Festival of Kerry and Rose of Tralee Festival, which was established in 1939 in an attempt to attract visitors away from Killarney, as well as Ireland's biggest selection of all-weather visitor attractions. Both Tralee and Killarney are popular among retirees, particularly from Dublin. Kerry is also said to be where you'll find Ireland's friendliest, most flamboyant and humorous people – as well as its wettest weather! In fact the Gulf Stream keeps the climate fairly mild, and snow and frost are rare.

The recent property boom has centred on Kerry, which boasts easy access (direct flights to Dublin as well as Luton and Manchester in the UK), some of the cleanest water and air in Europe, and 10,000 hectares (25,000 acres) of national park for golf, fishing and walking. Not surprisingly, resale property is scarce, particularly in coastal areas. Most of what's available is newly built, but even that is snapped up almost as soon as the mortar is dry – or even before. In Killarney, new three-bedroom semis average IR£140,000 and similar resale properties between IR£110,000 and IR£135,000. Better value is to be had in Tralee, where ex-local authority townhouses can be bought for IR£85,000. Residential development land costs between IR£250,000 and IR£300,000 per acre.

Limerick: Limerick was a county long before it became a 'nonsense' verse, although the tradition of inventing five-line stanzas is said to have originated in the 18th century in the drinking games of a group of would-be poets from the town of Croom. County Limerick itself is a peaceful farming area with some of the country's finest dairy cattle (it's also famous for its horses). The fertile pastures are dotted with the ruins of hundreds of castles and surrounded by hills and mountains. To the north is the River Shannon, which unofficially divides the south-west from the west of Ireland. Where the Shannon meets the Atlantic lies the ancient city of Limerick, the country's third largest city (after Dublin and Cork). Once felt to be rather drab, the city has recently had a substantial facelift and boasts smart clothes shops as well as a thriving arts centre and lively nightlife. Limerick is also the home of one of the most important collections of mediaeval artefacts in the world, the Hunt Collection, and has lately won worldwide renown as the setting of Frank McCourt's autobiographical novel Angela's Ashes. There's still high unemployment, but new industries have been established in and around the city; Dell computers, for example, are currently building a IR£20 million plant at Raheen. Colourful market towns are scattered throughout the county, notably Castleconnell, Kilfinane, Kilmallock and Newcastle West. Adare, with its old-world, thatched cottages and mediaeval churches, recalls a bygone way of life and claims to be Ireland's prettiest village.

House prices in Co. Limerick rose by an average of 20 per cent in 1999 and an acre of land can fetch IR£250,000. Limerick town has a number of residential developments, with three-bedroom semis ranging from IR£95,000 to IR£130,000.

Tipperary: "It's a long way to Tipperary" goes the song, but that rather depends on where you set out from. Tipperary is the most southerly of the inland counties of Ireland (Carlow, Cavan, Kildare, Kilkenny, Longford, Laois, Monaghan, Offaly, Roscommon and Westmeath also lack a coastline) and one of the most beautiful. Tipperary is rich in contrast with flat, fertile farmland (known as the Golden Vale) interspersed by low but spectacular mountains: the Silvermines and Devil's Bit in the north and the Galtee in the south. The River Suir is noted for its trout and Lough Derg on the river Shannon is Ireland's largest lake, while hunting is a popular pastime in other parts of Tipperary. Clonmel (in the south) means 'honeyed meadows' and has a prosperous air deriving from the abundance of food produced in the county.

Waterford: Waterford is a fertile county watered by three rivers, which come together at Waterford city, and is noted for its mountains, tiny lakes and pine forests, as well as an abundance of ruins. West Waterford's mountain passes are among the most beautiful scenery in Ireland, while the south-east coast is one of the sunniest parts of the country, offering miles of safe, sandy beaches. The capital, Waterford city, is most famous for its glass factory, which has been producing Waterford crystal for over 200 years. It's also a bustling maritime centre with regular visits from cruise ships, yachts and other vessels, not to mention its own sizeable fishing fleet.

House prices in Waterford rose by some 25 per cent in 1999, good starter homes making almost IR£110,000. Building land is now fetching IR£150,000 per acre.

Ulster

Ulster is Ireland's most northerly province, most of which is part of the United Kingdom. The counties of Antrim, Armagh, Down, Fermanagh, Londonderry and Tyrone form the region known today as Northern Ireland, which remained part of the UK when the Irish state was established in 1921, but Counties Cavan, Donegal and Monaghan are within the Republic.

Cavan: With a population of just 4,000, landlocked Cavan is another peaceful, unspoilt county (it's said to be Ireland's Garden of Eden), although the recent re-opening of the Ballinamore-Ballyconnell Canal (originally constructed in 1860 but only operational for nine years) between the Shannon and Erne waterways is attracting a good deal of tourist traffic. Cavan is a favourite of anglers because of the abundance of fish in its many beautiful lakes and rivers, winding between wooded hills. Ireland's longest river, the Shannon, has its source here, on the slopes of Cuilcagh in a pool known as the Shannon Pot.

Donegal: The most northerly county in Ireland and one of its largest, Donegal, is virtually cut off from the rest of the country by the Northern Irish county of Fermanagh. It has changed less during the 20th century than almost anywhere else in Ireland and has the largest Gaelic-speaking population of any county, although the Ulster dialect though has more in common with Scottish Gaelic than 'official' Leinster Irish and the county maintains strong links with Scotland: the buses even go to Glasgow (but not by road)! Donegal has something of everything found in the rest of the country: cliffs, mountains, heather-clad moors, bogs and fertile pastures. The coastal town of Killybegs, where the *Gaeltacht* begins, is untypical of the area, having developed into one of Europe's principal fishing ports, complete with fishmeal factory whose smell pervades one end of the town. They say that the best fish and chips in Ireland are to be had at Melly's opposite the harbour!

House prices in Donegal rose between 15 and 20 per cent in 1999, with starter homes reaching IR£100,000 and above. Two-bedroom apartments in the coastal resort of Bundoran, where some 700 new homes have recently been built, are fetching IR£140,000 and three-bedroom houses IR£170,000.

Monaghan: Neighbouring Monaghan is an undulating county where lakes alternate with gentle hills. Market towns, farms and quiet waterways make up the quintessentially Irish landscape, which is dotted with ancient monuments and ruined castles. Renowned as an angling centre, Monaghan also offers watersports, golf, riding and other outdoor pursuits, although it has no coastline. Monaghan is a peaceful place, yet it's just an hour's drive from Dublin in one direction and Belfast (in Northern Ireland) in the other, thus offering the best of several worlds.

RESEARCH

There's plenty of choice of property for sale in Ireland, but it's still a sellers' market in most areas. As when buying property anywhere, you should never be in too much of a hurry. It's a wise or lucky person who gets his choice absolutely right first time, which is why most experts recommend that you rent before buying unless you're absolutely certain what you want, how much you wish to pay and where you want to live. Have a good look around in your chosen area(s) and obtain an accurate picture of the kind of properties available, their relative prices and what you can expect to get for your money. However, before doing this, you should make a comprehensive list of what you want (and don't want) from a home, so that you can narrow the field and save time on wild goose chases. Alternatively, can buy a plot of land and have a house built to your own specifications. If, however, after discussing it at length with your partner, one of you insists on a new luxury apartment in Dublin and the other an 18th century farmhouse in the Connemara, the easiest solution may be to get a divorce!

To reduce the risk of making an expensive error when buying in an unfamiliar region, it's often prudent to rent a house for a period (see **Renting** on page 124), taking in the worst part of the year (weather-wise). This allows you to become familiar with the region and the weather, and gives you time to look around for a home at your leisure. There's no shortage of properties for sale in Ireland and, whatever you're looking for, you should have plenty to choose from. Wait until you find something you fall head over heels in love with and then think about it for another week or two before rushing to the altar! One of the advantages of buying property in Ireland is that there's usually another 'dream' home around the next corner – and the second or third dream home is often even better than the first. Better to miss the 'opportunity of a lifetime' than end up with an expensive pile of stones around your neck. However, don't dally too long, as good properties at the right price don't remain on the market for ever!

If you're looking for a holiday home, you may wish to investigate mobile homes or a scheme that limits your occupancy of a property to a number of weeks each year. These include shared ownership, leaseback, time-sharing and a holiday property bond (see **Timeshare & Part-Ownership Schemes** on page 145). Don't rush into any of these schemes without fully researching the market and before you're absolutely clear about what you want and what you can realistically expect to get for your money. The more research you do before buying a property in Ireland the better, which should (if possible) include advice from those who already own a home there, from whom you can usually obtain invaluable information (often based on their own mistakes). Many people set themselves impossible deadlines for choosing a property or business (e.g. a few days or a week) and often end up bitterly regretting their impulsive decision. Although it's a common practice, mixing a holiday with property purchase isn't a good idea, as most people are inclined to make poor decisions when their mind is set on play, rather than business.

Publications & Exhibitions: Outbound Publishing (1 Commercial Road, Eastbourne, East Sussex BN21 3XQ, UK ☎ 01323-726040) publish *World of Property*, a quarterly publication containing properties for sale in Ireland (and other countries) and organise property exhibitions in the south and north of England. Property is also advertised for sale in most newspapers and many magazines in Ireland and abroad (see **Appendix A** on page 194) and on the Internet.

AVOIDING PROBLEMS

The problems associated with buying property abroad have been highlighted in the last decade or so, during which the property market in many countries has gone from boom to bust and back. However, although the pitfalls must never be ignored, buying property in Ireland needn't be a gamble. There are hundreds of thousands of Irish homeowners – in fact a higher percentage of Irish people own their own homes than the inhabitants of any other European Union (EU) country – and the vast majority are happy with their purchases and encountered few or no problems when buying their homes. This should be borne in mind when you hear or read horror stories concerning foreign buyers in Ireland (not that you will hear many). The possible dangers have been highlighted not in order to discourage you, but simply to ensure that you go into a purchase with your eyes open and to help you avoid problems ('forewarned is forearmed').

Legal Advice: It cannot be emphasised too strongly that anyone planning to buy property in Ireland must take expert, independent legal advice. Never sign anything, or pay any money, until you have sought advice from a solicitor who's experienced in Irish property law. If you aren't prepared to do this, you shouldn't even think about buying property in Ireland! Most people purchasing property in Ireland obtain legal advice only after having paid a deposit and some take none at all. Trying to cut corners to save on legal costs is foolhardy in the extreme when tens or hundreds of thousands of pounds are at stake. You will find that the relatively small price (in comparison with the cost of a home) of obtaining legal advice is excellent value, if only for the peace of mind it affords. However, be careful who you engage, as some solicitors are part of the problem rather than the solution! Don't pick a solicitor at random, but hire one who has been highly recommended by someone you can trust.

Employing Professionals: There are professionals in all areas of Ireland, and a number of expatriate professionals (e.g. architects and surveyors) also practise there. However, don't assume that because you're dealing with a fellow countryman that he'll offer you a better deal or do a better job than an Irishman (the contrary is often true). You should always check the credentials of all professionals you employ, whatever their nationality. Note that it's *never* wise to rely solely on advice proffered by those with a financial interest in selling you a property, such as a developer or real estate agent, although their advice may be excellent and totally unbiased. You should also avoid 'cowboy' agents and anyone who does property deals on the side (such as someone you meet in a bar or restaurant), as dealing with them often leads to heartache.

Problems: Among the myriad problems that can be experienced by buyers are properties bought without a legal title, properties built illegally without planning permission, properties sold that are subject to embargoes, properties sold with forged deeds, properties with missing infrastructure, builders or developers going bust; developers' loans being undischarged after completion, undischarged mortgages from the previous owner, intermediaries disappearing with the seller's proceeds, overcharging by vendors (particularly when selling to foreigners), properties sold to more than one buyer, and even properties sold that don't exist! On the other hand, buyers must also accept their share of the blame. It isn't uncommon for buyers to 'leave their brains behind at the airport' and some do incredibly irresponsible things, such as literally handing over bags full of cash to agents or owners without any security. It's hardly surprising that they're sometimes defrauded! **However, it should be noted that Ireland is one of the safest countries in Europe in which to buy property**.

Mistakes: Common mistakes made by buyers in Ireland include buying in the wrong area (rent first!), buying a home that's unsaleable, buying a property for renovation and grossly underestimating the restoration costs, not having a full survey done on an old property, not taking legal advice, buying a property for business (e.g. to convert to self-catering accommodation) and being over-optimistic about the income, and taking on too large a mortgage. It's possible when buying a property directly from the vendor that he will suggest you pay part of the price with an 'under the table' cash payment, thus lowering the price declared to the tax authorities and reducing the vendor's capital gains tax liability. You'll also save money on taxes and fees, but will have a higher capital gains tax bill when you sell. If you're selling a property and the buyer refuses to make the 'illicit' payment after the contract has been signed, you have no legal redress! You should steer well clear of this practice, which is, of course, strictly illegal. Checks must be carried out both before signing a contract and before signing the deed of sale. Note that disputes over property deals can take years to resolve in the Irish courts, and you may never receive satisfaction.

Subrogation: One of the Irish laws that property buyers should be aware of is the law of subrogation, whereby property debts, including mortgages, service and management charges, remain with a property and are inherited by the buyer. This is an open invitation to dishonest sellers to 'cut and run'. It's possible to check whether there are any outstanding debts on a property and this should be done by your solicitor a few days before completion (see **Completion** on page 156). If annual bills for services or management charges have already been paid, they're usually divided between the vendor and buyer according to how much of the year is left.

Buying Off Plan: Many problems can arise when buying off plan, i.e. unbuilt properties, or a property on an unfinished development. A 'finished' property is a property where the building is complete in every detail (as confirmed by an architect), all communal services have been completed, and all infrastructure is in place such as roads, parking areas, external lighting, landscaping, water and waste, electricity and telephone services. A builder is supposed to provide buyers purchasing off plan in stage payments with an insurance policy or banker's 'termination' guarantee, which protects them against the builder going broke before construction is completed. Make sure that your builder offers such a guarantee.

Take Your Time: Many people have had their fingers burnt by rushing into property deals without proper care and consideration. It's all too easy to fall in love with the attractions of a home in Ireland and to sign a contract without giving it sufficient thought. If you aren't absolutely certain, don't allow yourself to be rushed into making a hasty decision, e.g. by fears of an imminent price rise or of losing the property to another buyer who has 'made an offer'. Although many people dream of buying a holiday or retirement home in Ireland, it's vital to do your homework thoroughly and avoid the 'dream sellers' (often fellow countrymen), who will happily prey on your ignorance and tell you anything in order to sell you a home.

CHOOSING THE LOCATION

The most important consideration when buying a home in Ireland is usually its location – or, as the old adage goes, the three most important points are location, location and location! A property in a reasonable condition in a popular area is likely to be a better investment than an exceptional property in a less attractive location. There's usually no point in buying a dream property in a terrible location.

Where you buy a property in Ireland will depend on a range of factors including your preferences, your financial resources and, not least, whether you plan to work or not. If you have a job in Ireland, the location of your home will probably be determined by its proximity to your place of employment. However, if you intend to look for employment or start a business, you must live in an area that allows you maximum scope. Unless you have good reason to believe otherwise, it would be foolish to rely on finding employment in a particular area. If, on the other hand, you're looking for a holiday or retirement home, the whole of Ireland is your oyster. The most popular areas are the south and west coasts, particularly Counties Waterford, Cork, Kerry and Galway. When seeking a permanent home, don't be too influenced by where you have spent an enjoyable holiday or two. A town or area that was adequate for a few weeks' holiday may be totally unsuitable for a permanent home, particularly regarding the proximity to shops, medical services, and sports and leisure facilities.

If you have little idea about where you wish to live, read as much as you can about the different regions of Ireland (see **Regions** on page 104) and spend some time looking around your areas of interest. Note that the lifestyle and cost of living can vary considerably from region to region (and even within a particular region). Before looking at properties, it's important to have a good idea of the kind of property you want and the price you wish to pay, and to draw up a shortlist of the areas and towns of interest. Most importantly, make a list of what you want and don't want in a property; if you don't do this, you're likely to be overwhelmed by the number of properties to be viewed.

The 'best' area to live in depends on a range of considerations including proximity to your place of work as well as to schools, shops, public transport, entertainment and sports facilities, places of worship, pubs, etc. There are beautiful areas to choose from throughout Ireland, most within easy travelling distance of a town or city. Don't, however, always believe the travelling times and distances stated in adverts and quoted by estate agents, but check for yourself. When looking for a home, bear in mind travelling times and costs to your place of work, shops and schools (and the local pub/restaurant). If you buy a remote country property, the distance to local amenities and services could become a problem, particularly if you plan to retire to Ireland. If you live in a remote rural area, you'll need to be much more self-sufficient than if you live in a town.

If possible, you should visit an area a number of times over a period of a few weeks, both on weekdays and at weekends, in order to get a feel for the neighbourhood (it's better to walk than drive around). A property seen on a balmy summer's day after a delicious lunch and a few pints of Guinness may not be nearly so attractive on a subsequent visit without the sunshine and warm inner glow. Ideally, you should also visit an area at different times of the year, e.g. in both summer and winter; somewhere that's wonderful in summer can be forbidding and inhospitable in winter. In any case, you should view a property a number of times before deciding to buy it. If you're unfamiliar with an area, most experts recommend that you rent for a period before deciding to buy (see **Renting** on page 124). This is particularly important if you're planning to buy a permanent or retirement home in an unfamiliar area. Many people change their minds after a while and it isn't unusual for buyers to move once or twice before settling down permanently.

If you'll be working in Ireland, obtain a small scale map of the area and decide the maximum distance you'll consider travelling to work, e.g. by drawing a circle with your work place in the middle. Mark the places that you've seen, at the same time making a list of the plus and minus points of each property. If you use an estate agent, he'll usually drive you around and you can return later to the properties that you like best at your leisure (provided that you've marked them on your map!). Note, however, that agents may be reluctant to give you the keys to visit a property on your own.

There are many points to consider regarding the location of a home. These can roughly be divided into the immediate surroundings and neighbourhood, and the general area or region. Take into account the present and future needs of all members of your family, including the following:

Climate: You won't have chosen Ireland for its year-round sunshine record. Nevertheless, some areas are drier than others and you may prefer to give yourself the best chance of avoiding a wet summer holiday. Bear in mind both the winter and summer climate, position of the sun, and the average daily sunshine and rainfall (see **Climate** on page 46). The orientation or aspect of a building is vital and, if you want morning or afternoon sun (or both), you must ensure that balconies, terraces and gardens are facing the right direction.

Floods & Storms: Check whether the area you're interested in is liable to natural disasters such as floods or storms. The north-west coast, for example, is subject to particularly high winds, and low lying areas near the coast or the River Shannon can be flooded. Properties in such areas may be expensive to insure.

Noise: Noise isn't usually a problem in Ireland, which is one of the quietest countries in Europe. Nevertheless, it's a consideration, particularly in urban areas. Although you cannot choose your neighbours, you can at least ensure that a property isn't located next to a busy road, industrial plant, commercial area, building site, discotheque, night club, bar or restaurant (where revelries may continue into the early hours). Look out for objectionable neighbouring properties which may be too close to the one you're considering and check whether nearby vacant land has been zoned for commercial activities. In 'communal' developments (e.g. apartment blocks and townhouse devlopments) some properties may be second homes that are let short-term, which means you may have to tolerate boisterous holidaymakers as neighbours during certain periods. In towns, traffic noise can continue all night!

Tourists: If you live in a popular tourist area, i.e. almost anywhere on the south-west coast, you'll be inundated with tourists in the summer. Not only will they jam the roads and pack the beaches and shops, but they'll also occupy your favourite table at your local bar or restaurant! Bear in mind that while a 'front-line' property on the beach sounds attractive and may be ideal for short holidays, it isn't always the best solution for permanent residence. Many beaches are crowded in the peak season, parking may be impossible, services stretched to breaking point, and the constant coming and going of tourists may drive you crazy. Some people prefer to move inland where it's generally less busy, you're isolated from the tourists and can also enjoy beautiful scenery. On the other hand, getting to and from isolated properties can be a slow business and minor roads can become virtually impassable in winter without a four-wheel-drive vehicle.

Neighbours: Do you wish to live in an area with many other expatriates or as far away from them as possible (which may not in fact be very far on parts of the south-west coast)? If you wish to integrate with the local community, you should avoid the foreign 'ghettos' and choose an Irish village or an area or development with mainly local inhabitants. Bear in mind that it may take time for you to become accepted in small communities, although residents in rural areas who make an effort to integrate into the local community are invariably warmly welcomed. If you're buying a permanent home, it's important to check on your prospective neighbours, particularly when buying an apartment. For example, are they noisy, sociable or absent for long periods? Do you think you'll get on with them? Good neighbours are invaluable, particularly when buying a holiday home in the country. On the other hand, if you wish to mix only with your compatriots, life in a mainly foreign community, or at least a cosmopolitan city such as Dublin or Galway, may be your ideal.

Town or Country? Do you wish to be in a town or do you prefer the country? Inland or by the sea? How about living on an island? Life on an island is more restricted and remote, e.g. you cannot jump into your car and drive to Cork or Galway or 'pop' over to Northern Ireland or the rest of the UK. If you buy a property in the country, you may have to tolerate poor public transport, long travelling distances to a town of any size, solitude and remoteness, and the high cost and amount of work involved in the upkeep of a country house and garden. You won't be able to pop to the local shops for fresh bread and milk, drop into the local bar for a glass of your favourite tipple with the locals, or have a choice of restaurants on your doorstep. In a town or large village, the weekly market will be just around the corner, the doctor and pharmacy close at hand and, if you need help or run into any problems, your neighbours will be nearby.

On the other hand, in the country you'll be closer to nature, will have more freedom (e.g. to make as much noise as you wish) and possibly complete privacy. Living in a remote area in the country will suit those looking for peace and quiet who don't want to involve themselves in the 'hustle and bustle' of town life (not that there's a lot of this in Irish rural towns!). If you're after peace and quiet, make sure that there isn't a busy road or railway line nearby or a local church within 'donging' distance! Note, however, that many people who buy a remote country home find that the peace of the countryside palls after a time and they yearn for the more exciting city life. If you've never lived in the country, it's wise to rent before buying. Note also that while it's cheaper to buy in a remote or unpopular location, it's usually much more difficult to find a buyer when you want to sell.

Garden: If you're planning to buy a country property with a large garden or plot of land, bear in mind the high cost and amount of work involved in its upkeep. If it's to be a second home, who will look after the house and garden when you're away? Do you want to spend your holidays mowing the lawn and cutting back the undergrowth? Do you want a home with a lot of outbuildings? What are you going to do with them? Can you afford to convert them into extra rooms or guest accommodation?

Work: How secure is your job or business and are you likely to move to another area in the near future? Can you find other work in the same area, if necessary? If there's a possibility that you'll need to move in a few years' time, you should rent or at least buy a property that will be relatively easy to sell and recoup the cost. Bear in mind also your partner's and children's jobs.

Schools: What about your children's present and future schooling? What is the quality of local schools? Note that, even if your family has no need of local schools, the value of a home is often influenced by the quality and location of schools.

Health: What local health and social services are provided? How far is the nearest hospital with an emergency department? Are there doctors and dentists in the area?

Shops: What shopping facilities are provided in the neighbourhood? How far is it to the nearest town with good shopping facilities? How would you get there if your car was out of order?

Leisure: What is the range and quality of local leisure, sports, community and cultural facilities? What is the proximity to sports facilities such as a beach, golf course or waterway? Bear in mind that properties in or close to coastal resorts are more expensive, although they also have the best letting potential.

Public Transport: Is proximity to public transport (e.g. an international airport, port or railway station) or access to a main road important? Don't believe all you're told about the distance or travelling times to the nearest airport, railway station, beach or town, but check it for yourself.

Parking: If you're planning to buy in a town or city, is there adequate private or free on-street parking for your family and visitors? Is it safe to park in the street? Note that in Dublin it's important to have secure off-street parking if you value your car. Traffic congestion is fast becoming a problem in the major cities and towns in Ireland. Bear in mind that an apartment or townhouse may be some distance from the nearest road or car park. How do you feel about carrying heavy shopping hundreds of metres to your home and possibly up several flights of stairs? If you're planning to buy an apartment above the ground floor, make sure the building has a lift.

Crime: What is the local crime rate? The incidence of housebreaking and burglary is higher in some areas than others, which also means more expensive home insurance. Check the crime rate in the local area, e.g. burglaries, housebreaking, stolen cars and violent crime. Is crime increasing or decreasing? Note that professional crooks like isolated houses, particularly those full of expensive furniture and other belongings that they can strip bare at their leisure. You're much less likely to be the victim of crime if you live in a village, where crime is virtually unknown (strangers stand out like sore thumbs in villages, where their every move is monitored by the local populace).

Local Council: Is the local council well run? What are the views of other residents? If the municipality is efficiently run, you can usually rely on good local social and sports services and facilities.

Radon: A final consideration when choosing the location of your property is the likelihood of its being affected by radon. Radon is a naturally occurring radioactive gas formed underground by the radioactive decay of uranium, which is present in small quantities in rocks and soils and is particularly prevalent in Ireland. It's estimated that more than half of the radiation dose received by the average person in Ireland is due to radon. For the majority of people, the radiation received from radon isn't high enough to be a cause for concern. Radon surfacing in the open air is quickly diluted to harmless concentrations. However, when it enters an enclosed space, such as a house, it can sometimes build up to dangerous concentrations. The acceptable limit for radon concentration (known as the 'reference level') is 200 becquerels per m^3 of air ($200Bq/m^3$). It has been shown that prolonged exposure to concentrations of radon above this level increases the chance of contracting lung cancer; in a minority of homes and other buildings in Ireland with very high radon levels, there's a significant health risk for occupants. To put this risk into perspective: whereas the average person in Ireland has a 3 per cent risk of contracting fatal lung cancer, someone living in a building which is above the reference level may have a 4 or 5 per cent risk of the same fate.

Recognising the possible danger of radon, the government has undertaken a survey of the whole country which identifies the areas of greatest risk. There are high risk areas in most parts of the country, but Counties Carlow and Sligo appear to have more such areas than other parts of the country. A copy of the survey and a leaflet entitled *Radon Radiation in Homes* can be obtained free of charge from the Radiological Protection Institute of Ireland (☎ 01-269 7766; 🖳 www.rpii.ie). Note also that building regulations introduced in December 1997 require all new houses to have a radon 'sump' and those in high risk areas a radon 'barrier'.

There are three important points to bear in mind when considering the possible effects of radon gas on your choice of property:

- The health danger of high radon levels is small, particularly if you're only spending short periods in your Irish home.

- Radon cannot be seen or smelt but it can easily be detected by special equipment. The necessary equipment can be hired from the Radiological Protection Institute for IR£15. However, readings should be spread over at least three months, so it may not be possible to obtain a reliable measurement before you buy a property.

- Even if a property is found to contain a high level of radon gas, there are ways of reducing it to a safer level. Various measures that can be taken are outlined in a guide, *Radon in Buildings* (price IR£5), available from Government Publications (☎ 01-679 3515 or 01-661 3111).

RENTING

If you're uncertain about exactly what sort of home you want and where you wish to live, it's prudent to rent for a period in order to reduce the risk of making a costly error. Renting long-term before buying is particularly prudent for anyone planning to live in Ireland permanently. If possible, you should rent a similar property to the one you're planning to buy, during the time of year when you plan to occupy it. Renting allows you to become familiar with the weather, the amenities and the local people; to meet other foreigners who have made their homes in Ireland and to share their experiences, and, not least, to discover the cost of living at first hand. Provided that you still find Ireland alluring, renting 'buys' you time to find your dream home. You may even wish to consider renting a home long-term (or even 'permanently') as an alternative to buying, as it saves tying up your capital and can be surprisingly inexpensive in many regions. People who are relocating to Ireland for up to five years often prefer to rent rather than buy. Some let their family homes abroad and rent one in Ireland – a few even make a profit!

If you're looking for a long-term rental, e.g. three to six months, it's best not to rent unseen, but to rent a holiday apartment for a week or two to allow yourself time to look around for a longer-term rental. Properties for rent are advertised in local newspapers and can also be found through property publications in many countries (see **Appendix A** for a list). Many estate agents in Ireland offer a long-term rental service and a number of agencies (listed under 'Auctioneers, Estate Agents & Valuers' in the Golden Pages) deal in long and short-term rentals (see below).

Some accommodation agencies charge a registration fee, while others take a percentage of the rental fee from the landlord so that their service is effectively free (although you may find yourself paying a higher rent as a result). In general, you should try to obtain a reference before signing up with an agency and, particularly if you're being asked to pay a registration fee, find out how likely the agency is to find you suitable accommodation, i.e. what sort of accommodation it has to offer and how frequently its lists are updated. You should also ask whether the agency is licensed (estate agents are required by law to be licensed and bonded, but the legal position regarding accommodation agencies is less clear), what services are provided in return for the fee, and whether you're entitled to a refund if the agency fails to find you accommodation within a reasonable period. Also ensure that you receive a receipt for any money you pay.

Rental prices have been adversely affected by the spiralling property market, and the availability of rental accommodation severely reduced by recent changes in taxation laws. The abolition of mortgage interest relief on residential investment property, which came into effect in April 1998, and the introduction of an anti-speculative property tax in June 2000, combined with increased demand for rented accommodation resulting from growth in employment opportunities, have created a shortage of rental property, in turn causing prices to rise even more steeply. In 1999 ,average rental prices increased by 13 per cent nationally and 15 per cent in Dublin, where not only are queues of prospective renters now common but the unpleasant practice of gazumping (see page 149) has also spread to the rental market, unscrupulous landlords reneging on agreements in order to pocket a few extra pounds per month.

With the Irish economy flourishing and both employment and university enrolment at record levels (note that September and October are especially busy times for renting in university towns), demand for rented accommodation is expected to continue to be high in 2001, although there are signs that investors are being attracted back into the rental market by the prospect of low interest rates and continually increasing property prices.

Most rental properties, whether long or short-term, are let furnished, and long-term unfurnished properties are particularly difficult to find. Standards of rented accommodation in Ireland are generally good. The Housing (Standards for Rented Houses) Regulations 1993 specified certain minimum requirements regarding structural condition, the provision of sinks, toilets, baths/showers, cooking and food storage facilities, the safety of electrical and gas installations, the adequacy of heating, lighting and ventilation; and the maintenance of communal areas – so you shouldn't be offered anything less than habitable.

A rental contract is necessary when renting any property in Ireland, whether long or short-term (except for holiday lettings), and must contain certain information. This includes the address of the accommodation, the names and addresses of the landlord and letting agent, the tenant's name, the length of the tenancy, the amount of rent and when and how it's to be paid, details of other charges that aren't included in the rental fee (e.g. telephone, electricity), the deposit to be paid and the conditions under which it may be returned, the basic rights of the tenant and the landlord, and an inventory of items included with the accommodation. In accordance with the Housing (Rent Books) Regulations 1993, your landlord must provide you with a rent book or written lease which specifies the above, and all rental or other payments must be recorded in the rent book or provided in writing.

With all rental agreements it's important to establish under what circumstances your landlord may have access to the accommodation and what maintenance or repair costs you're liable for. Also ensure that you have an emergency contact number for your landlord. If you require more information about rented accommodation in Ireland or experience a problem with a landlord, you should contact a Threshold Advice Centre in Cork, Galway or Dublin (☎ 01-872 6311). Threshold, a voluntary body funded by the Department of the Environment and local government, also publishes various information leaflets to help you find suitable accommodation and avoid the less reputable accommodation agencies.

Rent is usually payable monthly, in advance, and an initial deposit of one or two months' rent (one or two weeks' rent for a weekly tenancy) is also required as security. Landlords can legally raise the rent by as much and as often as they like, unless there's a specific agreement to the contrary (e.g. in your lease), but you must be given sufficient notice of any increases. This is at least a week for weekly tenancies and at least a month for monthly tenancies.

Long-Term Rentals: The usual minimum long-term rental period in Ireland is six months, although three-month lets can be found, and the maximum three years. Most rental contracts, however, are for nine or 12 months. Rental costs vary considerably depending on the size (number of bedrooms) and quality of a property, its age and the facilities provided. However, the most significant factor influencing rents is the region, the city and the neighbourhood. A one-bedroom apartment in the capital now costs upwards of IR£500 per month and as much as IR£750 in areas like Ballsbridge, whereas a similar unit can be rented in a small town for as little as IR£250 per month. (Note that in Ireland there's a distinction between 'flats' and 'apartments': a flat may be above a shop or office or in a converted old house, whereas an apartment is usually purpose-built.) Two-bedroom apartments in Dublin now start at IR£700 per month and houses at IR£1,200, although in some suburban areas, e.g. Lucan and Blanchardstown, three-bedroom semis can be rented for as little as IR£700 per month. In rural areas away from the main cities the rental for a three-bedroom house is as low as IR£300 per month. At the other end of the scale, quality homes are renting for between IR£1,500 and IR£2,000 per month in Cork city and between IR£2,500 and IR£5,000 per month in Dublin.

Note that, if you sign a lease, you're committing yourself to renting for that period, so don't sign one unless you're happy with all the terms and conditions. If you want to leave before the lease expires, you'll usually be held liable for the rent for the remaining period. However, if you can arrange for someone to take over the lease, the landlord may waive charges.

Agencies which deal mostly in long-term rentals include Accommodation Lettings in Dublin (☎ 01-496 2866), who offer a free list of accommodation for rent, Home Locators (☎ 01-679 5233), who produce a list of available accommodation in Dublin but charge you a IR£5 registration fee to view as many properties as you like within one month, and Express Accommodation (☎ 01-878 2100), who, for a fee of IR£50, will send you daily accommodation lists and keep looking until they find something suitable. In Cork city, Apartmentfinders (☎ 021-427 7718) offer a free service for long-term rentals, as do Marian Rose Properties (☎ 021-429 3333).

Short-Term Rentals: There's an abundance of properties for rent short-term in Ireland, including apartments, cottages, farmhouses, townhouses, bungalows, mansions, castles and even mobile homes. The best source of short-term rental accommodation in Ireland is the Tourist Board (*Bord Fáilte*), which publishes an annual *Self-Catering Accommodation Guide*. This can be obtained from Tourist Board offices for IR£5 or by post from *Bord Fáilte* (☎ 01-602 4000), price IR£6.50, or from the Irish Tourist Board in your home country). The guide lists around 3,000 premises nation-wide, classified by a star rating. Individual regions, e.g. Cork/Kerry, also publish holiday guides which include lists of self-catering accommodation. Short Term Solutions specialises in short-term rentals in Dublin, though mainly for business people (☎ 01-679 2222). Many hotels also offer lower rates for long stays during the low season (see **Hotels, Guesthouses & B&Bs** below).

Rents for short-term lets are usually higher pro rata than for longer lets, particularly in popular holiday areas, where many properties are let as self-catering holiday accommodation. However, many agents let self-catering properties in holiday areas at a considerable reduction during the 'low season', which may extend from September to June. In some cases the rental year is divided into as many as four seasons, e.g. November to March, April and October, June and September, and July/August, but in most cases there are three periods: July/August, May/June and September, and the rest of the year. Only a few owners charge the same rate all year round.

For an average two-bedroom holiday cottage in a popular area such as Kerry, you may pay between IR£125 and IR£175 per week in the low season, compared with up to IR£350 in mid-summer. In less popular areas, although the low season rate would be similar, you usually pay 'only' IR£225 to IR£275 in July or August. The price of urban accommodation varies even less with the time of year; for an ordinary two-bedroom apartment in Dublin or Cork you could expect to pay around IR£225 per week in low season and around IR£275 in the summer months. Rental fees usually include linen but exclude electricity and gas.

Hotels, Guesthouses & B&Bs: Hotel rates in Ireland vary according to the time of year, the standard of the establishment and its location. In hotel terms, there are usually only two seasons: high (July/August) and low (the rest of the year). Prices are generally between 30 and 40 per cent less in low season than in high season, and quite a few establishments close between November and March. Many hotels offer special deals for weekend stays (two nights), three nights mid-week (one night free) and seven nights 'partial board' including dinner and breakfast. Like self-catering accommodation, hotels and guesthouses are graded by the Irish Tourist Board using a star rating system. One star indicates basic facilities but also in many cases includes 'luxuries' such as a TV and shower room. The highest rating for hotels is five stars; the maximum for guesthouses (which tend to be smaller, family-run establishments) is four stars.

Hotels and guesthouses in large towns and cities and popular coastal areas tend to be more expensive than comparable establishments in other parts of Ireland, and rates in cities such as Dublin and Cork are similar to those in other major European cities. However, inexpensive hotels can be found in most towns, where a single room can be had for IR£30 or less and a double around £45 (usually without an en suite bath/shower room) in low season. Elsewhere, room rates start at around IR£20 and rarely rise above IR£90 per person per night. Hotels obviously aren't an economical long-term solution for home hunters, although there's usually little alternative if you need accommodation for only a short period.

Bed and breakfast accommodation is also widely available in Ireland. In fact, in some areas it seems as if every other house is offering 'B&B'. Rates start as low as IR£12 per person per night, the average being between IR£18 and IR£22.

Hostels: There are more than 170 hostels in Ireland (there are 18 in Dublin, for example, and nine in Cork), which offer cheap accommodation. They vary in size from half-a-dozen to 250 or more beds, the majority of which are in dormitories (separate ones for males and females!) but most hostels also offer twin, double and family rooms. Most hostels (137) are operated by Independent Holiday Hostels (IHH). The IHH is an independent co-operative but all its hostels are *Bord Fáilte* approved. Hostels are open all year round and admit people of all ages. No membership fee is payable and dormitory accommodation is available from IR£5 per person per night in low season, with the average around IR£7 to IR£9, although some hostels charge up to IR£25. You should expect to pay an extra IR£1 or so in high season and generally for hostels in the Dublin area. The supplement for a twin or double room is between 20 and 50 per cent. Further information and a list of hostels can be obtained from the IHH (☎ 01-836 4700; 💻 www.hostels-ireland.com).

The other 34 hostels belong to the Irish Youth Hostel Association (*An Óige* in Irish), which is a non-profit making organisation. To stay at IYHA hostels, you don't need to be a 'youth' or a member the association, but if you aren't a member you'll have to pay extra – charges vary from hostel to hostel. Annual membership costs IR£10 for adults or IR£20 for family membership and IR£40 for life membership. If you're a member of a foreign association which is affiliated to the International Youth Hostel Federation, you won't need to join the IYHA. Accommodation fees range from IR£3 to IR£10 per person per night (the average charge is IR£7.50). Unlike IHH hostels, IYHA hostels aren't open all year round, so you need to check opening dates. Booking can be made locally, at travel agents or via the Internet. Further details and a handbook listing all 34 hostels (price 30p) are obtainable from the IYHA (☎ 01-830 4555; 💻 www.irelandyha.org).

Home Exchange: An alternative to renting is to exchange your home abroad with one in Ireland for a period. This way you can experience home living in Ireland for a relatively small cost and may save yourself the expense of a long-term rental. Although there's an element of risk involved in exchanging your home with another family (depending on whether your swap is made in heaven or hell!), most agencies thoroughly vet clients and have a track record of successful swaps. There are home exchange agencies in many countries, many of which are members of the International Home Exchange Association (IHEA).

There are many home exchange companies in the USA, including HomeLink International (17,500 members in around 50 countries), Box 650, Key West, FL 33041, USA (☎ 305-294 7766 or 800-638 3841). Two long-established home exchange companies in Britain are HomeLink International, Linfield House, Gorse Hill Road, Virginia Water, Surrey GU25 4AS, UK (☎ 01344-842642; 💻 www.home link.org.uk), which publishes a directory of homes and holiday homes for exchange, and Home Base Holidays, 7 Park Avenue, London N13 5PG, UK (☎ 020-8886 8752; 💻 www.homebase-hols.com).

COST

Property prices started soaring throughout Ireland in the late '80s. In the decade from March 1988 to March 1998, new house prices increased by 123 per cent, compared with average wage increases of 32 per cent and a 27.5 per cent rise in the consumer price index. In the last two or three years of this period, property values rose on average an astonishing 25 per cent per year in some areas, while inflation was running at no more than 3 per cent. Price rises were particularly steep in Dublin and Galway cities, Co. Kerry and throughout Munster, where annual increases of 40 per cent and more were reported. As a result, there was a rush to buy property as an investment and substantial profits were made. In 1997, as many as a quarter of new properties were purchased by investors. This in turn made things difficult for homebuyers (particularly first-time buyers), who were faced not only with sharply rising prices but with a shortage of available houses. It wasn't unusual for people to queue overnight in order to be first in line for new properties being released onto the market. At one time, there were an estimated five purchasers for each property on the market.

Radical changes to the taxation laws in April 1998 'cooled' the market somewhat, but property prices continued to soar (by 31 per cent in 1998 and a further 22 per cent in 1999), forcing the government to introduce still more Draconian measures in early 2000 in an attempt to bring prices back under control. The principal changes in legislation were to stamp duty, capital gains tax and tax relief on rental property, all of which were substantially reduced in April 1998 and again in June 2000 as a result of the government-commissioned Bacon Report. These measures have discouraged investment, with the result that price rises have begun to slow: the rate of price increase was halved in the quarter March–June 2000, as was the demand for investment properties in most areas outside Dublin. Most experts believe that there won't be a crash for several reasons: Ireland's sound economic situation (average earnings are expected to rise by around 8 per cent per annum during 2001 and 2002); the large owner-occupier base; the reasonably tight controls which banks and building societies still impose on lending; the relatively low cost of maintaining property in Ireland; and for demographic reasons. The baby boom of the '60s and '70s means that some 110,000 Irish men and women aged between 28 and 34 (the average house-buying age) will be entering the property market between 1999 and 2004.

From the mid-'90s there has also been a marked swing towards the European practice of apartment living: over 20 per cent of all new properties built in 1997 were apartments, although since 1999 the amount of new building has diminished slightly. This means that the cost of apartments rose even more steeply than that of houses, particularly in Dublin and Galway, where prices increased by almost 25 per cent in 12 months between 1997 and 1998. The average price of a new apartment in these cities is now higher than that of a comparable new house. Note that a garage is rarely provided with apartments or townhouses in Ireland, although there may be a private parking space in an underground or surface car park. However, these are usually sold separately and can cost as much as IR£30,000 in Dublin!

Despite the current popularity of Ireland and the recent rise in property prices, a slice of the quiet life still needn't cost the earth, although the idyllic dream of a traditional thatched cottage on a bit of land overlooking the sea for IR£15,000 is very much a thing of the past. Small rural properties start at around IR£25,000, three-bedroom semis from around IR£55,000 and detached three-bedroom houses from IR£65,000. However, if you're after a property in one of the fashionable regions (such as the south-west) where there's strong demand from foreign buyers, you can expect to pay a premium of 50 per cent or more (see **Regions** on page 104).

Average property prices aren't necessarily an accurate indication of the relative values of specific kinds of property in different areas (there may be a greater number of cheaper or more expensive houses in one area than another), but they give some idea of the variation in values across the country. In general, the cost of apartments has risen more rapidly than that of houses. Average resale house prices rose by 62 per cent in the period June 1998–June 2000, compared with a 41 per cent increase in new house prices. The average cost of a new apartment rose by almost 80 per cent in the same period, compared with over 67 per cent for resale apartments. Outside Dublin, where prices continue to rise faster than anywhere else in Ireland, the sharpest increases in the last few years have been in Cork (houses and apartments), Waterford (houses), Galway (new apartments) and Limerick (resale apartments). After Dublin, the highest average house prices are now in Cork, and Waterford has overtaken Limerick; new apartments cost slightly more in Galway than in Cork and slightly more in Limerick than Waterford, but the average price of resale apartments in Limerick is now higher even than in Cork. Average property prices (in IR£) in Ireland in June 2000 were as follows:

Type of Property				Region			
	Whole Country	Dublin	Cork	Galway	Waterford	Limerick	Other Areas
New House	129,400	172,300	127,400	122,000	115,400	114,400	118,400
Resale House	149,100	196,700	130,600	130,500	110,600	106,300	122,900
New Apartment	168,400	207,500	142,200	154,600	112,000	112,600	116,300
Resale Apartment	160,200	189,400	124,100	114,300	106,900	127,000	128,100

Apart from obvious variables such as size, quality and land area, the most important factor influencing the price of a house is its location. Properties in the cities, particularly in and around Dublin and in Galway and Cork, can cost up to five or six times as much as equivalent properties in rural parts. There's also a considerable price variation between sought-after west coast areas such as Co. Kerry and less popular inland counties. For details of prices in different regions of Ireland, see **Regions** on page 104. Approximate prices outside Dublin are shown below:

Property	Price range (IR£'000)
1-bedroom apartment	15 to 100
2-bedroom apartment	25 to 130
3-bedroom apartment	50 to 160
2-bedroom cottage	30 to 105
3-bedroom cottage	44 to 130
2-bedroom townhouse	65 to 90
3-bedroom townhouse	90 to 120
4-bedroom townhouse	90 to 180
2-bedroom country house	30 to 135
3-bedroom country house	45 to 180
4/5-bedroom country house	60 to 375

The quality of properties obviously varies considerably in respect of materials, fixtures and fittings, and workmanship. You should therefore compare at least half a dozen properties in order to get a good idea of their relative values.

When property is advertised in Ireland, the number of rooms is usually stated but the floor area isn't, although the size of the plot or garden is generally specified. The dimensions of individual rooms are only given in the agent's details. If you're in any doubt about the size of rooms you should measure them yourself, rather than rely on the measurements provided by the vendor or agent, who may 'cheat' by measuring into alcoves and doorways.

FEES

Various fees are payable when buying a property in Ireland, which usually add a minimum of 5 per cent to the purchase price. Fees are considerably lower on new properties than resale properties, on which stamp duty must be paid. The fees payable when buying a property in Ireland include some or all of the following:

- stamp duty (except for first-time buyers and new properties);
- legal fees;
- deed registration fee;
- survey or valuation fee;
- ground rent (leasehold properties only);
- management fee (apartments only);
- VAT (certain commercial properties only);
- utility connection fees (new properties only);
- selling agent's fees (normally 'included' in the property price);
- mortgage costs, e.g. application fee, mortgage indemnity fee (on loans above a certain percentage of the purchase price), and life assurance or a mortgage protection policy.

Always ensure you know exactly what the total fees will be before signing a contract.

Stamp Duty: Stamp duty is the main fee involved when buying a home in Ireland. It's the tax on the purchase deed payable by the buyer when the sale is closed. The rates and criteria for stamp duty were changed in April 1988 and again in June 2000. New houses and apartments with a floor area of less than 125m^2 are still exempt from stamp duty. However, the duty will usually become payable if a property is let within five years of the date of purchase, which means that, if you purchase a new property as a holiday home with the intention of letting it for the rest of the year, you'll no longer avoid paying stamp duty.

In the case of new houses or apartments of 125m^2 or more, the stamp duty is calculated on the basis of the site value or 25 per cent of the combined value of the site and the building, whichever is greater. For example, if the total cost of the site and building is IR£200,000 (x 25 per cent = IR£50,000) and the site is worth IR£60,000, stamp duty will be payable on IR£60,000. In the case of resale properties, stamp duty is payable on the full value of the site and building.

There are now three scales of stamp duty rates on residential property, for first-time buyers, owner occupiers (i.e. those living in the property, other than first-time buyers) and investors (i.e. those purchasing a property other than their home for letting purposes):

Purchase Price (IR£)	Stamp Duty (%)		
	First-time Buyers	Owner Occupiers	Investors
up to 100,000	Nil	Nil	9
100,001–150,000	Nil	3	9
150,001–200,000	3	4	9
200,001–250,000	3.75	5	9
250,001–300,000	4.5	6	9
300,001–500,000	7.5	7.5	9
over 500,000	9	9	9

As well as having to pay 9 per cent stamp duty on all property purchases, investors are liable to a new tax introduced in June 2000, called an anti-speculative property tax. This is a 2 per cent levy on the value of the property payable for the first three years after purchase (purchases after 2002 will be exempt from this tax). Both stamp duty and anti-speculative property tax are paid to the Revenue Commissioners, but, whereas stamp duty is paid at the time of purchase, property tax is due at the same time as your income tax. This means that it's up to you to declare it on your annual tax return.

These rates apply only to residential property or to the value of the residential component of a mixed-use property (e.g. an apartment above a shop). On non-residential property and on the non-residential component of mixed-use property, the rates of stamp duty remain as follows:

Purchase Price (IR£)	Stamp Duty (%)
up to 5,000	0
5,001–10,000	1
10,001–15,000	2
15,001–25,000	3
25,001–50,000	4
50,001–60,000	5
over 60,000	6

Note that the cost of any fixtures and fittings (e.g. carpets and curtains) included in a purchase is taken into account when determining the stamp duty 'band'; for example, if (as an owner occupier) you purchased a house for IR£198,000 with fixtures and fittings worth an extra IR£3,000, you'd be liable for 5 per cent stamp duty instead of 4 per cent (which would mean that you were effectively paying more than IR£2,000 extra for the fixtures and fittings!). You can, of course, buy the fixtures and fittings separately.

There's a 50 per cent stamp duty relief on conveyances between certain classes of blood relative; for example, if you give a property worth IR£220,000 to your son or daughter, the stamp duty chargeable is 2.5 per cent instead of the usual 5 per cent. Transfers between parents and children of land (up to a value of IR£200,000) on which the children are to build their principal residence are exempt from stamp duty.

There's also a small stamp duty (1 per cent up to a maximum of IR£500) on mortgages above IR£20,000.

Legal Fees: Since the Competition Act, 1994, solicitors' fees for conveyance (see page 153) are no longer subject to a fixed scale of charges and you must agree them in writing in advance. Under section 68 of the Act, a solicitor is bound to notify a client in writing of the fee to be charged for a particular transaction or of the basis on which the fee will be calculated. The actual amount depends upon the work involved, although according to the Incorporated Law Society of Ireland you should expect to pay between 1 and 1.5 per cent of the property price. Note that Irish solicitors won't usually agree to undertake only part of the conveyance, e.g. checking the sales contract. Although engaging a solicitor and paying legal fees is optional, it's highly recommended. Legal fees are exclusive of disbursements and are subject to VAT at 20 per cent. Fees are usually paid on closing but before registration (see below). Registration can take a year for a new house and even longer for a very old, unregistered property. If there are problems with registration, you may be liable for additional solicitor's fees.

Deed Registration Fee: Your solicitor will pass on to you the charges relating to registration of the title deed to a property. There are two kinds of title in Ireland: registered and unregistered. Registered land was introduced by the local Registration of Title (Ireland) Act, 1891 and means that a record of the land is kept with the land registry. Registration, which is compulsory in all counties of Ireland, provides proof of ownership. When a property is sold, a Deed of Transfer is lodged with the land registry, and the Registrar simply deletes the vendor's name and substitutes the buyer's. The land registry recently went onto the Internet, so it's now possible to check ownership and other property details from the comfort of your computer terminal (though it's still wise to use a qualified solicitor).

In the case of unregistered land, all title documents must be inspected by your solicitor to establish ownership. Copies of these documents are lodged with the registry of deeds in accordance with the Registration of Deeds Act, 1707 in case there's a conflict of interest, e.g. if two people try to take out a mortgage on the same piece of land simultaneously. A deed of conveyance is used to transfer freehold unregistered land, a deed of assignment for leasehold unregistered land (see page 143). There's roughly an equal amount of registered and unregistered land in Ireland, although land in rural areas is more likely to be registered.

The fee for registration with the land registry varies according to the value of the property as follows:

Property Value (IR£)	Fee (IR£)
up to 10,000	100
10,001–20,000	150
20,001–40,000	200
40,001–200,000	300
200,001–300,000	400
over 300,000	500

In addition, you'll be charged for land registry searches (around IR£75), commissioners' fees (IR£10.50), and a copy folio and map (IR£9). In the case of registration with the registry of deeds, the fees will include searches (IR£50 to IR£80), commissioners' fees (IR£10.50), and memorials (copies) of the purchase deed and mortgage deed (IR£52).

Survey or Valuation Fee: If you employ a surveyor (see page 151) to inspect a building or plot of land before you offer to buy it (which is strongly advised), the fee will depend on the kind of survey, any special requirements and the value of the property. The cost of a valuation report (which is usually a minimum requirement of your mortgage lender) is usually between IR£1.30 and IR£1.50 per IR£1,000 of a property's value. So, for example, for a property valued at IR£100,000 you'll pay between IR£130 and IR£150. Some lending institutions make a fixed charge on a sliding scale according to the value of the property, which may be as little as IR£75 for a property worth up to IR£50,000 rising to IR£120 or more for a property worth over IR£100,000. The valuer's travelling expenses are sometimes added to the bill. If the mortgage is refused, the valuation fee is refunded.

The cost of a full structural survey is generally around IR£150 in addition to the valuation report fee but, if you use the same firm for both, you may be able to negotiate a reduced rate. Note that your mortgage lender may insist on a structural report if a property is over 100 years old.

Ground Rent: Title may be freehold, where the property is theoretically held forever free of rent, or leasehold, where it's held for anything from 250 to 9,999 years. In the case of leasehold property, it's normal for a nominal ground rent to be paid to a superior title holder, i.e. landlord. This is usually around IR£10 per year, but may be as little as a penny. There are even cases where the property is leased rent free.

Management Fee: If you're buying an apartment (or, in some cases, a house on an up-market estate), you'll usually be liable for annual management fees. Each apartment owner automatically becomes a member of the management company responsible for the insurance and upkeep of the common elements of the property, e.g. grounds, entrances, hallways, lifts and stairs. To cover the costs involved there's usually a fund to which each owner must contribute. The amount payable depends on a number of factors (e.g. the extent of the grounds and the age and condition of the property), but you should expect to pay in the region of IR£400 per year.

VAT: Under the Finance Act, 1997, VAT must be included in the price of new properties and doesn't apply to resale properties. However, commercial property transactions may be subject to VAT at 12.5 per cent, unless the property was developed before 31st October 1972 and hasn't been extended, altered or adapted since. The rules regarding VAT on property are complicated and you should take expert advice before completing any commercial property transactions, particularly as there can be serious implications if you make a mistake (see **Value Added Tax** on page 95).

Utility Connection Fees: If you buy a new property, you may need to pay for connection to electricity, gas and mains water supplies, as well as for the installation of meters. Your builder will usually provide electricity and gas connections and meters, and the cost of these should be included in your quotation. Provided that a property is within 15 metres of a gas main, there should be no charge for connection. If it's more than 15 metres from the nearest main, the charge should be IR£10 per metre.

In the case of electricity there's a fixed connection charge of IR£650 (plus VAT at 12.5 per cent) if the property is within a certain distance from the medium voltage network. If the property is further than the specified distance from the network, an additional charge will be made according to the work necessary and in some cases there's an extra charge even if the property is within the specified distance (see **Electricity** on page 163).

You must usually arrange your own water main connection, which can be expensive. Connection charges vary considerably from county to county; they may be as little as IR£80 or as much as IR£500 or more if major work needs to be done, e.g. roads dug up. You should make enquiries at your local city, county or borough council so that you know how much to budget for.

Selling Agent's Fees: Estate agents' fees are usually paid by the vendor. They are, however, usually allowed for in the asking price, so in effect are paid by the buyer. As a buyer you'd be responsible for a separate fee only if you retained an auctioneer to purchase a property on your behalf, in which case you should agree a fee in advance and confirm it in writing. The auctioneer's fee can vary between 1 and 3.5 per cent of the selling price, depending on the cost of the property and the type of contract, but it's usually around 2.5 per cent and is subject to VAT (at 20 per cent).

Mortgage Application Fee: Most banks and building societies charge a fee of around IR£50 or 0.5 per cent of the value of the loan when they grant a mortgage. This is known as a mortgage application (or acceptance or arrangement) fee. When shopping around for a mortgage, however, you should ask if the lending institution is prepared to waive the fee; with increasing competition for mortgages, many lenders will agree to do so. Note that mortgage lenders shouldn't ask you to pay any legal costs as they usually use your solicitor for their legal work. Check this with them before confirming your mortgage.

Mortgage Indemnity Fee: If you borrow more than 70 or 80 per cent (depending on the lending institution) of the purchase price, you must pay a mortgage indemnity fee (also called a mortgage indemnity bond) of around 3 per cent of the difference between the specified percentage of the purchase price and the amount borrowed, plus a 2 per cent government levy (see **Mortgages** on page 81). Some lenders spread the cost of the indemnity over the term of the mortgage, while others don't charge an indemnity fee but charge a higher rate of interest for loans above 80 per cent. If you're buying a property for investment, the indemnity fee is 4 per cent.

Mortgage Protection Policy: You'll need to obtain life assurance before your lender will agree to advance your mortgage; a mortgage protection policy is usually the minimum cover required. There are various plans available, costing around IR£4.50 per IR£100 of your monthly repayment, to which the policy fee will be added.

Running Costs: In addition to the fees associated with buying a property, you should take into account running costs. These include management fees (for apartments), garden maintenance (if necessary), and building and contents insurance (see **Household Insurance** on page 54). There are no local authority charges, 'rates' or 'poll taxes' for residential property in Ireland, but you will incur standing charges for utilities (electricity, gas and telephone). Water is free (unless you run a business from home) and the cost of refuse collection varies from nothing (in parts of Dublin and Co. Wicklow, for example) to IR£150, which is the maximum charge in most areas, irrespective of the location or size of the property. In a few places, however, the local authority charges more for larger properties; in Co. Mayo, for example, you could find yourself having to pay IR£300 or more and in Co. Limerick as much as IR£570 per year! If you're letting a property, you should also allow for property management fees, income tax on rental income and possibly a tax consultant's fees.

BUYING A NEW HOME

According to UN figures, Ireland has the highest rate of house building in Europe at 9.5 units per thousand people compared, for example, with 3.5 units per thousand in the UK and an EU average of 5 units per thousand. More than 46,500 new dwellings were built in 1999, compared with 30,500 in 1995. Despite this high rate of construction, new properties can barely keep pace with demand and many people are purchasing plots of land and having their own homes built to order (see **Building Your Own Home** on page 138). Most new properties in the main cities are apartments, whereas in rural areas the majority are detached bungalows, which are springing up almost everywhere you look. Prices of new properties vary considerably according to their location (see **Choosing the Location** on page 119) and quality, but it's often cheaper to buy a new home than an old property requiring modernisation, as the price is fixed; the cost of renovation can soar way beyond original estimates (as many people have discovered to their cost). If required, a new property can usually be let immediately and modern homes have good resale potential. On the other hand, new homes may be smaller than older properties and have less land.

A major advantage of buying new is that you don't have to pay stamp duty, although you'll incur connection charges for electricity, water and sometimes gas (see **Fees** on page 131). It's even possible to obtain a grant of IR£3,000 from the Department of the Environment towards the cost of a new house. However, a number of conditions must be met, which are principally as follows:

1. The total floor area must be between 38 and $125m^2$ (except in the case of houses specially adapted for the disabled).
2. Applicants mustn't have previously built or purchased another house in Ireland for their own occupation.
3. The house must be built in accordance with certain standards and practices.
4. The house must be built by a VAT registered contractor with a tax clearance certificate or, in the case of 'self-build' houses, at least IR£15,000 worth of VAT registered work must be carried out.
5. The house must be the applicant's principal residence.

Applications should be made well before any work begins in order to ensure that the plans comply with the appropriate requirements. Plans must be accompanied by various documents including a tax certificate, purchase contract, specifications, planning permission and a fire safety certificate. No payment will be made until all work has been satisfactorily completed and you're actually occupying the property. You'll then be given a certificate of provisional approval (by the Department of the Environment) which you should take to your lending institution. The grant will be paid on completion of your mortgage arrangements. You can give your builder or lending institution power of attorney to receive the grant on your behalf (in which case the DoE should send you a 'letter of undertaking' to confirm that they'll pay the third party). Further details of New House Grants can be obtained from the Department of the Environment (Housing Grants Section), Government Offices, Ballina, Co. Mayo (☎ 096-70677).

Note that new properties are also covered by a 10-year warranty called a 'Homebond' (see **Finding an Architect & Builder** on page 141) and it's against the law to sell a new house without one. The warranty is transferable to a new owner if a property is sold within the warranty period.

If you're considering buying a property in a large development, there's often a 'show house' that will give you a good idea of how the finished building will look (although not everything in the show house will be included in the price!). If you're buying 'off plan' (i.e. before a house has been built), you can usually choose your bathroom suite, kitchen, fireplace, wallpaper and paint, wall and floor tiles, some or all of which may be included in the price. You may even be able to alter the interior room layout, although this will increase the price. Note that you should make any changes or additions to a property during the design stage, such as including a more luxurious kitchen, a chimney or an additional shower room, which will cost much more to install later.

When a building is purchased off plan, payment is made in stages as building work progresses over a period of one to two years (see below). Note that it's imperative to ensure that each stage is completed satisfactorily before making payments. If you're unable to do this yourself, you should engage an independent representative (e.g. an architect) to do it for you.

The quality of new property in Ireland is variable, although all builders must conform to certain standards. The quality of a building and the materials used will be reflected in the price, so when comparing prices ensure that you're comparing similar quality. Cheaper properties aren't usually the best built, although there are exceptions. If you want a permanent rather than a holiday home, you're better off opting for quality. Average prices for new properties are around IR£40,000 for a small (75m²) three-bedroom bungalow, IR£42,000 to IR£50,000 for a medium size (95m²) three-bedroom bungalow and IR£50,000 to IR£60,000 for a 125m² four-bedroom house, excluding the cost of land.

Most builders include in the basic price a standard bathroom suite and kitchen sink unit, a back boiler and radiators, twin sockets in each room, floor and wall insulation. Some also include fitted wardrobes, an electric shower, ventilation units for bathroom and kitchen, and a fire alarm. Optional extras may include double glazing, oil or gas central heating and exterior paving. Items such as carpets, kitchen units and light fittings need to be installed separately by specialist contractors.

Resale 'New' Homes: Buying 'new' doesn't necessarily mean buying a brand new home of which you're the first occupant. There are many advantages to buying a modern resale home, which may include better value for money, an established development with a range of local services and facilities in place, individual design and style, fixtures and fittings and other extras included in the price, a mature garden, and possibly a larger plot of land. With a resale property, you can see exactly what you're getting for your money, most 'teething troubles' will have been resolved, and the previous owners may have made improvements or added extras such as a loft conversion or conservatory, which may not be fully reflected in the asking price. See also **Buying a Resale Home** on page 143.

Retirement Homes: Purpose-built retirement properties (or sheltered housing) are becoming more common in Ireland, although large purpose-built developments are rare. Some large older properties have been converted into retirement homes, but it's more usual for individual buyers to have properties specially built, taking into consideration the requirements of older people (e.g. access ramps, stair lifts and emergency systems).

Building Your Own Home

If you want to be far from the madd(en)ing crowd, you can buy a plot of land and have a house built to your own design and specifications or to a standard design provided by a builder. Note, however, that building permission is quite difficult to obtain, particularly in the south-west where it's strictly controlled by the local authorities. In general, building a home in Ireland, or anywhere else for that matter, isn't recommended for the timid. However, there are many excellent builders in Ireland who will build an individually designed house on your plot of land or will sell you a plot and build a house chosen from a range of standard designs.

The Cost: The cost of land in Ireland varies considerably (from around IR£10,000 to IR£100,000 or more for a standard half-acre plot) according to the area. Prices have escalated sharply in recent years in some areas, because of the demand for new homes. Land can represent up to half the cost of building a home, although it's still possible in many areas to buy a plot of land and build a bigger and better home for less than the cost of a resale property. And the more land you buy, the cheaper it is: for example, a 60-acre farm in County Cork could cost as little as IR£175,000. But when putting in your bid, don't forget the old Irish adage: "The wrath of God has nothing on the wrath of an Irishman outbid for land"!

Building your own home allows you not only to design it yourself, but to ensure that the quality of materials and workmanship is first class. Building costs are around IR£350 to IR£600 per m^2, depending on the quality and the area. There's no VAT on land purchased for building a home, but VAT at 12.5 per cent is payable on the building itself (it should be included in the prices quoted by builders).

Some builders offer 'package deals' which include the land and the cost of building a home. However, it isn't always wise to buy the building plot from the builder who's going to build your home, and you should shop around and compare separate land and building costs. If you do decide to buy a package deal from a builder, you should insist on separate contracts for the land and the building, and obtain the title deed for the land before signing a building contract (see below). In most cases, a plot of land is purchased and then a builder is contracted to build a house on it.

Buying a Building Plot: You must take the same care when buying land as you would when buying a home. The continued housing boom in Ireland means that plots of land are being snapped up as fast as they become available and you may need to negotiate directly with the vendor (in most cases a farmer) rather than buying through an estate agent. In this case, it's particularly important to ensure that the land has been approved for building and that the plot is large enough and suitable for the house you plan to build. You must check with the planning authority of the local county, borough or urban district council that's responsible for preparing and updating the development plan for the area. According to this plan, land is 'zoned' for particular use: residential, amenity, commercial or industrial. Some areas may be zoned for mixed use, but any development must be in accordance with the zoning. These plans are revised every five years (new strategic planning guidelines for the Dublin area were published in 1999, for example). Development plans may be consulted at the planning authority's office or at the local library.

You should also check with the planning officer whether there are restrictions on the type of building which may be constructed. In scenic areas, for example, there may be limits on a building's height. Some plots are unsuitable for building as they're too steep or require prohibitively expensive foundations. Also check that there aren't any obstructions such as high-tension electricity lines, water pipes or rights of way which may restrict building. Note that the cost of providing services to a property in a remote rural area can be prohibitive and it must have a reliable water supply. It's also worth checking whether a plot is in an area where there are high levels of radon gas (see **Radon** on page 123).

It may be possible to build on agricultural land, but it will depend on whether you're an EU citizen and whether the land has been zoned for house building. Although there are theoretically no restrictions on EU citizens purchasing land in Ireland, the authorities may insist that farm land is retained as such and not purchased for conversion into residential or commercial property. If you're a non-EU citizen, you may need written consent from the Land Commission to buy agricultural land, although obtaining such consent is more or less a formality and it's rarely, if ever, withheld. You will need to obtain Form NQ1 from the Department of Agriculture and Food. The minimum plot that can be built on is usually 2,000m^2 (half an acre) with a frontage of at least 60m (200ft).

Before buying land for building, you should obtain a land registry map to certify that the plot has been properly registered. Ensure also that the purchase contract is dependent on obtaining the necessary planning permission and check for yourself that the correct planning permission is obtained (don't simply leave it to the builder). If planning permission is flawed, you may have to pay extra to improve the local infrastructure; the property may even need to be demolished!

Planning Permission: Planning permission is required for building a house or an extension (e.g. conservatory) of more than 23m^2 (247ft^2), as well as for erecting a fence or wall more than 2m (6ft) high or a path or pond more than 1m (3ft) above the surrounding ground level. Certain internal constructions may also require planning permission. There's a set procedure for making a planning application. First you must place an advertisement in the local newspaper indicating your intentions, and your planning application must be submitted within two weeks of the appearance of the advertisement. The application must include two copies of the newspaper advertisement as well as a site location map (four copies), detailed drawings/ elevations (four copies), a site layout plan (four copies), a site notice (two copies) and the application fee of IR£47. Obviously, the cost of preparing drawings and plans will be far greater than the application fee itself.

You need to decide in advance whether to apply for outline planning permission first. This is a sort of agreement in principle, a way of 'testing the water' if you're unsure whether permission will be granted. The costs involved are less, but you cannot start building until full approval has been granted. Once outline planning permission has been given, you can submit detailed plans for approval. Alternatively, you can make a full application for planning permission from the start. This will save you time but, if it's refused, you'll have wasted money on producing plans and drawings. As they say, "you pays your money and you takes your choice", although by taking expert advice you can minimise the risk involved.

Once you've submitted your application for planning permission, the local authority has two months in which to make a decision, although they may ask for more details. There are three possible outcomes: permission is granted, permission is refused or permission is granted under certain conditions. If permission is granted, you have five years in which to complete the construction (note that the planning authorities are under no obligation to renew the permission after this period). However, it's important not to start building work until at least a month after the planning authority's decision to grant permission. During this time it's possible for other people to object to the planning application or to appeal against the planning authority's decision. The official 'grant of permission' is therefore not issued until one month after the initial decision. Even then, you may need to obtain other approvals before building can start, such as permission to connect to a public water main or sewer. Finally, building control regulations require the service of a commencement notice on the building control authority (which is generally the planning authority itself).

If planning permission is refused or you're dissatisfied with the authority's decision, you can appeal to *An Bord Pleanála*, a sort of planning appeal court, whose decision is final. Your appeal must be lodged within one month of the planning authority's decision. The penalties for carrying out work without the necessary planning permission are severe and include fines of up to IR£1 million and prison sentences of up to two years.

Bye-Law Approval: Even if you don't need planning permission, e.g. for an extension of less than 23m^2 (247ft^2), you may (depending on the area) need bye-law approval from the building control section of your local authority. You must obtain the appropriate application form and pay a small fee (around IR£30). The authorities are particularly concerned about safety standards (particularly in Cork city and parts of Co. Dublin), e.g. that a kitchen extension doesn't cover a main sewer, that an attic or loft conversion has adequate ventilation, and that extra toilets and bathrooms have proper plumbing and drainage. Note that even garden sheds must be constructed in accordance with the bye-laws relating to open spaces.

The authorities have two months to consider bye-law applications. Once you've obtained approval, you must notify them in writing when you intend to start work and when you've finished. It may seem a lot of bother for what may be only a minor alteration, but it's obviously in your interest to ensure that any work meets the required standards so that you're adding to the value of a property rather than subtracting from it. In fact, you may not be able to sell the property at all if you haven't obtained the necessary approval – prospective buyers may be unable to secure a loan if the planning documents aren't in order (they can apply for a retention order, i.e. permission to retain an unauthorised structure, but this can take a long time and there's no guarantee that it will be granted). Note also that it isn't possible to obtain retrospective bye-law approval. When buying, you should therefore ask your solicitor to check that the necessary approvals for alterations or extensions have been obtained (see **Conveyance** on page 153).

Finding an Architect & Builder: When looking for an architect and builder it's best to obtain recommendations from local people you can trust, e.g. neighbours or friends. Note that estate agents and other professionals aren't always the best people to ask, as they may receive a commission. You can also obtain valuable information from expatriates and from owners of properties in an area that you particularly like.

Architects' fees are usually calculated as a percentage of the total cost of the work (normally around 10 per cent), which doesn't encourage them to cut costs. You're advised to use an architect who's a member of the Royal Institute of the Architects of Ireland (RIAI), which requires a high standard of qualification and competence. The RIAI can supply you with a copy of its Conditions of Appointment for Domestic Work (price IR£5), which covers all aspects of the services offered by RIAI members (☎ 01-676 1703).

A good architect should be able to recommend a number of reliable builders, but you should also do your own research, as the most important consideration when building a home is the reputation (and financial standing) of the builder. However, you should be wary of an architect with his 'own' builder (or a builder with his own architect), as it's the architect's job to ensure that the builder does his work according to the plans and specifications (so you don't want their relationship to be too cosy). Inspect other homes a builder has built and check with the owners what problems they've had and whether they're satisfied. Bear in mind that building standards vary and you shouldn't assume that the lowest quotation is the best. Note that it's imperative that the builder has an insurance policy (or 'termination' guarantee) to cover you in the event that he goes bust before completing the property and its infrastructure. This must be specified in the contract.

There are few large building companies in Ireland, where most builders are more or less 'one man bands'. When choosing a builder, make sure that he's registered with Homebond, the scheme set up by the Construction Industry Federation and operated by the National House Building Guarantee Company. If a builder is a member of the Irish Home Builders' Association (IHBA), he'll automatically be Homebond registered. Homebond provides three types of guarantee: against the loss of a deposit in the event of the builder going bust; against water and smoke damage for two years after completion; and against major structural defects for ten years after completion. Note that banks and building societies require Homebond registration on new houses, which is certified by Homebond Certificate HB47. When you enter into an agreement with a builder, you should immediately receive the Homebond Form HB10 incorporating the guarantee, and you should ensure that your solicitor receives this document at the earliest possible stage. According to the IHBA, a significant number of houses are still being built without certification, particularly in the west and north-west, so if you're buying without finance from an Irish bank or building society, make sure you obtain the necessary Homebond certification. Queries relating to Homebond should be addressed to Homebond, Construction House, Canal Road, Dublin 6 (☎ 01-491 0210).

If you want a house built exactly to your specifications, you'll need to personally supervise it every step of the way or employ an architect to do so for you. Without close supervision, it's highly likely that your instructions *won't* be followed to the letter.

Contracts: You should obtain written quotations from a number of builders before signing a contract. Once you've chosen a builder, your architect will prepare the contract documents, which will include a 'form of contract' and a set of drawings and specifications. These will be sent to the builder for completion. The builder will then provide you with a programme for the job, indicating the projected start and finish dates, and evidence that he holds the insurance required under the contract. The contract should include a detailed building description and a list of the materials to be used (with references to the architect's plans), the exact location of the building on the plot, the building and payment schedule, which must be made in stages according to building progress, a penalty clause for late completion, the retention of a percentage (typically 10 per cent for domestic work) of the building costs for up to 12 months as a guarantee against defects, and and explanation of how any disputes will be settled.

Ensure that the contract includes all costs, including the architect's fees (unless contracted separately), landscaping (if applicable), all permits and licences, and the connection of utilities (electricity, gas, etc.) to the house, not just to the building site. The only extra is usually the cost of the mains water connection.

Before accepting a quotation, you should have it checked by a building consultant to confirm that it's a fair deal. You should check whether the quotation (which should include VAT at 12.5 per cent) is an estimate or a fixed price, as sometimes the cost can escalate wildly as a result of contract clauses and changes made during building work. A fixed price contract isn't usual in one-off projects, because the scope of the work required frequently changes during the project. It is, however, possible to have a fixed rate contract whereby the unit cost of each element in the project is fixed against inflation. It's vital to have a contract checked by a solicitor, as they're often heavily biased in the builder's favour.

Payment: You're usually expected to pay a deposit of up to 10 per cent of the agreed price. How the remainder of the cost is paid varies from one part of the country to another. In Dublin, for example, you usually pay the balance on completion, whereas in Cork you normally pay in instalments. Instalment payments may be made at fixed stages in the construction process, e.g. on completion of the external walls, the roof and the wiring. More often, however, the work is valued and paid for at fixed intervals, e.g. monthly. In either case, your architect will value the work as it proceeds and advise you, by way of 'architect's certificates of payment due', how much is owed to the builder. Make sure you have all work inspected by your architect before making any payments. In any case, Homebond's own inspectors will be required to see the work at certain stages (typically when the foundations have been opened, when the drains are available, and on completion).

When building work is nearing completion, your architect will carry out particular inspections and have the builder attend to any defective or outstanding work before 'practical completion' of the work is certified, half of the retention money released and the job handed over to you. At this stage you'll need to ensure continuity of insurance cover from the builder to yourself. After practical completion, there's a 'defects liability period', during which the builder will remedy defects without charge. This usually lasts between six and 12 months and, ideally, extends through a winter. At the end of the defects liability period and after the builder has made good any defects that have become apparent, the balance of the retention money is released; this constitutes 'final completion'.

Note that it's important to ensure that payments are made on time, otherwise you could forfeit all previous payments and the property could be sold to another buyer. See also **Avoiding Problems** on page 117, which particularly applies to buying off plan and buying unfinished properties.

Warranties: On completion of the work, your achitect must complete an 'opinion on compliance' with Planning and Building Regulations. This document is required to sell a property, and banks and building societies also usually insist on it before providing a mortgage.

A useful booklet entitled *A Home of Your Own Making* is published by AIB Bank in association with The Royal Institute of the Architects of Ireland.

BUYING A RESALE HOME

Resale (or secondhand) properties represent good value for money in Ireland and are often more attractive and interesting than new buildings. Another advantage of buying a resale property is that you can see exactly what you're getting for your money and will save on the cost of installing such things as telephone lines and connections to services. When buying a resale property in a development, you should ask the neighbours about any problems, planned developments and anything else that may affect your enjoyment of the property. Most residents are usually happy to tell you (unless of course they're trying to sell you their own property!)

If you want a property with abundant charm and character, a building for renovation or conversion, outbuildings or a large plot of land, you must usually buy an old property. Note, however, that old country homes such as farmhouses may be harder to find and you'll need to go to small local auctioneers rather than large national companies. Some old homes lack basic services such as electricity, a reliable water supply and sanitation. Because purchase prices are often low, many foreign buyers are deceived into believing that they're getting a wonderful bargain, without fully investigating renovation and modernisation costs (see **Renovation & Restoration** on page 158).

Occasionally, owners advertise their properties directly in a local paper or by simply putting a 'for sale' sign in the window. But, although you can save money by buying directly from an owner, particularly when he's forced to sell, you should always employ a solicitor to carry out the necessary checks (see **Conveyance** on page 153). If you're unsure of the value of a property, you should obtain a professional valuation (see **Inspections, Valuations & Surveys** on page 151).

Leasehold Properties

In Ireland, as in the UK, properties with common elements (whether buildings, amenities or land) shared with other properties are usually sold on a leasehold rather than freehold basis. Owners of leasehold properties not only own their homes, but also own a share of the common elements of a building or development, including foyers, hallways, passages, lifts, patios, gardens, roads, and leisure and sports facilities (such as a gymnasium or tennis court). This means that you'll become part of a management company responsible for the insurance and upkeep of the common elements of the property. Note that being part of a management company is usually to your advantage, in that you have some control over expenditure on the property, rather than it being determined *ad hoc* by an absentee landlord. When buying a leasehold property, however, you should check whether the company has a healthy reserve or 'sink fund' and whether any major expenditure (e.g. a new roof) is imminent. Otherwise, you could find yourself being asked for several thousand pounds shortly after moving in. When you come to sell your apartment, you hand over a share transfer form that transfers your membership of the management company to the buyer.

When considering buying a leasehold property, the first thing you should do is ascertain the length of the lease, i.e. how many years it has left to run. If it's a new apartment, this may be as many as 9,999 years, in which case you needn't worry too much about outliving your lease! However, if there are only, say, 80 years left, you should take into account that, if you re-sell the property in 10 or 20 years, it may be difficult to find a buyer (note that a lease cannot be extended). On the other hand, once the lease expires, the lessee acquires the right to purchase the freehold, in which case a short lease may be attractive (although this right applies only to owner-occupiers, not to investors).

Note that Landlord and Tenant legislation introduced in 1978 made it illegal to purchase a freehold property and resell part of it on a leasehold basis.

Advantages: The advantages of owning a leasehold property may include increased security (all new apartments must be fitted with full fire alarm systems and most have individual intercom-controlled access), a range of communal facilities, community living with frequent social contacts and the companionship of close neighbours, no garden maintenance, and fewer of the responsibilities of home ownership.

Disadvantages: The disadvantages of leasehold properties can include excessively high management fees (owners may have no control over increases), restrictive rules and regulations, a confining living and social environment and possible lack of privacy, noisy neighbours (particularly if neighbouring properties are rented to holidaymakers), limited living and storage space, expensive parking (or insufficient off-road parking), and acrimonious management meetings.

Research: Before buying a leasehold property, you should ask current owners a few questions – e.g. do they like living there; what are the fees and restrictions; how noisy are other residents; are the recreational facilities easy to access; would they buy there again (why or why not); and, most importantly, is the management company solvent and well run? You may also wish to check on your prospective neighbours and, if you're planning to buy an apartment above the ground floor, whether the building has a lift. Upper floor apartments may offer more security than ground floor apartments; those that have other apartments above and below them are generally noisier than ground or top floor apartments.

Cost: The recent fashion for apartment living in Ireland has caused prices to soar, and most apartments now cost more than similar size houses with extensive grounds (see **Costs** on page 128).

Management Fees: Owners of leasehold properties usually need to pay management fees for the upkeep of communal areas and for communal services. Charges are usually billed annually and are calculated according to each owner's share of the development or apartment building, rather than whether they're temporary or permanent residents. Shares may be calculated according to the size of properties, e.g. the owners of ten equal size properties would each pay 10 per cent of management fees. Fees vary enormously depending on the quality of the development, the extent of the grounds, the facilities provided, and the age and condition of the property. You may pay as little as IR£200 per year, but the average annual management fee is around IR£400. If the fee is very low, you should check whether it actually includes all management costs or whether you're liable to be stung for extra charges for any major repairs that need to be done. If you're buying an apartment from a previous owner, always ask to see a copy of the management charges for previous years.

TIMESHARE & PART-OWNERSHIP SCHEMES

If you're looking for a holiday home, you may wish to investigate a scheme that provides sole occupancy of a property for a number of weeks each year. Such schemes include co-ownership, leaseback, timesharing and a holiday property bond. Don't rush into any of these schemes without fully researching the market and before you're absolutely clear what you want and what you can realistically expect to get for your money.

Co-Ownership: Two or more people buying a property together are called co-owners. There are two kinds of co-ownership in Ireland: joint tenancy and tenancy in common. In a joint tenancy, all the co-owners own the property as one legal entity and, on the death of one co-owner, his interest accrues to the others by 'right of survivorship' (*jus accrescendi*). This kind of ownership is most usual with married couples but could be used by any group of people. In the case of tenancy in common, each co-owner owns an undivided share of the property, so that if he dies his interest becomes part of his estate (as specified in his will). This is generally the better option for business or commercial purchases.

Co-ownership allows you to recoup your investment in savings on holiday costs and still retain equity in the property. A common arrangement is a four-owner scheme (many consider four to be the optimum number of co-owners), where you buy a quarter of a property and can occupy it for up to three months a year. However, there's no reason why there cannot be as many as 12 co-owners, with a month's occupancy each per year (usually divided between high, mid and low seasons).

Co-ownership provides access to a size and quality of property that may otherwise be unaffordable; it's even possible to have a share in a substantial mansion, where a number of families could live simultaneously and hardly ever see each other if they didn't want to! Co-ownership can be a good choice for a family seeking a holiday home for a few weeks or months a year and has the added advantage that (because of the lower cost) a mortgage may be unnecessary. Co-ownership is usually much better value than a timeshare (see below) and needn't cost much more. Note, however, that a water-tight contract must be drawn up by an experienced solicitor to protect the co-owners' interests.

One of the best ways to establish a co-ownership, if you can afford it, is to buy a property yourself and offer shares to others. This overcomes the problems of finding other would-be owners and agreeing on a purchase in advance, which is difficult unless you're a few friends or relatives. Many people form an Irish company to buy and manage a property, which can in turn be owned by a company in the co-owners' home country, thus allowing any disputes to be dealt with under local law. Each co-owner receives a number of shares, depending on how much he has paid, which entitle him to a certain number of weeks' occupancy a year. Owners don't need to have equal shares and can all be made title holders. If a co-owner wishes to sell his shares, he must usually offer first refusal to the other co-owners, although, if they don't wish to buy them and a new co-owner cannot be found, the property will need to be sold.

Leaseback: Leaseback or sale-and-leaseback schemes are designed for those seeking a holiday home for a limited number of weeks each year. Properties sold under a leaseback scheme are usually located in the most popular areas, e.g. near golf courses or coastal resorts, where self-catering accommodation is in high demand. Buying a property through a leaseback scheme allows you to buy a new property at less than its true cost, e.g. 30 per cent less than the list price. In return for the discount, the property must be leased back to the developer, usually for around ten years, so that he can let it as self-catering holiday accommodation. You own the freehold of the property and the full price is shown in the title deed. You're also entitled to occupy the property for a period each year, usually six or eight weeks, spread over high, mid and low seasons. These weeks can usually be let to provide income or can sometimes be exchanged with accommodation in another resort (as with a timeshare scheme). The developer furnishes and manages the property and pays all the maintenance and bills (e.g. for utilities) during the term of the lease, even when you're occupying the property. Note that it's important to have a contract checked by a solicitor to ensure that you receive vacant possession at the end of the leaseback period *without* having to pay an indemnity charge, otherwise you could end up paying more than the property is worth.

Timesharing: Timesharing, also called 'holiday ownership', 'vacation ownership' and 'holidays for life', earned a poor reputation at one time, but it has improved in recent years. The Timeshare Council (UK) and its Irish counterpart, the Timeshare Council of Ireland, as members of the Organisation for Timeshare in Europe (OTE), have restored respectability to the concept, as its members are bound by a code of conduct that includes a requirement that buyers have secure occupancy rights and that their money is properly protected prior to the completion of a new property. Further details can be obtained from the OTE/Timeshare Council (UK ☎ 020-7291 0901).

Since April 1997, an EU Directive has required timeshare companies to disclose information about the vendor and the property, and, at least in the UK, to allow prospective buyers a 14-day 'cooling off period' during which they may cancel any sales agreement they have signed without penalty. Elsewhere in the EU, although timeshare companies are technically bound by the directive, if they flout it you'll need to seek redress from the government of the country where the timeshare is situated, which may not be something you want or can afford to do.

There are only three recognised timeshare resorts in Ireland: Fitzpatrick Castle near Dublin, Connemara Cottages west of Galway and Knocktopher Abbey in Co. Kilkenny. Only the last of these is officially 'approved' by the OTE and it's managed by Seasons Holidays (☎ 01994-427332). If you buy a timeshare at Knocktopher Abbey, you may also be entitled to use Seasons Holidays' other resorts in England,

Wales, Cornwall, Portugal, Spain, etc. If you want a wider choice of alternative resorts, you can join Resort Condominium International (UK ☎ 01536-310101; 🖳 www.rci.com) or Interval International (UK ☎ 020-8336 9300; 🖳 www.interval world.com). RCI has timeshares in Counties Dublin, Galway, Kilkenny and Cork; Interval's are in Kerry and Cork.

Most experts believe that there's little or no advantage in a timeshare compared with a normal holiday rental and that it's simply an expensive way to pay for your holidays in advance. It doesn't make sense to tie up your money for what amounts to a long-term reservation on an annual holiday (usually you don't actually 'own' anything). The average timeshare in Ireland costs around IR£4,000 for one week per year, to which must be added annual management fees, which can run into hundreds or even thousands of pounds.

Most financial advisers believe you're better off putting your money into a long-term investment, where you retain your capital and may even earn sufficient interest to pay for a few weeks' holiday each year. For example, IR£10,000 invested at just 5 per cent yields IR£500 a year, which, when added to the saving on management fees, is sufficient to pay for a week's holiday in a self-catering apartment almost anywhere!

Timeshares are often difficult or impossible to sell at any price and 'pledges' from timeshare companies to sell them for you or buy them back at the market price are just a sales ploy, as timeshare companies are only interested in selling timeshares. Note that there's no real resale market for timeshares and, if you need to sell, you're highly unlikely to get your money back. If you want to buy a timeshare, it's best to buy a resale privately from an existing owner or a timeshare resale broker, when they sell for a fraction of their original cost. When buying privately, you can usually drive a hard bargain and may even get a timeshare 'free', simply by assuming the current owner's maintenance contract.

Holiday Property Bond: A Holiday Property Bond is a good alternative to timesharing for those with a minimum of GB£2,000 to invest. Holiday Property Bond (operated by HPB Management Ltd, HPB House, Newmarket, Suffolk CB8 8EH, UK ☎ 01638-660066; 🖳 www.hpb.co.uk) owns more than 700 properties in more than a dozen countries, as well as 'tenancy' properties in a dozen more, including Ireland. The Bond is a life assurance bond, invested in holiday properties and in securities to generate income for management charges. Each GB£ invested is equal to one point and each week's stay in each property is assigned a points rating depending on its size, location and the time of year. There are no extra fees apart from a 'user' charge to cover cleaning and utility costs. Furthermore, there's a buy-back guarantee after two years, when an investment can be sold at the current market value. Whereas bond properties are owned by HPB Management, tenancy properties are privately-owned and leased by HPB for the exclusive use of bondholders, who pay fewer points but a slightly higher user charge than for bond properties. HPB has three tenancy properties in the Republic of Ireland, located in Co. Cork, Co.Waterford and the Connemara.

BUYING FOR INVESTMENT

In recent years, Irish property has been an excellent investment, although changes to tax legislation in 1998 and 2000 have made it somewhat less attractive to investors. There are various kinds of property investment. Your home is itself an investment, in that it provides you with rent-free accommodation. It may also yield a return in terms of increased value (a capital gain), although that gain may be difficult to realise unless you trade down or move to another area or country where similar property is less expensive. Of course, if you buy property other than for your own regular use (i.e. a property which isn't your principal home), you'll be in a position to benefit from a more tangible return on your investment. There are essentially four main categories of investment property:

- A holiday home, which can provide a return in a number of ways: it can give you and your family and friends rent-free accommodation while (you hope) maintaining its value; you may be able to let it to generate supplementary income; it may also produce a capital gain if property values rise faster than inflation (as they have in most parts of Ireland in recent years).
- A home for your children, which may also realise a capital gain.
- A business property, which could be anything from bed and breakfast accommodation to a car park. Particularly attractive are properties which qualify for tax relief (e.g. under various Renewal Schemes).
- A property purchased for pure investment.

Any property investment needs to be considered over the medium to long term. For example, over the 25 years from 1972 to 1996, an Irish property would have yielded an average pre-tax return of 15 per cent per annum compared with average inflation at 9 per cent. But the divergence was not a constant one and there were short periods during this time when the increase in property values failed to keep pace with inflation (i.e. 1974–1976, 1981–1986 and 1991–1992). You also need to take into account the tax implications of owning and selling property, particularly capital gains tax (see page 96). Before deciding to invest in any property, you should ask yourself the following questions:

- Can I afford to tie up capital in the medium to long term, i.e. at least five years?
- How likely is it that the value of the property will rise during this period?
- Will I be relying on a regular income from my investment? If so, how easy will it be to generate that income, e.g. to find tenants for a property?
- Am I aware of all the risks involved and how comfortable am I with taking those risks?
- Do I have enough information to make a rational decision?

BUYING AT AUCTION

Although sales by auction tend to make headlines in Ireland's property pages, only some 6 per cent of properties in Ireland (generally the more prestigious kind) are sold by public auction. Nevertheless, buying at auction is becoming more popular and the number of properties sold at auction is increasing by around 10 per cent per year. There were more than 250 auctions in the first quarter of 1998, although the majority take place in spring and summer. They're usually advertised three or four weeks in advance so that there's sufficient time for prospective buyers to make the necessary preparations.

Before bidding at an auction, you must ensure that you have the legal title of the property approved by a solicitor, obtain a structural survey by a qualified architect, engineer or building surveyor (if necessary), secure formal written loan approval (if required), which will require a mortgage valuation report by a qualified valuer, and have sufficient cash to pay a deposit (usually 10 per cent) on the day of the auction – the balance is payable on completion of the sale (usually five to eight weeks after the auction).

Bear in mind when bidding at auction that you bid unconditionally. If you're successful, your deposit is at risk if you cannot complete the purchase for any reason. Note also that guideline prices provided by agents prior to an auction tend to be deliberately conservative (in order to attract more prospective buyers). Although the IAVI (Irish Auctioneers & Valuers Institute) recommends that guidelines should be within 15 per cent of the anticipated reserve price, the actual selling price is often so much higher than the reserve figure that the guidelines are virtually meaningless. In any case, reserve prices aren't disclosed in advance of the auction. The auctioneer's fee is usually the same as for a private treaty sale (see page 135), but may vary with the value of the property or be subject to negotiation.

BUYING BY PRIVATE TREATY

Most property in Ireland is sold by private treaty. Under this method, a price is put on a property by the vendor which is usually subject to negotiation between him and prospective buyers. A number of sales occur outside the normal system of auctions and estate agents, and you won't find out about these unless you know where to look or have a well-connected 'agent' in Ireland. However, by far the majority of sales are conducted through estate agents (see below) and it's rare for developers to sell directly as in some other countries.

If several people are interested in buying a property, the selling agent may suggest a closed or private tender, whereby written or oral bids must be submitted by a set time on a 'best and final offer' basis. Normally in such cases, the highest bidder secures the property, but not always. If, for example, an offer is subject to the sale of another property, a lower offer from a first-time buyer or someone who's in a position to buy unconditionally may be accepted instead. In a private treaty sale, you must bear in mind that the purchase isn't secure until all the formal documentation has been signed and exchanged between the buyer and seller. Up to that point the seller may still accept a higher offer, in which case the original buyer is said to have been 'gazumped'. It is, in fact, the agent's duty to inform the seller of all offers received at any time during the selling process. Gazumping isn't as common in Ireland as it is in the UK (the Irish blame the British for 'exporting' this unethical practice), but it's happening more frequently nowadays.

'Starter' homes targeted at first-time buyers often sell within two weeks of coming on the market. Estate agents will usually be offered the asking price on the first viewing, but may then invite bids from other would-be buyers in an effort to increase the price. If a higher bid is accepted, your deposit will be returned, but there's nothing you can do to oblige the vendor to honour the agreement. You simply have to start looking for another property and try to put all thoughts of the one you thought you were buying out of your mind!

ESTATE AGENTS

The vast majority of property sales in Ireland, particularly those where overseas buyers are involved, are handled by estate agents, who are usually referred to as auctioneers. It's common for foreigners, particularly the British and Germans, to use an agent in their own country who works in conjunction with an Irish agent. Many Irish agents also advertise abroad, particularly in the publications listed in **Appendix A**, and in expatriate magazines and newspapers in Ireland. If you want to find an agent in a particular town or area, you can look under 'Auctioneers' in the local Golden Pages (available at main libraries in many countries).

Qualifications: Irish estate agents are regulated by law and must be professionally qualified and licensed. You should choose an agent who's a member of a professional association such as the IAVI, which is by far the largest professional body in Ireland, or the Institute of Professional Auctioneers and Valuers (IPAV). You should also ensure that an agent has a current auctioneer's licence, which IAVI members are obliged to display prominently in their offices. Licensed auctioneers are 'bonded' (i.e. provide security against claims) to the sum of IR£10,000 in the high court. To become an individual member of the IAVI, auctioneers must have undertaken relevant studies or passed the Institute's own exams. IAVI 'member firm status' is granted only to practices in which the majority of equity is held by qualified IAVI individual members; member firms are also subject to a disciplinary code and must have professional indemnity insurance, and the IAVI compensation fund (a deposit protection fund) applies only to IAVI members and (in the case of residential and land sales) associate member firms.

When you pay a deposit to an agent, it must (by law) be deposited in a separate client or current account, so that the agent derives no interest from the money. Note that the rules for Irish estate agents also apply to foreigners, who cannot sell property in Ireland without an Irish auctioneer's licence.

Fees: There are no government controls on agents' fees in Ireland, but the commission charged by most Irish agents is between 2 and 2.5 per cent. This fee is included in the sale price and effectively paid by the buyer. Foreign agents located abroad often work with Irish agents and share the standard commission, so vendors usually pay no more by using them. When buying, check whether you need to pay commission or any extras in addition to the sale price, apart from the normal fees and taxes associated with buying a property.

Viewing: If possible, you should decide where you want to live, what sort of property you want and your budget *before* visiting Ireland. Obtain details of as many properties as possible in your chosen area and price range, and make a shortlist of those you wish to view. The details provided by Irish estate agents can be sparse. Often there's no photograph and, even when there is, it usually doesn't do a property justice. Note that there are no national property listings in Ireland, where each agent has his own list of properties for sale and it's unusual for the same property to be listed with more than two agents. Irish agents who advertise in foreign journals or work closely with overseas agents may provide coloured photographs and a full description, particularly for the more expensive properties. The best agents provide an abundance of information. Agents vary in their efficiency and enthusiasm as well as in the number and variety of properties they have to offer. If an agent shows little interest in finding out exactly what you want, you should look elsewhere. If you're using a foreign agent, confirm (and reconfirm) that a particular property is still for sale and the price, before travelling to Ireland to view it.

Note that Irish estate agents don't usually require you to sign an agreement before showing you properties, although they may do so if you're buying at auction. In Ireland, you're usually shown properties personally by agents and won't be given the keys (particularly to furnished properties) or be expected to deal with tenants or vendors directly. You should make an appointment to see properties, as agents don't usually like people turning up 'on spec'. If you cannot keep an appointment, you should always call and cancel it. If you're on holiday, it's acceptable to drop in unannounced to have a look at what's on offer, but don't expect an agent to show you properties without an appointment. If you view properties during a holiday, it's best to do so at the beginning so that you can return later to inspect any you particularly like a second and third time. Irish estate agents are usually open during lunch hours and on Saturdays.

You should try to view as many properties as possible during the time available, but allow sufficient time to view each property thoroughly, to travel between properties, and for breaks for sustenance. Make sure you also allow plenty of talking time, which is always necessary in Ireland! Although it's important to see sufficient properties to form an accurate opinion of price and quality, don't see too many properties in one day (around six to eight is usually a manageable number), as it's easy to become confused over the merits of each property. If you're shown properties that don't meet your specifications, tell the agent immediately. You can also help an agent narrow the field by telling him exactly what's wrong with the properties you reject. It's wise to make notes of both the good *and* bad features and take lots of photographs of the properties you like, so that you're able to compare them later at your leisure (but keep a record of which photos are of which house!). It's also wise to mark properties on a map so that, should you wish to return later on your own, you can find them without getting lost (too often). The more a property appeals to you, the more you should look for faults and negative points; if you still like it after stressing all the negative points, it must have special appeal.

Most agents offer after sales services and will help you to engage a solicitor and arrange insurance, utilities, interior decorators and builders; many offer a full management and rental service on behalf of non-resident owners. Note, however, that agents may receive commissions for referrals, so you may not always receive impartial advice.

INSPECTIONS, VALUATIONS & SURVEYS

When you've found a property that you like, you should make an inspection of its condition. Obviously, the extent of this will depend on whether it's an old house in need of complete restoration, a property that has been partly or totally modernised, or a modern home. One of the problems with a property that has been restored is that you don't know how well the job has been done, particularly if the owner did it himself, although he may have had to obtain local bye-law approval (see page 140), in which case certain standards will have been met. If work has been carried out by local builders, you should ask to see the bills.

There are certain things you can test yourself, including the electrical system, plumbing, mains water, hot water boiler and central heating. Don't take someone's word that these are functional, but check them for yourself. If a property doesn't have electricity or mains water, check the nearest connection point and the cost of extending the service to the property, as it can be *very* expensive in some rural areas. If a property has a well or septic tank, you should have it tested. An old property may show visible signs of damage and decay, such as bulging or cracked walls, rising damp, missing roof slates (you can check with binoculars) and rotten woodwork. Common problems also include rusting water pipes and leaky plumbing, inadequate sewage disposal, poor wiring, humidity and rising damp (no damp-proof course), uneven flooring or no concrete base, subsidence, and cracked internal and external walls. Some of these problems are even evident in relatively new properties. In areas that are liable to flooding, storms or subsidence, you should check an old property after heavy rain, when any leaks should come to light. If you find or suspect problems, you should have a property checked by a builder or have a full structural survey carried out by a surveyor.

You should never make an offer on an old property before at least having it checked by a builder, who will also be able to tell you whether the price is too high, given any work that needs to be done. It's important to check who was the developer or builder of a relatively new property, as a builder with a good reputation is unlikely to have cut corners. Note that a property over ten years old will no longer be covered by a builder's warranty (see **Building Your Own Home** on page 138). If you require a mortgage to buy a property, the lending institution (e.g. bank or building society) will require at least a valuation report, which, as well as verifying the value of the property, will usually reveal any major defects. However, a valuation report won't necessarily tell you whether there are (or are likely to be) minor problems such as unsafe wiring or a leaking roof. Therefore it's prudent to obtain a full structural survey, which will reveal any major or minor defects in a property and indicate the likely cost of any repairs or renovations required. If serious problems are discovered that would be expensive to rectify, you may decide to look for another property or negotiate a reduction in the price with the vendor. Note that your mortgage lender may insist on a structural report if a property is over 100 years old.

You could ask the vendor to have a survey done at his expense, which, provided it gives the property a clean bill of health, will help him sell it even if you decide not to buy. However, it's unlikely that he will agree to this as buying property in Ireland is very much a case of *caveat emptor* (buyer beware)! You can employ a foreign surveyor practising in Ireland. However, an Irish surveyor may have a more intimate knowledge of local properties and building methods. If you employ a foreign surveyor, you must ensure that he's experienced in the idiosyncrasies of Irish properties and that he has professional indemnity insurance covering Ireland (which means you can happily sue him if he does a bad job!).

Always discuss with a surveyor exactly what will be included and, most importantly, excluded from a survey (you may need to pay extra to include certain checks and tests). A full structural survey should include the condition of all buildings, particularly the foundations, roofs, walls and woodwork, the plumbing, and the electrical and heating systems. A survey can be limited to a few items or even a single system, such as the wiring or plumbing in an old house. You should receive a written report on the structural condition of a property, including anything that could become a problem in the future. Some surveyors allow you to accompany them and provide a video film of their findings in addition to a written report. A fee of IR£300 or so for a full structural survey on an average size home is a small price to pay for the peace of mind it affords.

Land: Before buying a home with a plot of land, you should walk the boundaries and look for fences, driveways, roads, and the eaves of buildings that may be encroaching upon the property. If you're uncertain about the boundaries, you should have the land surveyed, which is recommended in any case when buying a property with a large plot of land. When buying a rural property in Ireland, you may be able to negotiate the amount of land you want included in the purchase. If a property is part of a larger plot owned by the vendor or the boundaries need to be redrawn, you'll have to hire a surveyor to measure the land and draw up a new cadastral plan. You should also ask your solicitor to check the local municipal plans to find out what the land can be used for and whether there are any rights of way across it.

CONVEYANCE

Conveyance (often improperly referred to as conveyancing) is the legal term for processing the paperwork involved in buying and selling a property and transferring the deeds of ownership. As this can be a complicated process, it's virtually essential to use a solicitor. Basically, the procedure is as follows. Once the selling price has been agreed between the vendor and the buyer, the vendor's solicitor prepares a contract and sends it to the buyer's solicitor, who checks the title and asks the buyer to sign the contract and pay a deposit to secure the property. If the buyer is obtaining a loan (mortgage), the contract will be subject to the loan being granted, which in turn will be subject to a satisfactory valuation report. Some selling agents insist that the valuation is carried out before negotiations are concluded, and provisional loan approval can now be secured quickly (within 72 hours), which means that the vendor's solicitor will generally refuse a contract that's subject to loan approval.

The buyer's solicitor will then draft the purchase deed and raise his queries (requisitions) on title before sending the deposit, draft deed and any objections with regard to title back to the vendor's solicitor. Note that at this stage the buyer has committed himself to buying (subject to satisfactory title) whereas the vendor isn't yet committed to selling. The requisitions (commonly referred to as 'searches') carried out usually include:

- a planning search, with the local planning office, to reveal whether there are plans to construct anything which would adversely affect the value, enjoyment or use of the property such as roads, railway lines, airports, shops or factories, and whether applications for planning permission in respect of the property have been lodged or refused;

- a compulsory purchase order search with the local authority to find out whether the land is subject to compulsory purchase by the state or local authority, e.g. for road building or widening;

- a licensing search (in the case of a hotel or pub).

The solicitor will also check:

● that the property belongs to the vendor or that he has legal authority to sell it. If the property is registered with the land registry, this is a simple matter. If it's with the registry of deeds, 30 years' title is usually regarded as 'sufficient' (note that the vendor's solicitor is obliged by law to disclose any relevant legal matters, although not physical matters, relating to the title of a property);

● that the property was built in accordance with the appropriate regulations, e.g. planning regulations, bye-laws, building standards;

● that there are no encumbrances (e.g. mortgages or loans) against the property or any outstanding debts such as gas, electricity or telephone bills and management fees (in the case of a leasehold property). Note that you *must* ensure that any debts against a property are cleared before you sign the deed of sale, as unpaid debts on a property in Ireland are inherited by the buyer;

● whether there are any remaining guarantees from which you can benefit, such as the Homebond 10-year warranty for new homes;

● that all the agreed fixtures and fittings included in the price you've negotiated are actually included in the legal documentation.

When he has received satisfactory replies to these queries, the buyer's solicitor will draft a deed transferring title in the property to the buyer and give the lending institution a certificate of title. If the vendor is happy with the contract, he will also sign it. The draft deed is then approved by the vendor's solicitor and returned for 'typing up' (engrossment) by the buyer's solicitor before being returned again to the vendor's solicitor for signing by the vendor (no wonder solicitors' fees are so high!).

The buyer's solicitor will also need to check whether capital gains tax (CGT) has been paid by the vendor (if applicable). If the purchase price is over IR£150,000, he will need to obtain a CGT clearance certificate; otherwise the buyer is obliged to submit 15 per cent of the purchase price to the Revenue Commissioners against the possibility of CGT being unpaid (the vendor will then have to obtain a refund of the same amount once the clearance certificate has been produced).

Warning: You shouldn't even think about buying (or selling) property in Ireland without taking expert, independent legal advice. You should certainly never sign anything or pay any money before doing so. Before hiring a solicitor, compare the fees charged by a number of practices and obtain quotations in writing. Always check what's included in the fee and whether it's 'full and binding' or just an estimate (a low basic rate may be supplemented by more expensive 'extras'). Note that you shouldn't use the vendor's solicitor, even if this would save you money, as he is primarily concerned with protecting the interests of the vendor and not the buyer. See also **Avoiding Problems** on page 117.

PURCHASE CONTRACTS

Your solicitor should draw up the purchase contract and ensure that it includes everything required, particularly any necessary conditional clauses. The basis of all house purchase contracts in Ireland is the 'Standard Incorporated Law Society' contract (copies are obtainable from the Law Society of Ireland), which is revised from time to time (the one in use dates from 1995). The particulars of the purchase (i.e. the address of the property, selling price, date of purchase, etc.) and any special conditions must be included in the contract, but its general conditions won't usually need to be amended (unless there's a major problem, such as planning permission not having been obtained). If you're buying a new property from a builder, there are also standard contracts that can be used, and there may be separate contracts for the purchase of the site and for the construction of the building. Note that, from the moment the signed contracts are exchanged, the sale becomes irrevocable.

Deposits: When you sign the contract for a new or resale property or a plot of land, you must pay a deposit. If you're buying a resale or a new finished property (i.e. not off plan) you usually pay a deposit of 10 per cent when signing the contract (the actual amount may be negotiable), the balance being paid on completion when the deed of sale is signed.

Conditional Clauses: Most contracts, whether for new or resale properties, contain a number of conditional clauses that must be met to ensure the validity of the contract. Conditions usually apply to events beyond the control of either the vendor or buyer, although almost anything the buyer agrees with the vendor can be included in a contract. If any of the conditions aren't met, the contract can be suspended or declared null and void, and the deposit returned. However, if you decide to withdraw from purchase and aren't covered by a clause in the contract, you'll forfeit your deposit and could be compelled to go through with the purchase. Note that, if you're buying anything from the vendor such as carpets, curtains or furniture, which are included in the purchase price, you should have them listed and attached as an addendum to the contract. Any fixtures and fittings present in a property when you view it (and agree to buy it) should still be there when you take possession, unless otherwise stated in the contract (see also **Completion** below). In most cases, however, the contract will be conditional only upon the buyer obtaining the necessary mortgage and (if applicable) planning permission being obtained.

Inheritance & Capital Gains Tax: Before registering the title deed, carefully consider the tax and inheritance consequences for those in whose name the deed will be registered. Property can be registered in a single name, both names of a couple or joint buyers, the name or names of children, giving the parents sole use during their lifetime, or in the name of an Irish or foreign company (see below). However you decide to register a property, it should be done at the time of purchase, as it will be more expensive (or even impossible) to change it later. Discuss the matter with your solicitor before signing a contract. See also **Capital Gains Tax** on page 96 and **Capital Acquisition Tax** on page 97.

Buying Through a Company: It's no longer possible to avoid Irish capital gains and inheritance tax by registering a property in the name of an offshore company, as land is regarded as a 'qualified asset', which is always taxable. If a property is owned by a company in a country which has a double taxation treaty with Ireland, you'll pay the full amount of capital gains tax due in Ireland (see page 91). If the rate of CGT in your country of residence is higher than in Ireland, you'll pay the difference in that country; if it's lower, you *won't* receive a refund! Buying an Irish property through an Irish company has advantages and disadvantages. You can save a considerable amount in stamp duty (see **Fees** on page 131), but you may have to pay CGT or income tax on the increased value of your shares and, if the company has been running for some time and has a complicated financial history, you may have difficulty finding a buyer who's willing to take it over. Before buying property through any sort of company, it's essential to obtain expert legal advice. See also **Avoiding Problems** on page 117 and **Conveyance** on page 153.

COMPLETION

Completion (or closing) is the name given to the signing of the final deed of sale, the date of which is usually five to eight weeks after signing the purchase contract, as stated in that contract (although it may be 'moveable'). The exact date will be set by the buyer's solicitor once his client's mortgage has been approved. Before closing, the buyer's solicitor will carry out the final searches on title, including:

- a land registry or registry of deeds search to ascertain whether there are any restrictions on title such as outstanding mortgages or rights of residence. In the case of registered land, there are some burdens which aren't subject to registration such as outstanding estate duty, succession duty, rent charges, land improvement charges, annuities, rights of the public and short-term tenancies. The vendor is usually required to swear an affidavit that none of these burdens affect the property;
- a company search (with the Companies Registration office) in the case of company purchases;
- a judgement search (at the Central Office of the High Court) to reveal any record of litigation (*lis pendens*) affecting the property and any debts owed by the vendor which don't affect the property directly, but indicate the possibility of the debt having been converted into a 'judgement mortgage' registered against the property;
- a bankruptcy search (if the vendor is bankrupt, the property will be held by an Official Assignee who cannot transfer good title);
- a sheriff and revenue sheriff search (in the case of leasehold property only) to disclose any debts owed by the vendor.

Completion involves the signing of the deed of purchase (the vendor must sign it prior to completion, the buyer within one month of completion), transferring ownership of the property, and the payment of the balance of the purchase price (less the deposit and, if applicable, the amount of a mortgage), plus other payments such as solicitor's fees, taxes and duties.

Final Checks: Property is sold subject to the condition that it's accepted in the state it's in at the time of completion; you should therefore be aware of anything that occurs between signing the purchase contract and completion. Before signing the deed of sale, it's important to check that the property hasn't fallen down or been damaged in any way, e.g. by a storm or vandals (or the previous owner!). If you've employed a solicitor or are buying through an agent, he should accompany you on this visit. You should also do a final inventory immediately prior to completion (the previous owner should have already vacated the property) to ensure that the vendor hasn't absconded with anything that was included in the price. You should have an inventory of the fixtures and fittings and anything that was included in the contract or purchased separately, e.g. carpets, light fittings or curtains, and check that they're present and in good order. This is particularly important if furniture and furnishings (and major appliances) were included in the price. You should also ensure that expensive items (such as kitchen appliances) haven't been substituted by inferior (possibly secondhand) items. Any fixtures and fittings (and garden plants and shrubs) present in a property when you viewed it should still be there when you take possession, unless otherwise stated in the contract.

If you find that anything is missing or damaged or isn't in working order, you should make a note and insist on immediate restitution such as an appropriate reduction in the amount to be paid. In such cases it's normal for your solicitor to delay the signing of the deed until the matter is settled, although an appropriate amount could be withheld from the vendor's proceeds to pay for repairs or replacements. You should refuse to go through with the purchase if you aren't completely satisfied, as it will be difficult or impossible to obtain redress later. If it isn't possible to complete the sale, you should consult your solicitor concerning your rights and the return of your deposit and any other fees already paid.

Power of Attorney: Either the vendor or the buyer may give a third party (e.g. a solicitor) power of attorney to sign the contract or deed on his behalf. This is quite common among foreign buyers and sellers and can be arranged by your solicitor (for a fee of around IR£200). If a couple buy a property in both their names, the wife can give the husband power of attorney (or vice versa). Note, however, that it can be dangerous to give someone power of attorney, and in most cases it's unnecessary. If you need to give power of attorney, you should make sure you give it to someone not only whom you can trust, but who knows you well, or you could find yourself bound to an agreement of which you don't approve.

Payment: The balance of the price after the deposit and any mortgages have been subtracted must be paid by banker's draft or bank transfer. Usually, the most convenient way is by banker's draft, which means that you'll have the payment in your possession (a bank cannot lose it!) and the solicitor can confirm it immediately. It also allows you to withhold payment if there's a last minute problem that cannot be resolved. Non-resident buyers no longer need a certificate from an Irish bank stating that the amount to be paid has been exchanged or converted from a foreign currency, although it must be reported to the Bank of Ireland in accordance with legislation relating to money laundering (see **Importing & Exporting Money** on page 75). Non-residents may also be required to confirm their tax situation (i.e. whether or not they're liable for income tax in Ireland). Note that even if the vendor and buyer are of the same foreign nationality, the final payment must be made in Irish pounds (or euro). After you've paid, your solicitor should give you a receipt and an unsigned copy of the purchase deed showing that you're the new owner of the property. You'll also receive the keys!

Registration: After stamping by the Revenue Commissioners (if stamp duty is payable), the title deed is lodged for registration with either the land registry or the registry of deeds and returned to the buyer or, if the property is mortgaged, to his lender who retains it for the duration of the mortgage. When the mortgage has been repaid, the lending institution issues a 'vacate' (a kind of receipt) confirming that the loan has been repaid and transferring title to the owner.

RENOVATION & RESTORATION

Some old country or village homes are in need of restoration, renovation or modernisation. Before buying a property requiring restoration or modernisation, you should consider the alternatives. An extra few thousand punts spent on a purchase may represent much better value for money than spending the money on building work. It's often cheaper to buy a restored or partly restored property than a ruin in need of total restoration, unless you're going to do most of the work yourself. If you aren't into do-it-yourself in a big way, you may be better off buying a new or recently built property, as the cost of restoration can be double or even treble the price of the original property. If you're planning to buy a property that needs restoration or renovation and aren't planning to do the work yourself, make sure you obtain a *realistic* estimate of the costs *before* signing a contract.

Bear in mind that, if you buy and restore a property with the intention of selling it for a profit, you must take into account not only the initial price and the restoration costs, but also the fees and taxes included in the purchase, plus capital gains tax if it's a second home (see page 96). It's often difficult to sell a renovated old property at a higher than average market price, irrespective of its added value. If you're buying for investment, you may be better off buying a new home, as the price of most restored properties doesn't reflect the cost and amount of work that went into them (and many people who have restored a 'ruin' would never do it again and advise others against it).

Inspections & Surveys: It's vital to check a property for any obvious faults, particularly an old property. Most importantly, a building must have sound walls, without which it may be cheaper to erect a new building! Almost any other problem can be fixed or overcome (at a price). A sound roof that doesn't leak is desirable, as ensuring that a building is waterproof is the number one priority if funds are limited. Don't believe a vendor or agent who tells you that a roof or anything else can be repaired or patched up, but obtain expert advice from a local builder. Sound roof timbers are also important, as they can be expensive to replace. Old buildings often need a damp-proof course, timber treatment, new windows and doors, a new roof or extensive roof repairs, a modern kitchen and bathroom, re-wiring and central heating. Electricity and mains water should preferably already be connected, as they can be expensive to extend to a property in a remote area. If a house doesn't have electricity or mains water, it's important to check the cost of extending these services to it. If you're seeking a waterside property, you should check the likelihood of floods and, if fairly frequent, you should ensure that a building has been designed with floods in mind, e.g. with electrical installations above flood level and solid tiled floors.

It may well be worthwhile having a full structural survey carried out (see **Inspections, Valuations & Surveys** on page 151), as major problems can even be found in relatively new properties, and spending a few hundred punts on a survey could save you thousands in repairs.

Planning Permission: If modernisation of an old building involves making external alterations, such as building an extension or installing larger windows or new doorways, you may need permission from your local planning authority. If you plan to do major restoration or building work, you should ensure that a conditional clause is included in the contract stating that the purchase is dependent on obtaining planning permission. You should allow at least two months for planning permission to be obtained and a further month for any objections to be raised, compared, for example, with just four weeks in the UK and Germany. You should never start any building work before you have official permission.

DIY or Builders? One of the first decisions you need to make regarding restoration or modernisation is whether to do all or most of the work yourself or have it done by professional builders or local artisans. Note that, when restoring a period property, it's imperative to have a sensitive approach to restoration. You shouldn't tackle jobs yourself or with friends unless you're sure you're doing them right. In general, you should aim to retain as many of a property's original features as possible and stick to local building materials, reflecting the style of the property. When renovations and 'improvements' have been botched, there's often little that can be done except to start again from scratch. It's important not to over-modernise an old property, so that its natural rustic charm and attraction is lost. Note that, even if you intend to do most of the work yourself, you'll still need to hire artisans for certain jobs.

Finding a Builder: When looking for a builder, you should obtain recommendations from local people you can trust, e.g. neighbours or friends. Note that estate agents or other professionals aren't always the best people to ask as they may receive commissions. Always obtain references from previous customers. It may be better to use a local building consortium or contractor rather than a number of independent tradesmen, particularly if you won't be around to supervise them (although it will cost you a bit more). On the other hand, if you supervise it yourself using local hand-picked craftsmen, you can save money and learn a great deal into the bargain.

Supervision: If you aren't on the spot and able to supervise work, you should hire a 'clerk of works' such as an architect to oversee a large job, or it could drag on for months or be left half-finished. This will add around 10 per cent to the total bill, but it's usually worth every penny. Be extremely careful whom you employ if you have work done in your absence, and ensure that your instructions are accurate in every detail. Always make certain that you (and your builder) understand exactly what has been agreed and if necessary draw up a written agreement (with drawings). It isn't unusual for foreign owners to receive huge bills for work done in their absence which shouldn't have been done at all!

Quotations: Before buying a home in Ireland requiring restoration or modernisation, it's essential to obtain an accurate estimate of the work and costs involved. You should obtain written estimates from at least two builders before employing anyone. Note that for quotations to be accurate you must detail the eact work required, e.g. for electrical work this would include the number of lights, points and switches, and the quality of materials to be used. If you have only a vague idea of what you want, you'll receive a vague and unreliable quotation. Make sure that a quotation includes everything you want done and that you fully understand it (if you don't, have it checked by someone who does). You should fix a date for the start and completion of work and, if you can get a builder to agree to it, include a penalty for failing to finish on time. After signing a contract, it's usual to pay a deposit, the amount of which depends on the size and cost of a job.

Cost: The cost of restoration depends on the work involved, the quality of materials used and the region. As a rough guide, you should expect the cost of totally renovating an old 'habitable' building to be at least equal to its purchase price and possibly much more. How much you spend on restoring a property will depend on your purpose and the depth of your pockets. If you're restoring a property as an investment, don't be tempted to spend more than you can hope to recoup when you sell it. On the other hand, if you're restoring a property as a holiday or permanent home, there's no limit to what you can do and how much money you can spend. Always keep an eye on your budget (which will inevitably be 25 per cent more or less than you actually spend – usually less!) and don't be in too much of a hurry. Some people take many years to restore a holiday home, particularly when they're doing most of the work themselves. It isn't unknown for buyers to embark on a grandiose renovation scheme, only to run out of money before it's completed and be forced to sell at a loss.

Note that, if you make major improvements to a property, you should be sure to obtain evidence of your expenditure (i.e. quotations, invoices and receipts) so that you can offset some or all of the costs against tax. See also **Buying a Resale Home** on page 143, **Inspections, Valuations & Surveys** on page 151, **Water & Waste** on page 169 and **Heating** on page 168.

MOVING HOUSE

After finding a home in Ireland, it usually only takes a few weeks to have your belongings shipped from within continental Europe. From anywhere else it varies considerably, e.g. around four weeks from the east coast of America, six weeks from the US west coast and the Far East, and around eight weeks from Australasia. Customs clearance is no longer necessary when shipping your household effects between European Union (EU) countries. When shipping your effects from a non-EU country to Ireland, you should enquire about customs formalities in advance. If you fail to follow the correct procedure, you can encounter problems and delays, and may even be erroneously charged duty or fined (see **Customs** on page 183). Shipping companies usually take care of the paperwork and ensure that the correct documents are provided and properly completed.

It's best to use a major shipping company with a good reputation. For international moves, you should use a company that's a member of the International Federation of Furniture Removers (FIDI) or the Overseas Moving Network International (OMNI), with experience in Ireland. Members of FIDI and OMNI usually subscribe to an advance payment scheme providing a guarantee, whereby, if a member fails to fulfil its commitments to a client, the job is completed at the agreed cost by another company or your money is refunded. Some shipping companies have subsidiaries or affiliates in Ireland, which may be useful if you encounter problems or need to make an insurance claim.

You should obtain at least three written quotations before choosing a shipping company, as rates vary considerably. Shipping companies should send a representative to provide a detailed quotation. Most companies will pack your belongings and provide packing cases and special containers, although this is naturally more expensive than packing them yourself. Ask a company how they pack fragile and valuable items, and whether the cost of packing cases, materials and insurance (see below) are included in a quotation. If you're doing your own packing, most shipping companies will provide packing crates and boxes. Shipments are charged by volume, e.g. per m^2 in Europe and per ft^2 in the USA. You should expect to pay between IR£2,500 and IR£5,000 to move the contents of a three to four bedroom house within western Europe, e.g. from continental Europe to Dublin. If you're flexible about the delivery date, shipping companies will usually quote a lower fee based on a 'part load', where the cost is shared with other deliveries. This can result in savings of 50 per cent or more compared with a 'special' delivery. However, whether you have an individual or shared delivery, always obtain the maximum transit period in writing, otherwise you may have to wait months for delivery!

Be sure to fully insure your belongings during shipping with a well established insurance company. Don't insure with a shipping company that has its own insurance as they will usually fight every penny of a claim. Insurance premiums are usually 1 to 2 per cent of the declared value of your goods, depending on the type of cover chosen. It's wise to make a photographic or video record of valuables for insurance purposes. Most insurance policies cover for 'all risks' on a replacement value basis. Note, however, that china, glass and other breakables can usually only be included in an all-risks policy when they're packed by the shipping company. Insurance usually covers total loss or loss of a particular crate only, rather than individual items (unless they were packed by the shipping company). If there are any broken or damaged items, they must be noted and listed before you sign the delivery bill (although it's obviously impractical to check everything on delivery). If you need to make a claim, be sure to read the small print, as some companies require clients to make a claim within a few days of delivery, although a week is usual. Send a claim by registered mail. Some insurance companies apply an excess of around 1 per cent of the total shipment value when assessing claims. This means that, if your shipment is valued at IR£20,000 and you make a claim for less than IR£200, you won't receive anything.

If you're unable to ship your belongings directly to Ireland, most companies will put them into storage and some offer a limited free storage period prior to shipment, e.g. 14 days. If you need to put your household effects into storage, it's imperative to have them fully insured, as warehouses have been known to burn down! Make a complete list of everything to be moved and give a copy to the shipping company. Don't include anything illegal (e.g. guns, bombs, drugs or pornography) with your belongings as customs checks can be rigorous and penalties severe. Provide the shipping company with *detailed* instructions for finding your Irish address from the nearest main road and a telephone number where you can be contacted.

After considering the shipping costs, you may decide to ship only selected items of furniture and personal effects, and buy new furniture in Ireland. If you're importing household goods from another European country, it's possible to rent a self-drive van or truck. Note, however, that if you rent a vehicle outside Ireland you'll usually need to return it to the country where it was hired. If you plan to transport your belongings to Ireland personally, check the customs requirements in the countries you'll pass through. Most people find it isn't wise to do their own move unless it's a simple job, e.g. a few items of furniture and personal effects only. It's no fun heaving beds and wardrobes up stairs and squeezing them into impossible spaces! If you're taking pets with you, you may need to ask your vet to tranquillise them, as many pets are frightened (even more than people) by the chaos and stress of moving house. They may also need several weeks or even months to become accustomed to their new surroundings (see **Pets** on page 62).

Bear in mind when moving home that everything that can go wrong often does. You should therefore allow plenty of time and try not to arrange your move to your new home on the same day as the previous owner is moving out. That's just asking for Murphy to intervene! Last but not least, if your Irish home has poor or impossible access for a large truck, you must inform the shipping company (the ground must also be firm enough to support a heavy vehicle). Note also that, if large items of furniture need to be taken in through an upstairs window, you may need to pay extra. See also **Customs** on page 183 and the **Checklists** on page 187.

HOME SECURITY

When moving into a new home, it's wise to replace the locks (or lock barrels) as soon as possible, as you have no idea how many keys are in circulation for the existing locks. This is true even for new homes, as builders often give keys to sub-contractors. In any case, it's prudent to change external lock barrels regularly, particularly if you let a home. If they aren't already fitted, you should buy high security locks (e.g. five-lever mortise deadlocks). Patio doors should be fitted with key operated locks and a stop should be fitted in the top of the door frame to prevent the doors from being lifted out. All ground floor windows should be fitted with key operated locks or bolts. Extra keys for high security locks cannot usually be cut at a local hardware store; if they're already fitted, you'll need to obtain details from the previous owner or your landlord. In areas with a higher risk of theft (e.g. Dublin) your insurance company may insist on extra security measures.

You may wish to have a security system fitted, which is usually the best way to deter thieves and may also reduce your household insurance (see **Household Insurance** on page 54). It should be fitted to Irish Standard 199 (1987) and include all external doors and windows, and internal infra-red security beams. It may also include a coded entry keypad (which can be frequently changed and is useful if you let) and 24-hour monitoring (with some systems it's even possible to monitor properties remotely from another country). With a monitored system, when a sensor detects smoke or forced entry or when a panic button is pushed, a signal is sent automatically to a 24-hour monitoring station. The person on duty will telephone to check whether it's a genuine alarm and, if he cannot contact anyone or the wrong password is given, someone will be sent to investigate. A few Irish developments and estates have security gates and are patrolled by security guards.

You can deter thieves by ensuring that your house is well lit at night and not conspicuously unoccupied. External security 'motion detector' or PIR lights (that switch on automatically when someone approaches), random timed switches for internal lights, radios and TVs, dummy security cameras, and tapes that play barking dogs (etc.) triggered by a light or heat detector may all help deter burglars. You may wish to fit grilles to your windows, the advantage of which is that they allow you to leave windows open without inviting criminals in (unless they're *very* slim). Note, however, that security grilles must be heavy duty, as the bars on cheap grilles can be prised apart. You can also fit UPVC (toughened clear plastic) security windows and doors, which can survive an attack with a sledge-hammer without damage, and external steel security blinds (which can be electrically operated), although these are expensive. A dog can be useful to deter intruders, although it should be kept inside where it cannot be given poisoned food. Irrespective of whether you actually have a dog, a warning sign showing the image of a fierce dog may act as a deterrent. Bear in mind that prevention is better than cure, as stolen property is rarely recovered.

If you leave your home unoccupied for more than a few days, cancel deliveries and advise your local police (*Garda*) station, leaving them a contact name and number in case anything happens while you're away. Ask neighbours to park their car in the drive and to pop in from time to time. If they're very friendly, they may even be persuaded to cut the lawn for you! If you have a holiday home in Ireland, it isn't wise to leave anything of great value (monetary or sentimental) there and you should have comprehensive insurance for your belongings (see **Household Insurance** on page 54). One 'foolproof' way to protect a home when you're away is to employ a house-sitter to look after it. This can be done for short periods or for six months (e.g. during the winter) or longer if you have a holiday home in Ireland. It isn't usually necessary to pay someone to house-sit for a period of six months or more, when you can usually find someone to do so in return for free accommodation. However, you must take care whom you engage and obtain references.

An important aspect of home security is ensuring that you have early warning of a fire, which is easily accomplished by installing smoke detectors. Battery-operated smoke detectors can be purchased for around IR£7 and should conform to Irish Standard 409 (1988). They should be tested periodically to ensure that they're working properly and the batteries should be replaced twice a year. Fire extinguishers and fire blankets are also recommended. A 2.5kg dry powder or multi-purpose chemical extinguisher (which should conform to Irish Standard 290 of 1986) is ideal for the average house. Fire blankets should comply with Irish Standard 415 (1988). You can also fit an electric gas-detector that activates an alarm when a gas leak is detected.

When closing a property for an extended period, e.g. over the winter, you should ensure that everything is switched off and that it's secure. If you vacate your home for a long period, you may also be obliged to notify a caretaker, landlord or your insurance company and leave a key with a caretaker or landlord in case of emergencies. If you have a robbery, you should report it immediately to your local police station, where you must make a statement. You'll receive a copy, which will be required by your insurance company if you make a claim.

ELECTRICITY

Ireland's national power company, the Electricity Supply Board (ESB), is one of the largest companies in Ireland. Within the last decade it has developed from a giant monopoly utility that was prohibited from making a profit into a competitive, profitable enterprise (soon to become a plc) offering some of the lowest domestic electricity prices in the EU. The Irish electricity supply market opened to competition in February 2000, but only the industrial sector has so far been affected; domestic supply is expected to remain ESB-controlled until 2003 and the electricity market will not be completely 'open' until 2005. The only exception is electricity from renewable sources (e.g. wind energy – see page 167), which means that consumers can already choose to 'go green'.

Mains electricity is available in virtually all parts of the country. There are no nuclear power stations in Ireland, where most electricity is generated by conventional coal, gas and oil burning stations. Ireland's seven hydroelectric stations and five peat stations produce around 5 and 15 per cent of the national supply respectively. ESB is committed to a IR£ billion capital investment in a five year 'Network Renewal Programme'.

Registration: Immediately after buying or renting a property (unless utilities are included in the rent), you must register with the ESB. This usually entails a visit to one of the company's 80 regional offices or 'shops'. If you're a resident owner, you need only verify that you've purchased a property for the supply to be re-registered in your name. If you're a non-resident owner or are renting a property, you'll be given three options: you can to pay a deposit, set up a direct debit with your bank or appoint a guarantor who's an existing ESB customer.

Wiring Standards: Most modern properties (i.e. less than about 20 years old) in Ireland have good electrical installations. However, if you buy a resale property to which the electricity supply has been disconnected for more than six months, you'll be required to obtain a certificate from a qualified electrician stating that the electricity installation meets the required safety standards (this may also be required by your mortgage lender). In any case, you should ensure that the electricity installation is in good condition before buying a house (e.g. through a survey), as rewiring can be expensive.

Connection Costs: If you buy a new property, you'll be liable for connection charges. If the property is within a large development, electricity connection will usually have been made and meters installed by the builder, so the cost of connection will be incorporated in the purchase price, but in individual properties you may need to arrange connection with the ESB. In that case, you'll have to pay a standard connection charge (known in ESB-speak as a 'capital contribution') of IR£731 including VAT at 12.5 per cent. Note that the ESB requires a completion certificate from a qualified electrician before connecting new houses. All electrical work must be registered with the Register of Electrical Contractors of Ireland (☎ 01-492 9966) and be carried out in accordance with the National Wiring Rules for Electrical Installations.

Meters: In an old apartment block there may be a common meter, the bill being shared among the apartment owners according to the size of their apartments. In modern developments each apartment usually has its own meter. It's obviously better to have your own meter, particularly if you own a holiday home that's occupied for a few months of the year only. Meters may be installed in a basement or be housed in a meter 'cupboard' in a stair well or outside a group of properties, e.g. in an apartment or townhouse development. You should have free access to your meter.

Plugs, Fuses & Bulbs

Depending on the country you're moving from, you may need new plugs or a lot of adapters. Plug adapters for most foreign electrical apparatus can be purchased in Ireland, although it's wise to bring some with you, plus extension cords and multi-plug extensions that can be fitted with Irish plugs. Most modern properties will have at least two sockets in each room, although there may be a shortage of electric points in older Irish homes. Most Irish plugs have three flat pins as in the UK, apart from shaving sockets, which are of the standard international two-pin kind. A transformer (see below) is needed to convert American appliances (unless they're dual-voltage) and some items, like clocks, won't work even with a transformer. Cordless telephones may not work either, and even TVs that do work are of limited use because of the different broadcasting standards in Ireland. As in the rest of Europe, most videos are in PAL format, so American video recorders won't be of any use either.

Small, low-wattage electrical appliances such as table lamps, TVs and computers, don't require an earth. However, plugs with an earth must always be used for high-wattage appliances such as fires, kettles, washing machines and refrigerators. These plugs must always be used with earthed sockets. Electrical appliances that are earthed have a three-core wire and must never be used with a two-pin plug without an earth socket. Always make sure that a plug is correctly and securely wired, as bad wiring can be fatal.

In modern properties, fuses are of the earth-trip type. When there's a short circuit or the system has been overloaded, a circuit breaker is tripped and the power supply is cut. If your electricity fails, you should suspect a fuse of tripping, particularly if you've just switched on an electrical appliance. Before reconnecting the power, switch off any high-power appliances such as a stove, oven, washing machine or dishwasher. Make sure you know where the trip switches are located and keep a torch handy so that you can find them in the dark (see **Power Supply** below).

Electric light bulbs in Ireland are generally of the bayonet kind, but screw fitting ('Edison') bulbs are also widely available. Bulbs for non-standard electrical appliances (i.e. appliances that aren't made for the Irish market) such as refrigerators and sewing machines may not be available in Ireland, so you should bring some spares with you.

Power Supply

The standard domestic electrical supply in Ireland is 230 volts AC with a frequency of 50 Hertz (cycles). Most shaving sockets also support 100 volts. Power cuts are rare. Nevertheless, if you use a computer, it's wise to fit an uninterrupted power supply (UPS) with a battery backup, which not only allows you time to shut down your computer and save your work after a power failure (the battery will continue to supply power for around 15 to 20 minutes), but also protects it from power surges. If the power keeps tripping off or fuses blow when you attempt to use a number of high-power appliances simultaneously, e.g. an electric kettle and a heater, it could mean that the wiring to the property is inadequate. You should never simply put in heavier fuses but get an electrician to check the wiring and if necessary 'uprate' it to your requirements.

Converters & Transformers

Assuming that you have a 230-volt power supply, if you have electrical equipment rated at 110 volts AC (for example, from the USA) you'll require a converter or a step-down transformer to convert the supply to 110 volts. However, some electrical appliances are fitted with a 110/220 volt switch. Check whether there is one (it may be inside the casing) and make sure that it's switched to 220 volts *before* connecting to the power supply. Converters can be used for heating appliances, but transformers are required for motorised appliances. Add the wattage of all the devices you intend to connect to a transformer and make sure that its power rating *exceeds* this sum.

Generally, all small, high-wattage electrical appliances, e.g. kettles, toasters, heaters and irons, need large transformers. Motors in large appliances, such as cookers, refrigerators, washing machines, driers and dishwashers, will need replacing or fitting with a large transformer. In most cases, it's simpler to buy new appliances in Ireland, which are of good quality and reasonably priced. Note also that the dimensions of cookers, microwave ovens, refrigerators, washing machines, driers and dishwashers purchased abroad may differ from those in Ireland and may not fit into a standard Irish kitchen.

An additional problem with some electrical equipment is the frequency rating, which in some countries, e.g. the USA, is designed to run at 60 Hertz (Hz) and not Europe's 50Hz. Electrical equipment *without* a motor is generally unaffected by the drop in frequency to 50Hz (except TVs). Equipment with a motor may run with a 20 per cent drop in speed; however, automatic washing machines, cookers, electric clocks, record players and tape recorders must be converted from the US 60Hz cycle to Ireland's 50Hz cycle. To find out, look at the label on the back of the equipment. If it says 50/60Hz it should be all right; if the label says 60Hz you can try it, but first ensure that the voltage is correct as outlined above. Bear in mind that the transformers and motors of electrical devices designed to run at 60Hz will run hotter at 50Hz, so make sure that apparatus has sufficient space around it to allow for cooling.

Tariffs

Electricity is charged by the 'unit' in Ireland. One unit is equivalent to a kilowatt/hour (kWh) of electricity. One kWh is roughly enough to run a refrigerator for 24 hours, a TV for 12 hours, an iron for two hours, a vacuum cleaner for an hour, a dishwasher for half an hour or an instant shower for five minutes. There's a bi-monthly standing charge of IR£4.24 for normal consumption plus 7.97p per kWh (unit). To save on electricity costs, you can switch to the 'NightSaver' tariff and run high-consumption appliances overnight, e.g. water heater, dishwasher and washing machine (which can be operated by timers). A family that uses a lot of water will find it pays to have a large water heater (e.g. 150 litres) and heat water overnight. If you use electricity for your heating, you can install night storage heaters that run on the night tariff. When you use electricity at night for storage heaters only, you pay an extra IR£0.81 standing charge but only 3.17p per unit for night usage. If you run other appliances during the night, you can pay a standing charge of IR£11.15 so that all night use is charged at 3.17p per unit. The night rate applies between 11pm and 8am in winter and between midnight and 9am in summer. VAT at 12.5 per cent is levied on all charges.

Electricity Bills

Electricity bills are sent out every two months, usually after meters have been read. If the ESB is unable to read your meter, you'll be charged for an estimated consumption. If the estimate is wildly inaccurate, you can submit a corrected reading (make sure you know how to read your electricity meter) and you'll be sent a revised bill. Normally only one estimated reading per year is permitted. Once you've received an accurate bill, you have 14 days in which to pay. If you fail to do so, your supply can be cut off without warning, although in practice no action is usually taken for up to six months. If your electricity supply is cut off, you must pay to have it reconnected.

It's best to pay all your utility bills by direct debit from an Irish bank account. If you own a holiday home in Ireland, you can have your bills sent to an address abroad. Bills should then be paid automatically on presentation to your bank, although some banks cannot be relied on 100 per cent. Both the electricity company and your bank should notify you when they have sent or paid a bill. Alternatively, you can pay bills at any of the authorised banks or at one of the ESB's own 'shops'. The ESB has four regional headquarters (Dublin, northern, mid-western and southern) – your electricity bill indicates which one serves your area. A free booklet entitled *Getting the most from Electricity* is available from the ESB.

Wind Energy

Ireland's exposure to the full force of Atlantic winds, especially along its western coast, means that it's the ideal place for 'wind farms', of which there are already around 20. Although wind energy presently accounts for only 3 per cent of Ireland's total electricity output, the government is committed to reducing carbon dioxide emissions and it's predicted that in the next 10–15 years as much as 20 per cent of electrical power could be wind-generated. The two major providers are Saorgus, which supplies exclusively to ESB, and Eirtricity, currently the only company selling 'green energy' directly to consumers.

GAS

Most people in Ireland use gas for hot water and central heating (see below) and many for cooking as well. Mains gas is available in most areas of Ireland and is supplied by *Bord Gáis*, the national supply company. When moving into a property with mains gas, you must contact your local *Bord Gáis* office (there's one in all main towns in Ireland) to register the account in your name. Connection to a new property should take around a week, but re-connection to a property that was previously supplied with gas can be done in a day. As with electricity, you're billed every two months and bills include VAT at 12.5 per cent. Like all utility bills, gas bills can be paid by direct debit from an Irish bank account. In fact, if you're a non-resident property owner or are renting a property and want to obtain a gas supply, you'll have to set up a direct debit or pay a deposit of IR£150 (IR£40 if you'll be using gas for a cooker and fire only) or ask someone who has been a customer of *Bord Gáis* for at least 14 months to act as guarantor and sign the form for you.

Tariffs: Mains gas is charged at a standard rate of 1.75p per kWh (*Bord Gáis* has 'frozen' its prices to residential customers until 2002). There's also a 'supply charge' of IR£22 per bi-monthly bill. If you're buying a new property, connection is free, provided that the property is within 15 metres of a gas main. If it's further, there's a connection charge of IR£10 per metre. The approximate costs of using gas in an average home are IR£1 per day for central heating, 75p per week for cooking and 6p per hour for a gas fire. It generally works out cheaper to heat your water using a gas boiler than to use an electric immersion heater.

In most areas of Ireland, gas bottles can be delivered by Calor Gas, who supply more than one in four homes. A few developments, such as the Eagle Valley housing estate in Enniskerry and apartment projects in Letterkenny and Wexford, are entirely Calor run. If you want to use bottled gas, you must first have your property inspected and decide whether to use bottles or have a tank installed. A 1,250 litre tank costs IR£195 to deliver and install and IR£60 per year to rent thereafter. The gas itself currently costs IR£1.55 per gallon. Bottles are available in various sizes; a standard 'yellow' bottle (11kg) costs IR£14 for a refill and a 34kg bottle IR£58 (there are also 47kg bottles). You must pay a non-returnable deposit (IR£5 for a yellow bottle, IR£22 for a 34kg bottle). You should keep a spare bottle handy and make sure you know how to change them (ask the previous owner or a neighbour to show you).

A bottle used just for cooking will last an average family around six to eight weeks. Bottles can be connected into 'banks'; a four-bottle bank is enough to run a complete central heating system. Calor Gas also install boilers (their Combi boiler provides central heating and instant hot water). If you opt for a condensing boiler, you may be able to reduce your annual fuel bills by up to 30 per cent. You must have your gas appliances serviced and inspected at least every five years. If you have a contract with Calor Gas, they'll do this for you or it will be done by your local authorised distributor. Calor's headquarters are in Dublin (☎ 01-450 5000) and they have depots in Cork, Claremorris (Co. Mayo), New Ross (Co. Wexford) and Sligo.

HEATING

Heating is essential in winter (and sometimes in summer!) in Ireland. Central heating systems may be powered by gas, electricity, oil or solid fuel (usually wood or peat). Note, however, that, whatever form of heating you use, it's important to have good insulation, without which up to 60 per cent of the heat generated can be lost through the walls and roof.

Gas: Gas central heating is by far the most common in Ireland. Even if you have no mains gas, it's possible to install a central heating system operating from a gas tank or bottles (see above). Stand-alone gas heaters using standard gas bottles cost around IR£90 and are an economical way of providing heating in all but the depths of winter. Note that gas heaters must be used only in rooms with adequate ventilation, and it can be dangerous to have too large a difference between indoor and outdoor temperatures.

Electricity: Electric central heating is rare in Ireland, as it's relatively expensive and requires good insulation. Stand-alone electric heaters are also expensive to run and are best suited to holiday homes. However, a system of night-storage heaters operating on the night tariff (see **Tariffs** on page 166) can be economical. If you rely on electricity for all your power and use the night tariff, you should expect to pay around IR£35–40 per month.

Oil: It's quite expensive to install an oil tank (around IR£165 for a 1,000 litre tank), and the price of oil and kerosene, which has lower emissions, has rocketed in the last few years (oil rose nearly 70 per cent in 2000) to 40p per litre. The tank will need refilling around twice a year depending on the amount you use (further details can be obtained from the South of Ireland Petroleum Company (☎ 021-431 4221).

Solid Fuel: Many people still have open fires in Ireland, particularly in rural areas, where wood or peat-burning fires and stoves are often connected to a central heating system.

WATER & WASTE

The provision of water and waste services in Ireland is the responsibility of the 88 local authorities, which must follow policies laid down by the Department of the Environment. The growth in the economy and tourism during the mid-'90s led to a huge increase in demand for water and waste services (over 7 per cent per annum in the years 1996–98), to which the government responded by spending IR£900 million (65 per cent of it coming from the EU Cohesion Fund) on water and waste services in the period 1994–99. A total of 61 major schemes were started in 1998, including the Dublin Bay Project, aimed at putting an end to the dumping of the capital's sewage into the Irish Sea, and schemes at Bantry, Drogheda, Dundalk, Leixlip, Mitchelstown (near Cork), Navan, Osberstown (near Dublin), Sligo, Tralee, Tuam (near Galway), Waterford, and Wexford. As part of its National Development Plan for 2000–06, the government has announced a IR£2.1 billion investment in a further 79 major water and sewerage schemes, covering every county in Ireland.

Check the Supply: One of the most important tasks before renting or buying a home in Ireland is to check the reliability of the local water supply (over a number of years). Ask your prospective neighbours and other local residents for information. It's essential to have the water supply checked and, if necessary, install your own water purification system. Domestic water in Ireland is currently free, so you won't need to worry about paying bills (or being cut off for failing to do so), but there has been recent pressure from the OECD to fit water meters to all new houses in line with its policy of 'eco-taxation'.

Over 80 per cent of Irish homes are connected to a public water supply, which is generally good; tap water can safely be drunk in most areas. The peaty nature of Irish soil causes occasional colouring of the water as well as slight alkalinity, but water everywhere is pleasantly 'soft' (which no doubt accounts for those rosy Irish complexions!). Of the remaining 20 per cent, mainly in rural areas, three-quarters have small private supplies (i.e. wells), while a quarter have so-called group water schemes, where a number of households manage their own supply. In some of these ,the water isn't purified or disinfected in any way, so there's a risk of contamination from sources such as septic tanks or animal slurry pits. Recognising this problem, the government has recently allocated a record IR£35 million to the upgrading of rural water supply systems with the aim of bringing all group water schemes up to standard by 2003. As part of this project, the subsidy available for operating such schemes has been increased from IR£75 to IR£155 per house.

Hot Water: Water heating in apartments may be provided by a central heating source for the whole building or apartments may have their own water heaters. If you install your own water heater, it should have a capacity of at least 75 litres. If you need to install a water heater (or fit a larger one), you should consider the merits of both electric and gas heaters. An electric water boiler with a capacity of 75 litres (sufficient for two people) costs between IR£100 and IR£200 and usually takes between 60 and 90 minutes to heat water to 40°C in winter. A gas flow-through water heater is more expensive to purchase and install than an electric boiler, but you get unlimited hot water immediately whenever you want it. Make sure that a gas heater has a capacity of 10 to 16 litres per minute if you want it for a shower. A gas heater costs between IR£75 to IR£200 (although there's little difference in quality between the cheaper and more expensive heaters), plus installation costs. Note that a gas water heater with a permanent flame may use up to 50 per cent more gas than one without. A resident family with a constant consumption is better off with an electric heater operating on the night tariff (see **Tariffs** on page 166), while non-residents using a property for short periods will find a self-igniting gas heater more economical.

Connection Costs: The connection of water supplies to new properties is a local matter in Ireland and is controlled by the county or urban district council (or in some cases the borough corporation). Connection charges vary considerably from county to county and even from village to village as private local schemes proliferate; they can be as low as IR£100 or as high as IR£600 and may be even higher if major works are necessary, e.g. roads need to be dug up. The good news is that there are no standing or consumption charges for domestic water anywhere in Ireland so, if you move into a property that already has a water supply, you won't have to pay a penny. However, if you run a business from home (or, for example, offer bed and breakfast), you may be liable for commercial water rates.

Sewage: There's no direct charge for sewage services in Ireland. Eighty-five per cent of properties, including the vast majority in urban areas, are connected to the mains sewage system. The remainder, mostly in rural areas, have septic tanks, which are emptied regularly by the local council.

REFUSE COLLECTION

Like water connection, refuse collection is managed locally and charges vary from county to county. In some places (e.g. parts of Dublin) there's no charge at all, while in others charges range from as little as IR£30 per year (in Kilkenny, for example) to IR£100 or more (e.g. in Counties Cork, Kerry and Mayo). In parts of Co. Limerick ,you can be faced with a bill of nearly IR£600! (Note, however, that you may claim tax relief of up to IR£150 on refuse collection charges.) In many areas, the service has been privatised and costs are falling as a result. In some remote parts, no refuse collection service is provided and residents must make their own arrangements (often with a local farmer) to dispose of household waste.

PROPERTY INCOME

Many people planning to buy a holiday home in Ireland are interested in owning a property that will provide them with an income, e.g. from letting, to cover the running costs and help with mortgage payments. Note, however, that you're highly unlikely to meet all your mortgage payments and running costs from rental income. Buyers who over-stretch their financial resources often find themselves on the rental treadmill, constantly struggling to raise sufficient income to cover their running costs and mortgage payments. Note that it's difficult to make a living providing holiday accommodation in most areas, as the season is too short and there's simply too much competition (the market is saturated in many regions). On the other hand, letting a home for just a few weeks in the summer can recoup your running costs and pay for your holidays.

If you're planning on holiday lets, don't overestimate the length of the season, which can be as little as eight weeks, i.e. the summer holiday period. The letting season is longest in the main cities, particularly Dublin (where properties have year-round letting potential). Note that buying property in Ireland (and in most other countries) isn't always a good investment compared with the return on income that can be achieved by investing elsewhere. Most experts recommend that you don't purchase a home in Ireland if you need to rely heavily on rental income to pay for it.

Regulations & Restrictions: If you let a property in Ireland other than for holidays, you must register it with the Housing Division of your local authority within a month of the first letting. You'll need to apply in writing on a form provided by the local authority, giving the address of the property, a description, your name and address (or that of your agent), the tenant's name, the amount of rent, and how and when it's to be paid. There's an annual registration fee of IR£40 for each property for as long as it's let. A rent book isn't necessary for holiday letting, nor does the property need to comply with the Housing (Standards for Rented Houses) Regulations 1993. If you use a letting agency, the agency should apply for the necessary permits and pay income tax on your behalf.

Location: If income from your Irish home is a priority, you should buy a property with this in mind. To maximise rental income, a property should be located as close as possible to main attractions and/or the coast, and be suitably furnished and professionally managed.

Rents: Rental rates vary considerably depending on the season, the region, and the size and quality of a property. A small, one or two-bedroom apartment (i.e. 50 to 75m$\approx$) which lets for IR£250 a month in per rural area (outside the main tourist season) could be worth between IR£500 and IR£1,200 per month in Dublin. A three-bedroom house in the country might rent for IR£300 per month, while a similar property in a small town could generate IR£700 per month. A five-bedroom suburban house could rent for anything between IR£1,500 and IR£5,000 per month depending on the location. Rents for short-term lets are usually higher (pro rata) than for longer lets, particularly in popular holiday areas, where many properties are let as self-catering holiday accommodation. However, many agents let self-catering properties in holiday areas at a considerable reduction during the low season, which may extend from October to April. The high season generally includes the months of July and August only. The mid-season usually comprises May, June and September, when rents are around 25 per cent lower than in high season; low season rates are usually 50 per cent or more below high season rates. Some owners divide the rental year into as many as four seasons, e.g. November to March, April and October, June and September, and July/August. Only a few owners charge the same rate all year round. Note that rental rates normally include linen, but gas and electricity are usually charged extra.

Furnishings & Keys: If you let a property, don't fill it with expensive furnishings or valuable belongings. Although theft is rare, items will certainly get damaged or broken over time. When furnishing a property that you plan to let, you should choose hard-wearing, dark coloured carpets that won't show the stains, and buy durable furniture and furnishings. Two-bedroom properties usually have a settee in the living room which converts into a double bed. Properties should be well equipped with cooking utensils, crockery and cutlery, and it's also usual to provide bed linen and towels. You may also need a cot or high chair for young children. Depending on the price and quality of a property, your guests may also expect central heating, a washing machine, dishwasher, microwave, TV and covered parking (in urban areas). Some owners provide bicycles, games and books, etc. It isn't usual to have a telephone in rental homes, although you could install a pay-phone or one that will receive incoming calls only.

You'll need several sets of keys, which will inevitably get lost at some time. If you employ a management company, their address should be on the key fob, not the address of the house. If you let a home yourself, you can use a 'key-finder' service, whereby lost keys can be returned to the key-finder company by anyone finding them. You should ensure that you get 'lost' keys returned or you may need to change the lock barrels (in any case it's prudent to change them annually if you let a home). You don't need to provide clients with keys to all the external doors, only the front door (the others can be left in your home). If you arrange your own lets, you can post keys to clients in your home country; otherwise they can be collected from a caretaker in Ireland. It's also possible to install a key-pad entry system and change the code after each let.

Letting Agents: If you're letting a second home, the most important decision is whether to let it yourself or use a letting agent (or agents). If you don't have much spare time, you're better off using an agent, who will take care of everything and save you the time and expense of advertising and finding clients. An agent will charge a commission of 10 to 25 per cent of the gross rental income, although some of this can be recouped through higher rents. The largest holiday letting agent in Ireland is the Irish Tourist Board (ITB), which publishes an annual *Self-Catering Accommodation Guide* listing some 3,000 ITB approved properties throughout the country. If you want your property listed in the *Guide*, you must contact the regional tourist office local to the property. Inspections are carried out in February and March for the following year's brochure, so you'll need to plan well ahead. A free booklet listing the requirements for inclusion is available from the ITB. Then either you can have your own name and address listed, so that all enquiries come directly to you, or the property can be included on the Tourist Board's computerised booking system (and on its website), whereby the ITB handles all bookings for you and takes a commission of 10 per cent (clients pay a booking fee of IR£5 plus a deposit equal to one-third of the rental fee). Either way, you'll have to pay an annual 'approval fee' of IR£220.

If you're using any other agent, you should ask the following questions: What sort of people do they let to? Where do they advertise? Do they have contracts with holiday and travel companies? Are you expected to contribute towards marketing costs? Are you free to let the property yourself and use it when you wish? The larger companies market homes via newspapers, magazines, overseas agents and colour brochures, and have representatives in a number of countries.

Note that, when letting an apartment short-term, you must check that it's permitted under the terms of the lease; you may also have to notify your insurance company.

Doing Your Own Letting: Some owners prefer to let a property to family, friends, colleagues and acquaintances, which gives them more control (with luck, the property will also be better looked after). In fact, the best way to get a high volume of lets is usually to do it yourself, although many owners use a letting agency in addition to doing their own marketing in their home country. If you wish to let a property yourself, there's a wide range of Irish and foreign newspapers and magazines in which you can advertise, e.g. *Dalton's Weekly* and newspapers such as *The Sunday Times* and *Sunday Telegraph* in Britain. Many of the English-language newspapers and magazines listed in **Appendix A** also include advertisements from property owners. You'll need to experiment to find the best publications and days of the week or months to advertise.

You can also advertise among friends and colleagues, in company and club magazines (which may even be free), and on notice boards in companies, stores and public places. The more marketing you do, the more income you're likely to earn. It also pays to work with other local people in the same business and to send surplus guests to competitors (they will usually reciprocate). It isn't necessary to just advertise locally or stick to your home country; you can extend your marketing abroad or advertise on the Internet. It's usually necessary to have a telephone answering machine and it's advantageous to have a fax machine and be on the Internet (for e-mail enquiries).

To get an idea of the rent you should charge, simply ring a few letting agents and ask them what it would cost to rent a property such as yours at the time of year you plan to let it. They're likely to quote the highest rent you can charge. You should also check advertisements in newspapers and magazines. Set a realistic rent, as there's a lot of competition, and add a returnable deposit (e.g. IR£100) as security against loss (of keys, etc.) or breakages. A booking deposit should be refundable up to six weeks before the letting period and it's usual to have a minimum two-week rental in July and August. You'll need a simple agreement form which includes the dates of arrival and departure and approximate times. Note that, if you plan to let to non-English speaking clients, you may need to have the letting agreement translated into foreign languages.

If you plan to let a home yourself, you'll need to decide how to handle enquiries about flights and car rentals. It's easier to let clients arrange such things themselves, but you should be able to offer advice and put them in touch with airlines, ferry companies, travel agents and car rental companies (see **Car Rental** on page 41). You'll also need to decide whether you want to let to smokers and accept pets and young children (some people don't let to families with children under five years of age because of the risk of bed-wetting). It's best to provide linen (some agents provide a linen hire service), which is expected in Ireland, and to include electricity in the rental fee.

You should produce a colour brochure containing external/internal pictures (or a single-colour brochure with full-colour photographs affixed to it, although this doesn't look so professional), important details, the exact location and how to get there (with a map), information regarding local attractions, and the name, address and telephone number of your local caretaker or letting agent. You should enclose a stamped, addressed envelope when sending out leaflets. You should make your home look as attractive as possible in a brochure without distorting or misrepresenting the facts. Advertise honestly and don't over-sell your property.

Local Information: You should also provide an information pack (in your home) for clients, explaining how things work (such as heating and appliances), security measures, what not to do, where to shop, recommended restaurants, local emergency numbers and health services such as doctors, hospitals and dentists, and assistance such as a general repairman, plumber and electrician. If you allow young children and pets, you should make a point of emphasising any dangers, such as falling into a river or lake. It's also beneficial to have a visitors' book, in which your clients can write their comments and recommendations. If you want to impress your guests, you may wish to arrange for fresh flowers, fruit, a bottle of wine and a grocery pack to greet them on their arrival. It's little touches like this that ensure repeat business and recommendations. If you go 'the extra mile', it will pay off and you may even find after the first year or two that you rarely need to advertise. Many people return to the same property each year and you should do an annual mail-shot to previous clients and send them some brochures. Word-of-mouth advertising is the cheapest and always the best.

Caretaker: If you own a second home in Ireland, you'll find it beneficial or even essential to employ a local caretaker, irrespective of whether you let it. You may also need to employ a gardener. You can have your caretaker prepare the house for your family and guests as well as looking after it when it isn't in use. If you have a holiday home in Ireland, it's wise to have your caretaker check it periodically (e.g. weekly) and to give him authority to effect minor repairs. If you let a property yourself, your caretaker can arrange for (or do) cleaning, linen changes, maintenance and repairs, gardening and bill paying. If you employ a caretaker or housekeeper, you should expect to pay at least the minimum Irish hourly wage (currently £4.70 per hour for adults).

Increasing Rental Income: It's possible to increase rental income outside the high season by offering special interest or package holidays, which could be organised in conjunction with other local businesses in order to broaden the appeal and cater for larger parties. These may include activities such as golf, fishing, cycling or hiking, cookery or gastronomy, cultural or historical tours, and courses in arts and crafts such as painting, sculpture, photography and writing. You don't need to be an expert or conduct courses yourself, but can employ someone to do it for you. It's also worth finding out when local festivals take place, so that you can offer accommodation to coincide with them.

Long-term Lets: As used here, 'long-term' refers to lets of between one and six months, usually outside the high season. Make sure that you use the correct contract. Although the law is on your side, you should be aware that, if a tenant with a long-term rental contract refuses to leave, it may take months to have him evicted. Note also that, if you receive rent and accept a lessee without protest, you're deemed under Irish law to have entered into a landlord-tenant relationship, even if there's no written contract. Most people who let all year round have low, medium and high season rates. Rates are naturally much lower for winter lets, although less so in urban areas (see **Doing Your Own Letting** on page 172). The tenant usually pays for electricity and heating. Note that central heating is essential if you want to let long-term.

Most Irish auctioneers also act as long-term letting agents and produce their own lists of accommodation, which are usually updated frequently (sometimes twice a week). Agents may be quite selective in taking on new properties, but they'll generally accept more than they refuse. Take care when selecting an agent. Always ask him to substantiate rental income claims and occupancy rates by showing you examples of actual income received from other properties. Ask for the names of satisfied customers and check with them. Also make sure that your income is deposited in an interest-bearing escrow account and paid regularly or, even better ,choose an agent with a bonding scheme who pays you the rent *before* the arrival of guests (some do). It's absolutely essential to employ a reliable and honest (preferably long-established) company. Note that anyone can set up a holiday letting agency and there are a number of 'cowboy' operators.

If you're letting a property long-term (in this case one year or longer), you may wish to use a property management service, which is offered by most estate agents. This can include finding suitable tenants and checking their references (bank credit, etc.), drawing up a lease and producing an inventory, transferring accounts for gas, electricity, cable TV, etc. into the tenant's name, setting up standing orders for rental payments, inspecting the property periodically (e.g. every three months), and reporting to the landlord. Charges for property management vary, but are usually either a proportion of the annual letting fee (e.g. five weeks' rent or 10 per cent).

Closing For The Winter: Before closing a property for the winter, you should turn off the water at the mains (required by insurance companies) and drain all pipes, remove all fuses (except the one for a security alarm if you have one), empty the food cupboards and the refrigerator/freezer, disconnect gas cylinders, and empty dustbins. You should also leave interior doors and a few small windows (with grilles or secure shutters) open to provide some ventilation. Lock all exterior doors and shutters and secure anything valuable against theft or leave it with a neighbour or friend. Check whether any essential work needs to be done before you leave and, if so, arrange for it to be done in your absence. Most importantly, leave a set of keys with a neighbour or have a caretaker check your home periodically. See also **Renting** on page 124 and **Income Tax for Property Owners** on page 93.

SELLING A HOME

Although this book is primarily concerned with buying a home in Ireland, you may wish to sell your home at some time in the future. Before offering your Irish home for sale, you should investigate the property market. For example, unless you're forced to, it definitely isn't wise to sell during a property slump when prices are depressed. It may be better to let your home long-term and wait until the market has recovered. It's also unwise to sell in the early years after purchase, when you'll probably make a loss, unless the property was an absolute bargain or the market is booming.

Having decided to sell a property, your first choice will be whether to sell it yourself or use the services of an estate agent. Although the majority of properties in Ireland are sold through estate agents, a significant number of people sell their own homes (or attempt to). If you need to sell a property before buying a new one, this must be included as a conditional clause (see page 155) in the contract for a new home.

Your next decision will be whether to sell at auction or by private treaty. Generally, only expensive properties are sold at auction, although, if you think there will be considerable demand for your property, there's no reason why you shouldn't try to sell it at auction. You should, of course, advise your solicitor of your intention to sell and give him the title deeds. If there's still a mortgage outstanding on the property, you'll have to sign an authorisation for your solicitor to obtain the deeds from your lending institution so that he can prepare the sales contract. This can take up to two weeks.

A recent survey indicated that the easiest properties to sell are small houses close to town centres (particularly in Dublin), apartments in period houses and newish homes under IR£200,000; hardest to sell are four and five-bedroom suburban houses which have not been renovated, large houses whose grounds have been sold off for new homes, new detached houses in the IR£750,000+ price bracket, and one-off '70s houses in streets of older properties. Another survey indicated that the average terrace house sells for 8 per cent more than the asking price, whereas detached properties tend to go for 4 per cent less and apartments within 1 per cent. The same survey revealed that the average property is viewed by 13 prospective buyers: detached houses tend to sell after ten viewings, semi-detached and terrace houses after 12 or 13, and apartments after 15 or 16.

Price: It's important to bear in mind that (like everything) property has a market price, and the best way of ensuring a fast sale (or any sale) is to ask a realistic price. Although Ireland is very much a seller's market at the moment, it's naturally easier to sell a cheaper property (e.g. one priced below IR£75,000) than an expensive one. However, there's also a strong and constant demand for exceptional homes priced at over IR£500,000, particularly those that have unusual features or are in a popular area or a superb location.

If your home is fairly standard for the area, you can ascertain its value by comparing the prices of other homes on the market or those that have recently been sold. Most agents will provide a free appraisal of a home's value in the expectation that you'll sell it through them. However, don't believe everything they tell you, as they may over-price it simply to encourage you. You can also hire a professional valuer (e.g. a surveyor) to determine the market value. Note that you should be prepared to drop the price slightly (e.g. 5 or 10 per cent) and should set it accordingly, but you shouldn't grossly over-price a home, as it will deter buyers. Don't reject an offer out of hand unless it's ridiculously low, as you may be able to get a prospective buyer to raise his offer. When selling a second home in Ireland, you may wish to include the furnishings and major appliances in the sale. You should add an appropriate amount to the price to cover the value of the furnishings or use them as an inducement to a prospective buyer at a later stage.

Presentation: The secret to selling a home quickly lies in its presentation (assuming that it's competitively priced). First impressions (both exterior and interior) are vital when marketing a property and it's important to present it in its best light to make it as attractive as possible to potential buyers. It may pay to invest in new interior decoration, new carpets, exterior paint and landscaping. A few plants and flowers can also work wonders. Note that, when decorating a home for resale, it's important to be conservative and not to do anything radical (such as install a red or black bathroom suite or paint the walls purple). White is a good neutral colour for walls, woodwork and tiles.

It may also pay you to carry out some modernisation such as installing a new kitchen or bathroom, as these are of vital importance (particularly kitchens) when selling a home. Note, however, that, although modernisation may be necessary to sell an old home, it's easy to spend more than you could hope to recoup on the sale price. If you're using an agent, you can ask him what you should (or need) to do to help sell your home. If a home is in poor repair, this must be reflected in the asking price and, if major work is needed which you cannot afford, you should obtain a quotation (or two) and offer to reduce the price accordingly. Note that, while you have a duty under Irish law to inform a prospective buyer of any legal issues affecting the title of the property, you aren't obliged to disclose any defects which aren't readily apparent. It's up to the buyer to discover them – *caveat emptor*!

Selling Your Home Yourself: While certainly not for everyone, selling your own home is a viable option for many people and is particularly recommended when selling an attractive home at a *realistic* price in a favourable market. The principal advantage, of course, is that you'll save yourself an estate agent's fee of 2 or 2.5 per cent. You can use this saving to offer the property at a more appealing price, which could be an important factor if you're after a fast sale. How you market your home will depend on the kind of property, the price and the country or area from where you expect your buyer to come. For example, if your property isn't of a type and style or in an area that's desirable to local people, it's usually a waste of time advertising it in the local press.

Marketing: Marketing is the key to selling your home. The first step is to have a professional looking 'For Sale' sign made (showing your telephone number) and erect it in the garden or place it in a window. Do some research into the best newspapers and magazines for advertising your property (see **Appendix A**), and place an advertisement in those that look the most promising. You could also have a leaflet printed (with pictures) extolling the virtues of your property and drop it into local letter boxes or have it distributed with a local newspaper (many people buy a new home in the vicinity of their present home). You may also need a 'fact sheet' printed (if your home's vital statistics aren't included in the leaflet mentioned above) and could offer a finder's fee, e.g. IR£500, to anyone who finds you a buyer. Don't forget to market your home among local companies, schools and organisations, particularly if they have many itinerant employees. Finally, it may help to provide information about local financing sources for potential buyers. With a bit of effort and practice, you may even make a better job of marketing your home than an estate agent! Unless you're in a hurry to sell, set yourself a realistic time limit for success, after which you can try an agent. When selling a home yourself, you'll need to draw up a contract or engage a solicitor to do so for you.

Using An Agent: Most owners prefer to use the services of an agent or agents, either in Ireland or in their home country, when selling a home in Ireland. If you purchased the property through an agent, it's often best to use the same agent when selling, as he will already be familiar with it and may still have the details on file. You should take particular care when selecting an agent, as they vary considerably in their enthusiasm and standard of service (the best way to investigate agents is by posing as a buyer). Note that many agents cover a fairly small area, so you should take care to choose one who regularly sells properties in your area and price range. If you own a property in an area popular with foreign buyers, it may be worthwhile using an overseas agent or advertising in foreign newspapers and magazines, such as the English-language publications listed in **Appendix A**.

Agents' Contracts: Before he can offer a property for sale, an Irish agent requires a signed authorisation from the owner in the form of an exclusive or non-exclusive contract. An exclusive contract (known as 'sole agency') gives a single agent the right to sell a property, while a non-exclusive contract allows you to deal with any number of agents and to negotiate directly with private individuals. In Ireland, the normal procedure is for the property to be placed with a maximum of two agents. You may think it's to your advantage to place it with as many agents as possible, but in practice, if they know they're one of several, they'll put little effort into finding you a buyer. In most cases two agents will happily communicate with each other to ensure that they aren't duplicating their efforts. Some agents, however, will insist on a sole agency contract. Note that, if you sign an exclusive contract, you must pay the agent's commission even if you sell your home yourself! Don't forget to ask an agent how your property will be marketed and to check regularly that he's actively seeking a buyer. Agents' contracts are usually for three months but can be extended.

Agents' Fees: When selling a property in Ireland, the agent's commission is usually paid by the vendor and included in the purchase price. Fees vary between around 2 and 2.5 per cent, depending on the price of a property, and may be lower with an exclusive contract than with a non-exclusive contract. Shop around for the best deal, as there's fierce competition among agents to sell good properties. Check the contract and make sure that you understand what you're signing. Contracts state the level of the agent's commission and what it includes. Generally you shouldn't pay any additional fees unless you require extra services (e.g. advertising, which is usually charged to the vendor) and you should never pay the agent's commission before a sale is completed and you've been paid.

Capital Gains Tax: Note that anyone selling a second home in Ireland must pay capital gains tax (see page 96). When a non-resident sells a property in Ireland for more than IR£150,000, 15 per cent of the price must be retained by the buyer (the solicitor will ensure that this is done) and paid to the Revenue Commissioners as a deposit against tax due. Note that, if you're resident in Ireland and are selling your principal home and buying another in Ireland, you must sell your existing home before buying a new one in order to benefit from the CGT concession for residents. One way round this if you need to buy a new home before you've sold your current one, is to buy it on a private contract and not register it until after you've sold your present home (obtain legal advice).

Warning: As when buying a home in Ireland, you must be very careful whom you deal with when selling a home. Make sure that you're paid with a certified banker's draft before signing over your property to a buyer as, once the deed of purchase has been signed, the property belongs to the buyer, whether you've been paid or not. Be extremely careful if you plan to use an intermediary, as it isn't uncommon for a 'middle man' to disappear with the proceeds! Never agree to accept part of the sale price 'under the table'; if the buyer refuses to pay the extra money, there's nothing you can do about it (at least legally). Sellers occasionally end up with no property and no money! All sales should be conducted through a solicitor. See also **Estate Agents** on page 135.

5.

ARRIVAL & SETTLING IN

On arrival in Ireland, your first task will be to negotiate immigration and customs. Fortunately, this presents few problems for most people, particularly European Union (EU) nationals. Note, however, that non-EU nationals coming to Ireland for any purpose other than as visitors may require a visa (see page 19).

In addition to information about immigration and customs, this chapter contains checklists of tasks to be completed before or soon after arrival in Ireland and when moving house, plus suggestions for finding local help and information.

IMMIGRATION

Ireland is one of the least bureaucratic countries in Europe when it comes to immigration 'red tape'. There's little of the 'fill-it-out-in-triplicate' system found in countries such as France, Italy and Spain. In fact, Irish immigration laws have traditionally been so lax (more people have always wanted to leave Ireland than go there!) that many African and East European *émigrés*, attracted by Ireland's new-found prosperity and generous welfare handouts, are knocking at her door and requesting asylum. Compared with a mere 39 applications for asylum in 1992, there were some 6,000 in 1998. The largest and most visible group are Romanians, and other substantial contingents come from Algeria, Nigeria, Somalia and Zaire. Nine out of ten of these asylum seekers aren't eligible for work or residence permits and are eventually sent back to where they came from (or to the UK). The number of what the Immigration Office calls 'registered aliens' (i.e. immigrants from non-EU countries who are entitled to live and work in Ireland) has also increased dramatically in the last few years: from 15,800 in 1996 to 29,600 in 1999, the largest numbers coming from the USA and China, with substantial numbers from Australia, India, Malaysia, Nigeria and Pakistan.

Those arriving from EU countries are free to enter Ireland; there are nevertheless certain formalities that must be observed. If you arrive in Ireland from the UK, there are usually no immigration checks or passport controls at the port of entry into Ireland. The Irish Republic and Great Britain are part of a 'Common Travel Area', which means that foreigners travelling to Ireland via the UK must meet British immigration requirements and will then be free to enter Ireland. If you're a British citizen arriving in Ireland from Britain, you don't require a passport, although it's wise to take some form of identity with you, in case you're required to complete any formalities (e.g. when hiring a car). All other nationals require a valid passport (or national identity card) and in some cases a visa. However, citizens of many non-EU countries, including Australia, Canada, New Zealand, South Africa and the USA, don't require visas (see page 19). If you're taking your car with you, ensure that you have its registration document, an insurance certificate valid for Ireland and your driving licence, and that the car has a nationality sticker on the back.

If you're a non-EU national and arrive in Ireland by air or sea from outside the EU, you must go through immigration for non-EU citizens. Non-EU citizens are required to complete immigration registration cards, which are provided on aircraft and ferries. If you need a visa to enter Ireland and attempt to enter without one, you'll be refused entry. Some people may wish to get a stamp in their passport as confirmation of their date of entry. If you're a non-EU national coming to Ireland to work, study or live, you may be asked to produce evidence such as a work permit or or confirmation of enrolment on a course, proof of accommodation, a health insurance certificate, a return ticket and evidence of sufficient financial resources, e.g. cash, traveller's cheques and credit cards. The onus is on visitors to show that they're genuine and that they don't intend to breach Irish immigration laws. Immigration officials aren't required to prove that you'll breach those laws and can refuse you entry on the grounds of suspicion only.

CUSTOMS

Permanent Residence – EU Residents

Household Effects: The Single European Act, which came into effect on 1st January 1993, created a single trading market and changed the rules regarding customs for EU residents. The shipment of personal (household) effects to Ireland from another EU member state is no longer subject to customs formalities on the basis that duty and VAT will already have been paid in the country of origin.

Vehicles: If you're importing a vehicle from another EU member state as part of your transfer of residence, you must present form C&E 1077 as well as the appropriate VRT (Vehicle Registration Tax) form, which must be completed at the Vehicle Registration Office of the county where you plan to live not later than the next working day following the vehicle's arrival in Ireland. In order to qualify for relief, you must be able to show that you've owned and used the vehicle outside Ireland for at least six months before the date of your transfer of residence; you'll therefore need to produce appropriate documentation such as the vehicle's registration document and an insurance certificate. In addition, you may not dispose of, hire or lend the vehicle to anyone during the 12 months following its registration in Ireland.

Permanent Residence – Non-EU Residents

Household Effects: Non-EU nationals planning to take up permanent residence in Ireland are permitted, under certain conditions, to import household and personal effects free of duty or taxes. This excludes property that's intended for commercial use, with the exception of portable 'tools of the trade' in the case of people such as artists, doctors, solicitors and barristers. However, other self-employed people transferring their business activities to Ireland may be eligible for relief from import duty (you should make enquires with Irish Customs and Excise).

You must have owned all such goods for at least six months and had your normal place of residence outside the EU for a continuous period of at least 12 months prior to your move (relief may also be granted if you can prove that it was your intention to reside outside the EU continuously for 12 months). Note that 'normal residence' is considered to be the place where you live for at least 185 days in each year. You'll therefore need to produce documentary evidence such as relevant sales invoices or receipts, proof of residence abroad and transfer of residence to Ireland, and evidence of the of your home in your previous country of residence and of employment in Ireland (if applicable).

You must declare all property at the place of importation on form C&E 1076, which should include an inventory of all items imported, except used clothes, toiletries and accessories. If you use a shipping company to transport your belongings to Ireland, they'll usually provide all the necessary forms and take care of the paperwork. Always keep a copy of all forms and communications with customs officials (both in Ireland and in your previous country of residence). Note that, if the paperwork isn't in order, your belongings may end up incarcerated in an Irish customs storage depot. If you personally import your belongings, you may need to employ a customs agent at the point of entry to clear them. You should also keep an official record of the export of valuables from any country, in case you wish to re-import them later. Another form, C&E 136 or CU 56, is required for any articles of gold or silver plate which you're bringing with you.

You may import personal effects (excluding vehicles) not more than six months in advance of or one year after your arrival, and you may not sell or otherwise dispose of them during the year following their importation unless you pay import taxes.

Vehicles: If you're importing a vehicle on transfer of residence from outside the EU, you may also qualify for relief from customs duty, VAT and VRT. The vehicle must be registered on its arrival in Ireland and have been owned and used by you for at least six months prior to your transfer of residence. You must include details of the vehicle on form C&E 1076 and present a completed copy of form VRT4 (cars) or VRT5 (motorcycles). You must also produce documentary evidence of ownership, usage and taxes paid in your country of origin, e.g. the vehicle registration document, an insurance certificate and a sales invoice. In addition, you may not dispose of, hire or lend the vehicle to anyone during the 12 months following its registration in Ireland. You must import the vehicle within 12 months of your transfer of residence.

Secondary Residence

The criteria regarding customs duty relief on the importation from non-EU countries of household effects (i.e. furniture, furnishings and equipment) also apply to a secondary residence. However, you're required to have owned or rented your secondary residence for at least two years and to undertake not to let it to any third party. In practice, this means that most non-EU nationals will be unlikely to be able to furnish a second home in Ireland with duty-free imported goods and may as well buy new furnishings locally. There's no VAT relief on goods imported to furnish a secondary residence.

Visitors

Certain goods may be temporarily imported (i.e. for a period of up to two years) into Ireland without payment of customs duty or VAT. This applies to private cars, camping vehicles (including trailers or caravans), motorcycles, aircraft and personal effects, for which no import formalities apply. Other goods may be temporarily imported on completion of Form C&E 1047. In this case, security for the duties and taxes normally payable will be required; this will be returned to you when you produce evidence of re-export. However, any goods and pets (see page 62) that you're carrying mustn't be subject to any prohibitions or restrictions (see below). Customs officials may stop anyone for a spot check, e.g. for drugs or illegal immigrants.

Prohibited & Restricted Goods

There are, of course, restrictions on the quantities of certain goods you're permitted to import into Ireland, and certain others may require a licence or be prohibited. This applies in particular to firearms and ammunition, certain plants and foodstuffs, dangerous drugs and pornography. For example, if you're planning to import sporting guns into Ireland, you must obtain a certificate from the Irish consulate in your country of origin (you'll be required to produce a valid firearms certificate) and present it to customs officials on arrival. If you're unsure whether particular goods are prohibited or restricted, you should check with Irish Customs before your departure. A full list of prohibited and restricted goods is set out in Part 2 of the *Customs and Excise Tariff of Ireland*.

Alcohol and Tobacco: If you're coming from another EU country, you may import a limited amount of alcoholic and tobacco products without paying import duty, provided you've paid the relevant tax in the country of origin, i.e. they aren't duty-free. The limits are 110 litres of beer, 90 litres of wine (of which only 60 litres may be sparkling wine or Champagne), 20 litres of fortified wine (e.g. port or sherry), 10 litres of spirits, 800 cigarettes, 400 cigarillos, 200 cigars and 1kg of tobacco. If you want to exceed these limits, you'll need evidence that it's all for your own use! If you're coming from a non-EU country, the limits are two litres of still wine, two litres of fortified wine or one litre of spirits, 200 cigarettes, 100 cigarillos, 50 cigars and 250g of tobacco, but in this case the goods may have been obtained duty-free.

Perfume: Perfume and certain kinds of gifts and new goods are also subject to restrictions, which vary according to whether you're resident in the EU and whether the goods were purchased in an EU country.

Currency: There are no restrictions on the import or export of Irish or foreign bank notes or securities, although, if you enter or leave Ireland with a large amount of currency (see **Importing & Exporting Money** on page 75), you must make a declaration to Irish customs.

Plants: To import certain kinds of plants into Ireland, you must obtain a licence or a 'plant passport'. There are no prohibited plants within the EU, although some require a passport. Plants from outside the EU may need a licence from the Department of Agriculture. Note also that you may not be allowed to import hay or straw, so these shouldn't be used to pack personal effects. To find out whether a licence is required, contact the Plant Health Section of the DoA (☎ 01-607 2089). Licences are issued free of charge.

Food: Certain kinds of food may not be taken into the Republic, e.g. pet food must be tinned and pre-cooked and have been manufactured in the EU (even then only a limited amount may be imported).

Illegal Drugs: Visitors arriving in Ireland from 'exotic' regions, e.g. Africa, South America, and the Middle and Far East, may find themselves under close scrutiny from customs and security officials looking for illegal drugs.

Value Added Tax (VAT)

VAT is levied on goods imported from outside the EU, in addition to any customs and excise duties which may be payable. In general, goods are liable to VAT at the same rate as applies to the sale of similar goods within Ireland (e.g. vehicles are subject to VAT at 20 per cent). VAT is also payable on import duty and on the transportation, handling and insurance costs of goods as they're conveyed to their final destination (i.e. your home). VAT is usually due at the same time as customs duty, but payment may be deferred, subject to the approval of the Revenue Commissioners. The criteria for relief from VAT aren't the same as those for relief from import duty. For example, relief from VAT cannot be obtained for personal effects imported for a secondary residence.

If you require general information about Irish customs regulations or have specific questions, contact the Customs Procedures section of the Revenue Commissioners (☎ 01-679 2777). Copies of the forms mentioned above can be obtained from any Irish Customs and Excise or vehicle registration office.

RESIDENCE PERMITS

Non-UK nationals must report to the police within three months and obtain a residence permit from the Department of Justice, Equality and Law Reform (see page 19). Unless you're retired or otherwise financially independent, the duration of the residence permit will be governed by the length of your employment or course (in the case of students) up to a maximum of five years. If you're employed in Ireland, the permit must be completed by your employer, who must also submit a letter detailing the nature and period of employment. If you're a student, retired or financially independent, you'll be required to show that you have private health insurance. In addition, anyone applying for a residence permit may be required to undergo a medical examination. If you intend to stay for less than a year but more than three months, you'll be issued with a temporary residence permit.

FINDING HELP

One of the major problems facing new arrivals in Ireland is how and where to obtain help with day-to-day problems such as finding accommodation, schooling, insurance and so on. In addition to the comprehensive information provided in this book, you'll also need detailed *local* information. How successful you are at finding local help depends on your employer, the town or area where you live (e.g. residents of large towns and cities are far better served than those living in rural areas), your nationality and your English (or Irish) language proficiency. An additional problem is that much of the available information isn't intended for foreigners and their particular needs. You may find that your friends and colleagues can help by offering advice based on their own experiences and mistakes. But take care! Although they mean well, you're likely to receive as much misleading and conflicting information as helpful advice (it may not be wrong, but often won't apply to your particular situation).

Your local city or county hall may be a good source of information, but you may well be sent on a wild goose chase from department to department. Apart from assisting with routine everyday matters, the town hall can be helpful when applying for an Irish driving licence and other official documents. One of the best places to obtain expert and impartial advice is at a Citizen's Information Centre (CIC), which provide free, confidential information on virtually any subject. There are CICs in most Irish towns, but opening times vary (many are open only in the morning). A wealth of valuable information is available in the major cities and towns, where foreigners are served by embassies and consulates. These will usually provide their nationals with local information including details of solicitors, doctors, schools, and social and expatriate organisations. Contacts can also be made through many expatriate magazines and newspapers (see **Appendix A**).

CHECKLISTS

The checklists on the following pages include tasks which you may need to complete before and after arrival in Ireland, and when moving your home permanently to Ireland.

Before Arrival

● Check that your family's passports are valid.
● Obtain a visa, if necessary, for all your family members (see page 19). Obviously, this *must* be done before arrival in Ireland.
● Arrange health and travel insurance for yourself and your family (see page 57). This is essential if you aren't already covered by an international health insurance policy and won't be covered by Irish social welfare.
● If you don't already have one, it's a good idea to obtain an international credit or charge card.
● Obtain an international driving licence if necessary (see page 38).
● Open a bank account in Ireland (see page 79) and transfer funds. You can open an account with many Irish banks while abroad, although it's best done in person in Ireland.
● It pays to obtain some Irish currency before arrival; this will save you having to queue to change money at the port or airport (and you'll probably get a better exchange rate abroad).
● If you plan to become a permanent resident, you may also need to do the following:
  – Arrange schooling for your children.
  – Organise the shipment of your personal and household effects.
  – Obtain as many credit references as possible, e.g. from banks, mortgage companies, credit card companies, credit agencies, companies with which you've had accounts, and from professionals such as solicitors and accountants. These will help you when opening bank accounts, setting up a business in Ireland and obtaining credit.

If you're planning to become a permanent resident in Ireland, don't forget to take all your family's official documents with you. These may include birth certificates, driving licences, marriage certificate, divorce papers or death certificate (if a widow or widower), educational diplomas and professional certificates, employment references and *curricula vitae*, school records and student ID cards, medical and dental records, bank account and credit card details, insurance policies (plus records of no-claims bonuses), and receipts for any valuables. You'll also need the documents necessary to obtain a residence permit (see page 19) plus certified copies, and numerous passport-size photographs (students should take at least a dozen).

After Arrival

The following checklist contains a summary of the tasks to be completed after arrival in Ireland (if not done before):

- On arrival at an Irish airport or port, have your visa cancelled and your passport stamped, as applicable.
- If you aren't taking a car with you, you may wish to rent (see page 41) or buy one locally.
- Open a cheque account (see page 79) at a local bank and give the details to your employer (if applicable) and any companies that you plan to pay by direct debit or standing order (such as utility and property management companies).
- Arrange all necessary insurance, such as health, car, household and third-party liability.
- Contact offices and organisations to obtain local information (see **Finding Help** on page 186).
- Make courtesy calls on your neighbours and local shops (etc.) within a few weeks of your arrival. This is particularly important in small villages and rural areas if you want to be accepted and integrate into the local community.
- If you plan to become a permanent resident in Ireland, you'll need to do the following within a few weeks of your arrival (if not done before):
  - Apply for a residence permit at the Department of Justice, Equality and Law Reform within 90 days of your arrival.
  - Register with the Aliens Registration Office in Dublin.
  - If necessary, apply for an Irish driving licence (see page 38).
  - Find a local doctor and dentist.
  - Arrange schooling for your children.

Moving House

When moving permanently to Ireland, there are many things to be considered and a 'million' people to be informed. Even if you plan to spend only a few months a year in Ireland, it may still be necessary to inform a number of people and companies in your home country. The checklists below are designed to make the task easier and help prevent an ulcer or a nervous breakdown (provided, of course, that you don't leave everything to the last minute). See also **Moving House** on page 160.

- If you live in rented accommodation, you'll need to give your landlord notice (check your contract).
- Arrange to store or dispose of everything you aren't taking with you (e.g. car and furniture). If you're selling a home or business, you should obtain expert legal

advice, as you may be able to save tax by establishing a trust or other legal entity. Note that, if you own more than one property, you may need to pay capital gains tax on any profits from the sale of second and subsequent homes.

- Arrange shipment of your furniture and belongings by booking a shipping company well in advance (see page 160). International shipping companies usually provide a wealth of information and can advise on a wide range of matters concerning an international relocation. (There are also specialist companies, such as RSI in Dublin, that offer a complete relocation service.) Find out the exact procedure for shipping your belongings to Ireland from your local Irish embassy or consulate.

- If you have a car that you're exporting to Ireland, you'll need to complete the relevant paperwork in your home country and re-register it in Ireland after your arrival. Contact your local Irish embassy or consulate for information.

- Check whether you need a 'green card', an international driving licence or a translation of your foreign driving licence(s) for Ireland. Note that some foreigners are required to take a driving test before they can buy and register a car in Ireland.

- Check whether you're entitled to a rebate on your road tax, car and other insurance. Obtain a letter from your motor insurance company confirming your no-claims bonus.

- Arrange inoculations and shipment for any pets that you're taking with you (see page 62).

- You may qualify for a rebate on your tax and social security contributions. If you're leaving a country permanently and have been a member of a company or state pension scheme, you may be entitled to a refund or be able to transfer to another pension scheme or continue payments to qualify for a full (or larger) pension when you retire. Contact your company personnel office, local tax office or pension company for information.

- It's wise to arrange health, dental and optical check-ups for your family before leaving your home country. Obtain a copy of all health records and a statement from your private health insurance company stating your present level of cover.

- Terminate any outstanding loan, lease or hire purchase contracts and pay all bills (allow plenty of time, as some companies are slow to respond).

- Return any library books and anything borrowed.

- Inform the following:
  - your employers (e.g. give notice or arrange leave of absence) or clients if you're self-employed;
  - your local town hall or council (you may be entitled to a refund on your local property or utilities taxes);
  - your electricity, gas, water and telephone companies (contact them well in advance, particularly if you need to get a deposit refunded);
  - your insurance companies (e.g. health, car, home contents and private pension), banks, post office (if you have a post office account) and other financial institutions, credit card, charge card and hire purchase companies,

your stockbroker, solicitor and accountant, and local businesses with which you have accounts;

– your family doctor, dentist and other health practitioners, e.g. vets (health records should be transferred to your new doctor, dentist and vet in Ireland, if applicable);

– your children's schools (try to give a term's notice and obtain a copy of any relevant school reports or records from your children's current schools);

– all regular correspondents, business associates, social and sports clubs, professional and trade journals, and friends and relatives (give them your new address and telephone number and arrange to have your mail and phone calls redirected by the post office or a friend).

– If it was necessary to register with the police in your home country (or present country of residence), you should inform them that you're moving abroad

● If you have a driving licence or car, you'll need to give the local vehicle registration office your new address in Ireland and, in some countries, return your car's registration plates.

● If you'll be living in Ireland for an extended period (but not permanently), you may wish to give someone 'power of attorney' over your financial affairs in your home country so that they can act for you in your absence. This can be for a fixed or unlimited period and can be for a specific purpose only. Note, however, that you should always take expert legal advice before doing this!

● Finally, allow plenty of time to get to the airport or port, register your luggage, and clear security and immigration.

As they say in Ireland, "May the ground rise to meet you"!

APPENDICES

APPENDIX A: USEFUL ADDRESSES

Embassies & Consulates

Foreign embassies and consulates in Ireland are located in Dublin and Cork, and are listed under 'Diplomatic and Consular Missions' in telephone books. Note that business hours vary considerably and all embassies close on their national holidays and on Ireland's public holidays. Always telephone to check the business hours before visiting. Embassies and consulates in Dublin are listed below:

Argentina: 15 Ailesbury Drive, Dublin 4 (☎ 01-269 1546).

Australia: Fitzwilton House, Wilton Terrace, Dublin 2 (☎ 01-676 1517).

Austria: 15 Ailesbury Court, 93 Ailesbury Road, Dublin 4 (☎ 01-269 4577).

Belgium: Shrewsbury House, Shrewsbury Road, Dublin 4 (☎ 01-269 2082).

Brazil: Europe House, Harcourt Street, Dublin 4 (☎ 01-475 6000).

Bulgaria: 22 Burlington Road, Dublin 4 (☎ 01-660 3293).

Canada: 65 St. Stephen's Green, Dublin 2 (☎ 01-478 1988).

China: 40 Ailesbury Road, Dublin 4 (☎ 01-269 1707).

Czech Republic: 57 Northumberland Road, Dublin 4 (☎ 01-668 1135).

Denmark: 121 St. Stephen's Green, Dublin 2 (☎ 01-475 6404).

Egypt: 12 Clyde Road, Ballsbridge, Dublin 4 (☎ 01-660 6566).

Finland: Stokes Place, St. Stephen's Green, Dublin 2 (☎ 01-478 1344).

France: 36 Ailesbury Road, Dublin 4 (☎ 01-260 1666).

Germany: 31 Trimleston Avenue, Booterstown (☎ 01-269 3011).

Greece: 1 Upper Pembroke Street, Dublin 2 (☎ 01-676 7254).

Hungary: 2 Fitzwilliam Place, Dublin 4 (☎ 01-661 2902).

India: 6 Lesson Park, Dublin 6 (☎ 01-497 0843).

Iran: 72 Mount Merrion Avenue, Blackrock (☎ 01-288 0252).

Israel: 122 Pembroke Road, Dublin 4 (☎ 01-668 0303).

Italy: 63 Northumberland Road, Dublin 4 (☎ 01-660 1744).

Japan: Merrion Centre, Nutley Lane, Dublin 4 (☎ 01-269 4244).

Korea: 15 Clyde Road, Dublin 4 (☎ 01-660 8800).

Mexico: 43 Ailesbury Road, Dublin 4 (☎ 01-260 0699).

Morocco: 53 Raglan Road, Ballsbridge, Dublin 4 (☎ 01-660 9449).

Netherlands: 160 Merrion Road, Dublin 4 (☎ 01-269 3444).

Nigeria: 56 Leeson Park, Dublin 6 (☎ 01-660 4366).

Norway: 34 Molesworth Street, Dublin 2 (☎ 01-662 1800).

Poland: 5 Ailesbury Road, Dublin 4 (☎ 01-283 0855).

Portugal: Knocksinna House, Foxrock, Dublin 18 (☎ 01-289 4416).

Romania: 47 Ailesbury Road, Dublin 4 (☎ 01-668 1336).

Russia: 186 Orwell Road, Dublin 14 (☎ 01-269 2852).

South Africa: Earlsfort Centre, Dublin 2 (☎ 01-661 5553).
Spain: S17a Merlyn Park, Dublin 4 (☎ 01-269 1640).
Sweden: Sun Alliance House, Dawson Street, Dublin 2 (☎ 01-671 5822).
Switzerland: 6 Ailesbury Road, Dublin 4 (☎ 01-269 2515).
Turkey: 11 Clyde Road, Ballsbridge, Dublin 4 (☎ 01-668 5240).
United Kingdom: 31 Merrion Road, Dublin 4 (☎ 01-205 3700).
USA: 42 Elgin Road, Dublin 4 (☎ 01-668 8777).

Government

Central Statistics Office, Ardee Road, Dublin 6 (☎ 01-497 7144) and Skehard Road, Cork (☎ 021-435 9000).
Collector General (Taxes), Sarsfield House, Limerick (☎ 061-310310).
Customs Procedures, A Branch, Castle House, South Great St George's Street, Dublin 2 (☎ 01-679 2777).
Department of Agriculture and Food, Agriculture House, Kildare Street, Dublin 2 (☎ 01-607 2000).
Department of Enterprise, Trade and Employment, 65A Adelaide Road, Dublin 2 (☎ 01-661 4444).
Department of the Environment, Customs House, Customs House Quay, Dublin 1 (☎ 01-888 2000).
Department of Foreign Affairs, 80 St Stephen's Green, Dublin 2 (☎ 01-478 0822).
Department of Health and Children, Hawkins House, Hawkins Street, Dublin 2 (☎ 01-635 4000).
Department of Justice, Equality and Law Reform, 72/76 St Stephen's Green, Dublin 2 (☎ 01-602 8202).
Department of Social, Community and Family Affairs, Store Street, Dublin 1 (☎ 01-874 8444).
National Social Service Board, Hume House, Ballsbridge, Dublin 4 (☎ 01-605 9000).
Revenue Commissioners, Central Information Office, Dublin (☎ 01-878 0000).

Business

Chambers of Commerce of Ireland, 22 Merrion Square, Dublin 2 (☎ 01-661 2888).
Companies Office, Parnell House, 14 Parnell Square, Dublin 1 (☎ 01-804 5200).
Forbairt, Wilton Park House, Wilton Place, Dublin 2 (☎ 01-808 2000).
Passport Office, Setanta Centre, Molesworth Street, Dublin 2 (☎ 01-679 7600)
Shannon Development, Shannon, Co. Clare (☎ 061-361555).
Small Firms Association, Confederation House, 84–86 Lower Baggot Street, Dublin 2 (☎ 01-660 1011).

The **Small Business and Services Division of the Department of Enterprise, Trade and Employment** (☎ 01-661 4444).

Training & Employment Authority (FÁS), 27/33 Upper Baggot Street, Dublin 4 (☎ 01-607 0500).

VAT Enquiries, Findlater House, 28/32 Upper O'Connell Street, Dublin 1 (☎ 01-874 6821).

Property

Calor Gas, Long Mile Road, Dublin 12 (☎ 01-450 5000).

Construction Industry Federation, Construction House, Canal Road, Dublin 6 (☎ 01-497 7487).

Eircom, St Stephen's Green, Dublin 2 (☎ 01-671 4444).

Electricity Supply Board, Fleet Street, Dublin 2 (☎ 01-677 2961).

Gas Board (*Bord Gáis*), D'Olier Street, Dublin 2 (☎ 01-602 1212).

Irish Brokers Association, 87 Merrion Square, Dublin 2 (☎ 01-661 3067).

Irish Home Builders Association, Construction House, Canal Road, Dublin 6 (☎ 01-497 7487).

Land Registry, Nassau Building, Setanta Centre, Nassau Street, Dublin 2 (☎ 01-670 7500).

Register of Electrical Contractors of Ireland, Parnell Avenue, Harold's Cross, Dublin 12 (☎ 01-454 5820).

Royal Institute of Architects of Ireland, 8 Merrion Square, Dublin 2 (☎ 01-676 1703).

Society of Chartered Surveyors, 5 Wilton Place, Dublin 2 (☎ 01-676 5500).

Timeshare Council of Ireland, PO Box 78, Waterford.

Publications

Examiner/Evening Echo, 96 Lower Baggot Street, Dublin 2 (☎ 01-661 2733).

Home Buyers' Guide, MAP Publications, 3 Lower Abbey Street, Dublin 1 (☎ 01-878 6622). Available free from estate agents, architects, property developers, the Irish **Home Builders' Association**, and central and local authorities (or it can be purchased at Eason bookshops or on subscription).

The Irish Times, 10–16 D'Olier St, Dublin 2 (☎ 01-679 2022).

Image, Image Publications Ltd, 22 Crofton Road, Dun Laoghaire (☎ 01-280 8415).

International Property Magazine, 2a Station Road, Gidea Park, Romford, Essex RM2 6DA, UK. Monthly magazine.

Irish Independent/Evening Herald, 90 Middle Abbey St, Dublin 1 (☎ 01-705 5333).

Phoenix Magazine, 44 Lower Baggot Street, Dublin 2 (☎ 01-661 1062).

The Star, Star House, 62A Terenure Road North, Dublin 6 (☎ 01-490 1228).

World of Property, Outbound Publishing, 1 Commercial Road, Eastbourne, East Sussex BN21 3XQ, UK (☎ 01323-412001). Quarterly magazine.

Miscellaneous

BUPA Ireland, 121 Fitzwilliam Square, Dublin 2 (☎ 01-662 7662) and Mill Island, Fermoy, Co. Cork (☎ 025-42121).

Car Rental Council of Ireland, 5 Upper Pembroke Street, Dublin 2 (☎ 01-676 1690).

Disability Federation of Ireland, 2 Sandyford Office Park, Dublin 18 (☎ 01-295 9344).

Dublin Bus (*Bus Átha Cliath*), 59 Upper O'Connell Street, Dublin 1 (☎ 01-872 000; passenger information 01-873 4222).

Excellence Ireland, Merrion Hall, Strand Road, Sandymount, Dublin 4 (☎ 01-269 5255)

Irish Co-operative Society Ltd. (ICOS), Plunkett House, 84 Merrion Square, Dublin 2 (☎ 01-676 4783/6).

Irish League of Credit Unions, 33/41 Lower Mount Street, Dublin 2 (☎ 01-614 6700).

Irish Rail (*Iarnród Éireann*), Connolly Station, Dublin 1 (☎ 01-836 3333).

Irish Tourist Board (*Bord Fáilte Éireann*), Baggot Street, Dublin 2 (☎ 01-602 4000).

Law Society of Ireland, Blackhall Place, Dublin 7 (☎ 01-671 0711).

National Disability Authority (*Comhairle*), 44 North Great George's Street, Dublin 1 (☎ 01-874 7503).

Pensions Board (*An Bord Pinsean*), Holbrook House, Holles Street, Dublin 2 (☎ 01-676 2622).

Police (*Garda Síochána*), Phoenix Park, Dublin 8 (☎ 01-677 1156).

Radio and Television Ireland (*Radio Telefís Éireann*), Dublin 4 (☎ 01-208 3111).

Voluntary Health Insurance Board (VHI), VHI House, Lower Abbey Street, Dublin 1 (☎ 01-872 4499).

APPENDIX B: FURTHER READING

The books listed below are just a small selection of the many books written for those planning to buy a home or work in Ireland. Some titles may be out of print, but you may still be able to find a copy in a bookshop or library. Books prefixed with an asterisk (*) are recommended by the author.

Tourist Guides & Travel Literature

Around Ireland with a Fridge, Tony Hawkes (Ebury)
***Baedeker's Ireland** (Baedeker)
Berlitz Pocket Guides: Ireland (Macmillan)
Discover Ireland, Martin Gostelow (Berlitz)
***Dublin: The Miniguide**, Dan Richardson (Rough Guides)
***Fodor's Exploring Ireland** (Fodor)
***Fodor's Ireland (Fodor's Gold Guides)** (Fodor)
***Frommer's Guilde to Ireland from $50 a Day** (Pocket books)
***Frommer's Ireland** (Frommer)
***Ireland**, Catharine Day (Cadogan Books)
Ireland, a Bicycle and a Tin Whistle, David A. Wilson (Blackstaff)
Ireland: A Cultural Encyclopaedia (Thames and Hudson)
***Ireland: A Travel Survival Kit**, Tom Smallman (Vacation Work)
***Ireland: The Rough Guide**, Sean Doran (The Rough Guides)
***Let's Go: Britain & Ireland** (Pan)
***Lonely Planet: Ireland**, Tom Smallman & Sean Sheehan (Lonely Planet)
***Michelin Green Guide to Ireland** (Michelin)
***Round Ireland in Low Gear**, Eric Newby (Picador)
***The Time Out Guide to Dublin** (Time Out)

Architecture & Gardens

150 Years of Architecture in Ireland, John Graby (Eblana Editions)
20th Century Architecture in Ireland, Annette Becker & Wilfred Wang (Prestel)
Buildings of Irish Towns, Patrick & Maura Shaffrey (O'Brien Press)
***Daily Telegraph Gardener's Guide to Britain and Ireland** (Dorling Kindersly)
***A Field Guide to the Buildings of Ireland**, Sean Rothery (Lilliput)
A Guide to Irish Houses, Mark Bence-Jones (Constable)
***In the Houses of Ireland**, Marianne Heron & Walter Pfeiffer (Thames & Hudson)
Irish Castles and Castellated Houses, Harold G. Leask (Dundalgan)
Irish Cottages, Joe Reynolds (Real Ireland Design)
***Irish Country Houses**, Terence Reeves-Smith (Appletree)

Irish Countryside Buildings, Patrick & Maura Shaffrey (O'Brien Press)
Irish Gardens, Terence Reeves-Smith (Appletree)
***In an Irish House**, David Davidson & Molly Keane (Weidenfeld & Nicolson)
Irish Houses (Gill & Macmillan)
Irish Houses and Gardens, Sean O'Reilly (Aurum Press)
New Irish Architecture, John Oregan (Gandon)
Vanishing Country Houses of Ireland, Knight of Glin (Irish Georgian Society)

Accommodation

***Bed and Breakfast in Ireland**, Elsie Dillard (Appletree)
Bed & Breakfast: Great Britain and Ireland (RAC Guides)
Bridgestone 100 Best Places to Stay in Ireland, Mckenna (Estragon)
***The Good Hotel Guide: Great Britain & Ireland**, Hilary Rubinstein & Caroline Raphael (Ebury)
Ireland Self Catering Guide (Jarrold)
***The Irish Bed and Breakfast Book**, Frank & Fran Sullivan (Pelican)
***Karen Brown's Charming Inns and B&Bs: Ireland**, June Brown & Barbara Tapp (Fodor)
***Les Routiers Guide to Great Britain and Ireland** (Les Routiers)
***Michelin Red Hotel and Restaurant Guide: Great Britain and Ireland** (Michelin)
***Special Places to Stay in Ireland**, Simon Greenwood (Alastair Sawday)
Stilwell's Ireland: Bed and Breakfast, Tim Stilwell (Stilwell)

Miscellaneous

Enterprise Ireland: A Directory of Sources of Assistance for Entrepreneurs and Small Business Owners (Oak Tree Press)
Home Away from Home: The Yanks in Ireland, Mary Pat Kelly (Stackpole)
***Irish Traditional Cooking**, Darina Allen (K. Cathie)
Laying Down the Law, Olive Brennan (Oak Tree Press)
***Living and Working in Ireland**, Joe Laredo (Survival Books)
Local Ireland Almanac and Yearbook of Facts, ed. Helen Curley (Local Ireland)
***Moving to Ireland**, Eileen McKay (Brent Irish Advisory Service)
Moving to Ireland: A Guide to Living and Investing, Brendan Connolly & Peter Steadman (Windrow & Greene)
***Real Irish Cookery**, Mary Caherty (Hale)
***Starting a Business in Ireland**, Brian O'Kane (Oak Tree Press)
***Taste of Ireland: In Food and Pictures**, Theodora Fitzgibbon (Weidenfeld)
***Your Guide to Irish Law**, Mary Faulkner, Gerry Kelly & Padraig Turley (Gill Macmillan)

APPENDIX C: MAP OF PROVINCES & COUNTIES

The map of Ireland opposite shows the four provinces (or regions) and 26 counties of Ireland, which are listed below. Note that most of the province of Ulster, with the exception of the counties of Cavan, Donegal and Monaghan, is part of the United Kingdom. The counties of Antrim, Armagh, Down, Fermanagh, Londonderry and Tyrone, which aren't shown on the map opposite, form the region know today as Northern Ireland, which remained part of the United Kingdom when the Republic of Ireland was established in 1921. A map of Ireland showing the main towns and geographical features is shown on page 6.

Province	Counties
Connacht	Galway
	Leitrim
	Mayo
	Roscommon
	Sligo
	Waterford
Munster	Clare
	Cork
	Kerry
	Limerick
	Tipperary
Leinster	Carlow
	Dublin
	Kildare
	Kilkenny
	Laois
	Longford
	Louth
	Meath
	Offaly
	Westmeath
	Wexford
	Wicklow
Ulster	Cavan
	Donegal
	Monaghan

U L S T E R

Northern Ireland

Donegal

ULSTER

Monaghan

Cavan

Sligo

Leitrim

Mayo

C O N N A C H T

Roscommon

Longford

Louth

Meath

Westmeath

Galway

Offaly

Kildare

Dublin

L E I N S T E R

Laois

Wicklow

Clare

Carlow

Tipperary

Kilkenny

Limerick

Wexford

M U N S T E R

Kerry

Waterford

Cork

APPENDIX D: WEIGHTS & MEASURES

Ireland uses the metric system of measurement. Nationals of a few countries (including the Americans and British) who are more familiar with the imperial system will find the tables on the following pages useful. Some comparisons shown are approximate only, but are close enough for most everyday use. In addition to the variety of measurement systems used, clothing sizes often vary considerably depending on the manufacturer (as we all know only too well). Try all clothes on before buying and don't be afraid to return something if, when you try it on at home, you decide it doesn't fit (most shops will exchange goods or give a refund).

Women's Clothes

Continental	34	36	38	40	42	44	46	48	50	52
UK	8	10	12	14	16	18	20	22	24	26
USA	6	8	10	12	14	16	18	20	22	24

Pullovers

	Women's						Men's					
Continental	40	42	44	46	48	50	44	46	48	50	52	54
UK	34	36	38	40	42	44	34	36	38	40	42	44
USA	34	36	38	40	42	44	sm	medium	large			xl

Note: sm = small, xl = extra large

Men's Shirts

Continental	36	37	38	39	40	41	42	43	44	46
UK/USA	14	14	15	15	16	16	17	17	18	-

Men's Underwear

Continental	5	6	7	8	9	10
UK	34	36	38	40	42	44
USA	small	medium		large	extra large	

Children's Clothes

Continental	92	104	116	128	140	152
UK	16/18	20/22	24/26	28/30	32/34	36/38
USA	2	4	6	8	10	12

Children's Shoes

Continental	18	19	20	21	22	23	24	25	26	27	28	29	30	31	32
UK/USA	2	3	4	4	5	6	7	7	8	9	10	11	11	12	13

Continental	33	34	35	36	37	38
UK/USA	1	2	2	3	4	5

Shoes (Women's and Men's)

Continental	35	35	36	37	37	38	39	39	40	40	41	42	42	43	44	44
UK	2	3	3	4	4	5	5	6	6	7	7	8	8	9	9	10
USA	4	4	5	5	6	6	7	7	8	8	9	9	10	10	11	11

Weight

Avoirdupois	Metric	Metric	Avoirdupois
1 oz	28.35 g	1 g	0.035 oz
1 pound*	454 g	100 g	3.5 oz
1 cwt	50.8 kg	250 g	9 oz
1 ton	1,016 kg	500g	18 oz
1 tonne	2,205 pounds	1 kg	2.2 pounds

* A metric 'pound' is 500g, g = gramme, kg = kilogramme

Length

British/US	Metric	Metric	British/US
1 inch	2.54 cm	1 cm	0.39 inch
1 foot	30.48 cm	1 m	3 feet 3.25 inches
1 yard	91.44 cm	1 km	0.62 mile
1 mile	1.6 km	8 km	5 miles

Note: cm = centimetre, m = metre, km = kilometre

Capacity

Imperial	Metric	Metric	Imperial
1 pint (USA)	0.47 litre	1 litre	1.76 UK pints
1 pint (UK)	0.57 litre	1 litre	0.26 US gallons
1 gallon (USA)	3.78 litre	1 litre	0.22 UK gallon
1 gallon (UK)	4.54 litre	1 litre	35.21 fluid oz

Square Measure

British/US	Metric	Metric	British/US
1 square inch	0.45 sq. cm	1 sq. cm	0.15 sq. inches
1 square foot	0.09 sq.m	1 sq. m	10.76 sq. feet
1 square yard	0.84 sq. m	1 sq. m	1. 2 sq. yards
1 acre	0.4 hectares	1 hectare	2.47 acres
1 square mile	259 hectares	1 sq. km	0.39 sq. mile

Temperature

° Celsius	° Fahrenheit	
0	32	freezing point of water
5	41	
10	50	
15	59	
20	68	
25	77	
30	86	
35	95	
40	104	

Note: The boiling point of water is 100°C / 212°F.

Oven Temperature

Gas	Electric	
	°F	°C
-	225–250	110–120
1	275	140
2	300	150
3	325	160
4	350	180
5	375	190
6	400	200
7	425	220
8	450	230
9	475	240

For a quick conversion, the Celsius temperature is approximately half the Fahrenheit temperature.

Temperature Conversion

Celsius to Fahrenheit: multiply by 9, divide by 5 and add 32.
Fahrenheit to Celsius: subtract 32, multiply by 5 and divide by 9.

Body Temperature

Normal body temperature (if you're alive and well) is 98.4° Fahrenheit, which equals 37° Celsius.

APPENDIX E: GLOSSARY

Acceptance: Agreeing to an offer on a property, which constitutes a contract.

Acceptance Fee: See *Mortgage Application Fee*.

Administration Fee: See *Vacate*.

Advance: The mortgage loan.

Amortisation: The gradual process of systematically reducing debt in equal payments (as in a *mortgage*) comprising both *principal* and interest, until the debt is paid in full.

Annual Percentage Rate (APR): Everything financed in a loan package (interest, loan fees and other charges), expressed as a percentage of the loan amount.

Annuity Mortgage: A *mortgage* loan in which both the capital and the interest are repaid over a fixed or variable term. Also called a repayment mortgage.

Arrangement Fee: See *Mortgage Application Fee*.

Auctioneer: A person licensed to represent buyers and sellers in property transactions. Also called an estate agent.

Broker: A more or less independent agency through which you can seek the most appropriate or economical financial service or product (e.g. insurance, *mortgage*).

Building(s) Insurance: An insurance policy that protects homeowners from damage to their home. Required by lenders (*premiums* are usually included in monthly *mortgage* payments).

Buy-Back: An agreement between a seller and a purchaser that the seller will repurchase a *security* within a specified time at a predetermined price.

Cap: The maximum rate by which a *variable rate mortgage* can change, either annually or over the *term* of the *mortgage*.

Clearing Fee: A charge arising from the clearing of a cheque paid to a lending institution on *redemption* of a *mortgage*.

Closing: The final procedure in a property transaction when documents are executed and recorded, funds are disbursed and the *title* transferred from the *vendor* to the buyer. Also called *completion* or settlement.

Closing Costs: Costs the buyer must pay at the time of closing in addition to the *deposit*, including solicitor's fees, *mortgage indemnity fee* and *buildings insurance*.

Closing Statement: A statement prepared by a solicitor detailing the closing costs for both the seller and the buyer.

Collateral: The *title deeds* of a property pledged as *security* against the repayment of a loan.

Common Elements: The parts of a property (e.g. apartment or flat) that aren't individually owned and in which all owners have an indivisible interest.

Completion: The final legal transfer of ownership of a property. See also *closing*.

Contents Insurance: An insurance policy protecting a homeowner from loss or damage to personal property (possibly outside as well as in a home).

Conveyance: The act of transferring the *title* of a property and also the document (such as a *deed*) used to transfer ownership. Also called conveyancing.

Conveyancer: Solicitor who undertakes *conveyance*.

County Development Plan: A plan drawn up by a county council for the use of land over a period of five years. See also *Zoning*.

Deed: A written legal document that conveys *title* to property.

Deed of Assignment: A *deed* used to transfer *leasehold unregistered land*.

Deed of Conveyance: A *deed* used to transfer *freehold unregistered land*.

Deed of Mortgage: A *deed* used to transfer title in a property to the *mortgagee*.

Deed of Transfer: A *deed* used to transfer *registered land*.

Deed Restriction: A clause in a *deed* that restricts the use of land.

Deferred Start Mortgage: A type of *mortgage* whereby no repayments are made for the first one to three months of the *term*. Only available with *repayment mortgages*.

Deposit: The amount that needs to be paid in cash in order to obtain a *mortgage*, e.g. if you have an 80 per cent *mortgage*, you must make a 20 per cent deposit.

Disbursements: Fees such as *stamp duty*, *land registry* and *search* fees which are incurred by the *conveyancer*.

Earnest Money: Funds paid with an offer to show good faith to complete a purchase. Earnest money is placed by a broker in an *escrow* account until *closing*, when it becomes part of the *deposit* or *closing costs*.

Easement: The interest, privilege or right that a party has in the land of another party, e.g. rights of way.

Encumbrance: Any right or interest in a property that affects its value such as outstanding loans, unpaid taxes, *easements* and *deed restrictions*.

Endowment Mortgage: A type of *mortgage* loan in which repayments are combined with savings through a life assurance policy. By the end of the mortgage *term*, the value of the endowment policy should have grown

sufficiently to repay the *mortgage* and (hopefully) will leave the *mortgagor* with a surplus.

Equity: The value a property owner has after the deduction of outstanding *liens* such as a mortgage, e.g. if a property is valued at IR£100,000 and the amount outstanding on a mortgage is IR£50,000, the owner has IR£50,000 equity.

Equity Loan: A second *mortgage* where the owner borrows against his *equity* in a property.

Escrow: A procedure in which documents of cash and property are put in the care of a third party, other than the buyer or seller, pending completion of agreed conditions and terms in sales contracts. An escrow company performs escrow services.

Estate Agent: See *Auctioneer*.

Fixed Rate Mortgage: A *mortgage* with a fixed *interest rate*, usually over a period of up to five years.

Flexible Month Mortgage: A type of *mortgage* whereby no repayments are made in one or two months of a year.

Foreclosure: Legal proceedings instigated by a lender to deprive a person of ownership rights when *mortgage* payments haven't been maintained. Also called repossession.

Freehold: The highest interest in a property that can be held by an individual. In theory, the owner is free to do with the property as he wishes. In practice, certain constraints (e.g. *planning permission*) are placed on this right.

Freeholder: One who owns *freehold*.

FSBO: An abbreviation for 'For Sale By Owner', when a home is being sold without the assistance of an *auctioneer*.

Funding Fee: A fee incurred by the *mortgagor* when switching from a *fixed rate* to a *variable rate mortgage* before the end of the *fixed rate* period.

Gazump: Renege on an *acceptance* in order to accept a higher offer.

Ground Rent: An annual fee payable by the *leaseholder* to the *freeholder*.

Interest Rate: A percentage that when multiplied by the *principal* determines the amount of money that the *principal* earns over a period of time (usually one year).

Joint Tenancy: Property ownership by two (e.g. a married couple) or more persons with an undivided interest and the right of survivorship, where if one owner dies the property automatically passes to the joint owner(s).

Land Registry: A public record of property and its ownership.

Lease: Permission to own or rent property for a limited period.

Leasehold: Ownership of property but not the land on which it stands. Leasehold ownership is restricted to a number of years and creates a landlord-tenant relationship between the *lessor* (*freeholder*) and the *lessee*.

Leaseholder: One who owns a *leasehold* property.

Lessee: Person to whom a *lease* is granted.

Lessor: Person who grants a *lease*.

Lien: A charge against property making it *security* for a debt such as a mortgage.

Management Company: An organisation which a buyer must usually join when buying a property such as a flat or apartment with *common elements*.

Market Value: The current value of a property compared with similar properties, generally accepted to be the highest price a buyer will pay and the lowest price a vendor will accept.

Mortgage: A written instrument that creates a *lien* against a property as security against the repayment of a loan.

Mortgage Application Fee: A fee charged by the lender for evaluating,

preparing and submitting a proposed *mortgage* loan. Also called an acceptance or arrangement fee.

Mortgage Indemnity Fee: A charge paid by the borrower (usually as part of the *closing costs*) to obtain financing, particularly when borrowing more than a certain percentage of the purchase price. Also called a mortgage indemnity bond.

Mortgage Protection Plan: Insurance against *foreclosure* in the event of job loss, major accident, illness or death.

Mortgagee: One who holds a *lien* or *title* to a property as *security* for a debt, i.e. the lender.

Mortgagor: One who pledges property as *security* for a loan, i.e. the borrower.

Offer: A bid to buy a property at a specified price.

Pension Mortgage: A type of *mortgage* loan in which the repayments cover only the interest on the loan, while separate payments are made into a personal pension plan. They are usually available only to those who are self-employed or whose employer doesn't offer an occupational pension scheme.

Planning Permission: Permission granted by a local planning authority to erect or alter a building.

Power of Attorney: Authority to act on behalf of another.

Premium: Payment in respect of a *mortgage* or insurance policy.

Principal: The amount of money borrowed to buy a property and the amount still owed. Also one who owns or will use a property.

Principal and Interest Payment: A periodic (usually monthly) *mortgage* repayment that includes interest charges ,plus an amount applied to the *amortisation* of the *principal* balance.

Private Treaty Sale: A method of selling a property by agreement between the vendor and the purchaser, either directly or through an *auctioneer*.

Provisional Loan Approval: A service offered by lenders whereby they provide provisional approval of a loan (for a maximum sum) thus establishing a buyer's price range, strengthening his buying position and shortening the loan approval period.

Redemption: Full repayment of a *mortgage* loan.

Redemption Fee: A fee incurred by the *mortgagor* when redeeming a loan (or part of it) before the end of the *term*.

Refinance: To replace an old loan with a new one, either to reduce the *interest rate*, secure better terms or increase the amount borrowed.

Register of Deeds: A public record of *unregistered land*.

Registration Fee: A fee payable by a purchaser to have *title deeds* registered in the *Land Registry* or the *Register of Deeds*.

Registered Land: Land which is recorded in the *Land Registry*.

Repayment Mortgage: See *Annuity Mortgage*.

Repossession: See *Foreclosure*.

Searches: Enquiries made by or on behalf of a purchaser to ensure proper *title* to a property.

Security: Assets such as house *deeds* pledged in support of a loan.

Semi: Semi-detached house.

Settlement: See *Closing*.

Sole Agency: An agreement giving an *auctioneer* the exclusive right to sell a property and to collect a commission if the property is sold by anyone else during the term of the agreement.

Stamp Duty: A tax payable on the purchase of property.

Survey (or **Structural Survey**): A thorough examination of the condition of a property before purchase, performed by a professional surveyor. You can make a purchase contingent on a satisfactory survey.

Term: The life-span of a *mortgage*, which can be either fixed (e.g. 15 or 25 years) or variable according to the rate of repayment.

Tenancy in Common: A form of ownership in which two or more people buy a property jointly, but with no right of survivorship. Owners are free to will their share to anyone they choose, which is the main difference between this and *joint tenancy*. Often used by friends or relatives buying together.

Title: The right of possession and evidence of ownership.

Title Search: A professional scrutiny of public records to establish the chain of ownership of a property and record any outstanding *liens*, *mortgage*, *encumbrances* or other factors that may restrict clear *title*.

Unregistered Land: Land which isn't recorded in the *Land Registry*.

Vacate: An official receipt by the *mortgagee* acknowledging that a *mortgage* has been paid off and effecting the transfer of *title* from the *mortgagee* to the *mortgagor*.

Valuation: The professional examination of a property to determine its *market value*.

Variable Rate Mortgage: A *mortgage* loan whose *interest rate* changes in accordance with prevailing interest rates.

Vendor: Person selling a property.

Zoning: The procedure that classifies land and property according to usage, e.g. residential, commercial or industrial, in accordance with a *county development plan*.

INDEX

U

V

W

LIVING AND WORKING IN IRELAND

Living and Working in Ireland is essential reading for anyone planning to spend some time there, including holiday-home owners, retirees, visitors, business people, migrants, students and even extraterrestrials! It's packed with over 500 pages of important and useful information designed to help you **avoid costly mistakes and save both time and money.** Topics covered include how to:

- find a job with a good salary & conditions
- obtain a residence permit
- avoid and overcome problems
- find your dream home
- get the best education for your family
- make the best use of public transport
- endure motoring in Ireland
- obtain the best health treatment
- stretch your punts (and euro) further
- make the most of your leisure time
- enjoy the Irish sporting life
- find the best shopping bargains
- insure yourself against most eventualities
- use post office and telephone services
- do numerous other things not listed above

Living and Working in Ireland is the most comprehensive and up-to-date source of practical information available about everyday life in Ireland. It isn't, however, a boring text book, but an interesting and entertaining guide written in a highly readable style.

Buy this book and discover what it's <u>really</u> like to live and work in Ireland.

Order your copies today by phone, fax, mail or e-mail from: Survival Books, PO Box 146, Wetherby, West Yorks. LS23 6XZ, United Kingdom (☎/▤ +44-1937-843523, ✉ orders@survival books.net, 💻 www.survivalbooks.net).

BUYING A HOME IN BRITAIN

Buying a Home in Britain is essential reading for anyone planning to purchase property in Britain and is designed to guide you through the jungle and make it a pleasant and enjoyable experience. Most importantly, it is packed with vital information to help you avoid the sort of disasters that can turn your dream home into a nightmare! Topics covered include:

- Choosing the Region
- Finding the Right Home & Location
- Estate Agents
- Finance, Mortgages & Taxes
- Home Security
- Utilities, Heating & Air-conditioning
- Moving House & Settling In
- Renting & Letting
- Permits & Visas
- Travelling & Communications
- Health & Insurance
- Renting a Car & Driving
- Retirement & Starting & Business
- And Much, Much More!

Buying a Home in Britain is the most comprehensive and up-to date source of information available about buying property in Britain. Whether you want a manor, farmhouse, townhouse or an apartment, a holiday or a permanent home, this book will help make your dreams come true.

Buy this book and save yourself time, trouble and money!

Order your copies today by phone, fax, mail or e-mail from Survival Books, PO Box 146, Wetherby, West Yorks. LS23 6XZ United Kingdom (☎/▤ +44-1937-843523, ✉ orders@surviva books.net, ▤ www.survivalbooks.net).

<u>ORDER FORM – ALIEN'S / BUYING A HOME SERIES</u>

Qty.	Title	Price (incl. p&p)*			Total
		UK	Europe	World	
	The Alien's Guide to America	Autumn 2001			
	The Alien's Guide to Britain	£5.95	£6.95	£8.45	
	The Alien's Guide to France	£5.95	£6.95	£8.45	
	Buying a Home Abroad	£11.45	£12.95	£14.95	
	Buying a Home in Britain	£11.45	£12.95	£14.95	
	Buying a Home in Florida	£11.45	£12.95	£14.95	
	Buying a Home in France	£11.45	£12.95	£14.95	
	Buying a Home in Greece & Cyprus	£11.45	£12.95	£14.95	
	Buying a Home in Ireland	£11.45	£12.95	£14.95	
	Buying a Home in Italy	£11.45	£12.95	£14.95	
	Buying a Home in Portugal	£11.45	£12.95	£14.95	
	Buying a Home in Spain	£11.45	£12.95	£14.95	
	Rioja and its Wines	£11.45	£12.95	£14.95	
	The Wines of Spain	£11.45	£12.95	£14.95	
				Total	

Order your copies today by phone, fax, mail or e-mail from: Survival Books, PO Box 146, Wetherby, West Yorks. LS23 6XZ, United Kingdom (☎/▤ +44-1937-843523, ✉ orders@survival books.net, ▣ www.survivalbooks.net). If you aren't entirely satisfied, simply return them to us within 14 days for a full and unconditional refund.

Cheque enclosed/please charge my Delta/Mastercard/Switch/Visa* card

Card No. _ _ _ _   _ _ _ _   _ _ _ _   _ _ _ _

Expiry date _____   **Issue number (Switch only)** _____

Signature _____   **Tel. No.** _____

NAME _____

ADDRESS _____

_____

_____

* Delete as applicable (price includes postage – airmail for Europe/world).

ORDER FORM – LIVING & WORKING SERIES

Qty.	Title	Price (incl. p&p)*			Total
		UK	Europe	World	
	Living & Working Abroad	£14.95	£16.95	£20.45	
	Living & Working in America	£14.95	£16.95	£20.45	
	Living & Working in Australia	£14.95	£16.95	£20.45	
	Living & Working in Britain	£14.95	£16.95	£20.45	
	Living & Working in Canada	£14.95	£16.95	£20.45	
	Living & Working in France	£14.95	£16.95	£20.45	
	Living & Working in Germany	£14.95	£16.95	£20.45	
	Living & Working in Ireland	£14.95	£16.95	£20.45	
	Living & Working in Italy	£14.95	£16.95	£20.45	
	Living & Working in London	£11.45	£12.95	£14.95	
	Living & Working in New Zealand	£14.95	£16.95	£20.45	
	Living & Working in Spain	£14.95	£16.95	£20.45	
	Living & Working in Switzerland	£14.95	£16.95	£20.45	
				Total	

Order your copies today by phone, fax, mail or e-mail from: Survival Books, PO Box 146, Wetherby, West Yorks. LS23 6XZ, United Kingdom (☎/▤ +44-1937-843523, ✉ orders@survival books.net, 💻 www.survivalbooks.net). If you aren't entirely satisfied, simply return them to us within 14 days for a full and unconditional refund.

Cheque enclosed/please charge my Delta/Mastercard/Switch/Visa* card

Card No. _ _ _ _   _ _ _ _   _ _ _ _   _ _ _ _

Expiry date_____   **Issue number (Switch only)** _____

Signature _____   **Tel. No.** _____

NAME _____

ADDRESS _____

_____

_____

* Delete as applicable (price includes postage – airmail for Europe/world).

NOTES

NOTES

<u>NOTES</u>

NOTES

<u>NOTES</u>

NOTES